Fathers
After
Divorce

Fathers After Divorce: Building a new life and becoming a successful separated parent

This edition first published in 1998 in Australia by
Finch Publishing Pty Limited, ACN 057 285 248,
PO Box 120, Lane Cove, NSW 1595, Australia

01 00 99 98 7 6 5 4 3 2 1

National Library of Australia
Cataloguing-in-Publication entry

Green, Michael, 1939– .
Fathers after divorce: building a new life and becoming a
successful separated parent.

Bibliography.
Includes index.
ISBN 1 876451 00 9.

1. Divorced fathers—Conduct of life. 2. Fatherhood.
3. Father and child. I. Title.

306.8742

Illustrations by Phil Somerville
Cover design by Steve Miller/Miller Hare
Cover photograph by Skeet Booth/Peepshow
Text designed and typeset by DOCUPRO
Edited by Devon Mills
Editorial assistance from Ella Martin
Index by Carolyn Conlon
Printed by Southwood Press

Fathers After Divorce

Building a new life and becoming
a successful separated parent

Michael Green

Illustrations by Phil Somerville

FINCH PUBLISHING
SYDNEY

Words of Thanks

Heartfelt thanks to all the men and women who in so many ways contributed to this book. Your comments and anecdotes have enlivened the text. I will remember you with gratitude and admiration.

After I had written the rough (very rough!) draft of this book I had several copies run off. I asked Maureen, Peter, Dennise, Sue, Marjan, Greg, Janne, Michael, Julie, Aart, Susan, Helen, Michael, Kay, Ian, Gail, Ros, David, Justin and, of course, Joan, what they all thought of it. Well, thankfully, they told me!

Thanks to them and their perceptive comments I was able to refine my thinking and rewrite the book. I was able to accommodate most of their suggestions and I am deeply grateful for their input. While they may not all agree with everything in the finished product, they may take consolation in the thought that they were instrumental in helping to rid it of my more outlandish ideas!

Special thanks go to Marjan and Sue (who assisted me in locating research material) and to Donna and Alison. I am particularly grateful to Michael McMahon for his insightful suggestions, and to Anne McMurray, Bettina Arndt, Sue Langford, Peter Jordan, Janne Gibson and Michael Hawton for their contributions. I am indebted to Justin Dowd who has been a tower of strength and a careful commentator. A big thank you also to Maureen Coffey and all at Books On Oxford.

Without Rex Finch's gentle persuasion and skilful management, this book would not have seen the light of day. His positive and stimulating insights have comforted me through the long and arduous process of writing. He deserves a medal.

Loving thanks to Joan who taught me to use the computer, who edited and printed the early drafts, and who was a never-ending source of encouragement.

Contents

The Separated Man Today

I really loved my wife and children. For six years I worked three jobs to buy the things we wanted. Suddenly she suggested a trial separation and counselling. I did not know it but she had formed another relationship. I was shellshocked. I lay in bed for two days and cried. I cried at work. I thought about suicide. At first we separated under the same roof, but soon she became abusive and asked me to move out. I lived with my parents. I was really depressed. I thought I'd never get over it.

Jim

What happens to men after separation and divorce? Those men *who are left by their wives* just cannot believe it has happened to them. They have difficulty in coping with everything that follows: the legal consequences, division of property, child support, and especially contact with their children.

Those *who leave their wives* wrestle with guilt, the attitude of relatives and friends, explanations at work, and enormous concern over the effects of the separation on their children.

Most men suffer a decline in health and happiness, particularly at the time of separation. Their performance at work falls off. Sometimes they lose their jobs. They can't sleep, they turn easily to drugs and drink, and some to suicide.

For many life becomes a daily struggle, financially and emotionally. They struggle to set themselves up in decent accommodation, to pay for their own upkeep and for that of their children. They struggle to stay in touch with their children. The pain of the separation is intense.

Most feel that everything is against them: their ex-wives, the legal system, society itself. Some men remain angry and bitter for years.

What's it like for *you* right now? Are you still bruised after a bitter separation and divorce? Are you recently separated and still in a complete swim about where your life will go now? Perhaps you have been separated for a while and aren't sure how to rebuild parts of your life.

In this book we will look at issues such as these.

Even though my own separation and divorce occurred some years ago, parts of what I went through are still vivid. I'm here to tell you that you *can* survive and enjoy a new life. Throughout the book you will hear from many men who confirm that.

Decision!

I was expressing this same thought about life after divorce in a discussion with a group of separated men. One of them asked: *'How did you get over it?'* I rambled on for a while in my attempt to answer when finally another man in the group said: *'Look, what you did was: **you made a positive decision!**'*

He was right. After my separation I found myself stuck in a period of unhappiness and frustration. I said to myself one day: *'I am not a bad person. I only have one life and I have a right to a happy life. No one is going to spoil it. I will try to be happy and to live my life peacefully.'*

Of course, things did not improve overnight. But I'm convinced that the **decision to move on** provided the kickstart for my recovery.

Some figures

About one-fifth of Australian fathers live without their children.[1] This means that in Australia in 1997/98 there are over 400,000 fathers living apart from their children.[2]

In 1996 Australia had over five million families. Over half a million were one-parent families with dependent children to age 17. In the same year over one million children lived with a parent who had separated, 88 percent of them with their mothers. On these figures[3] it appears that about one million children do not live with their fathers.

In New Zealand, of a total 950,000 families, there are 168,000 one-parent families, and over 28,000 of these are headed by a man.[4]

In the United States half of all first marriages end in divorce. About 40 percent of American children experience parental divorce before they are eighteen. The number of single men with custody of their children has risen to just under two million.[5]

Men and women

For many men separation and divorce are a tragedy from which they struggle to recover. Some never make it. They become lost to depression, ill health, job loss, alienation and suicide.[6]

In emphasising this, I am not suggesting that divorce is easy for women and that they do not go through their own forms of suffering and even despair. However, it does seem that they employ healthier coping mechanisms and adjust more successfully to the changes involved in separation. Their experience of pain is, I believe, different from that of men. Custodial parents face enormous difficulties, particularly in the day-to-day care of the children and with the burden of being the nurturing parent. *They could do with a lot more help from the absent parent!*

Lost men

Often in the eyes of others, and sometimes in his own, the lone father is looked on as an *oddity*. Why is this so? The separated male feels lost, betrayed, hurt, all at sea and very lonely. It's as if he has been washed up on an island and has to start life again without too many resources. He may have lost his identity, his points of reference; he no longer feels a real father or a real husband. His life is without meaning. He's not good at domestic chores, and pretty hopeless at organising his own family and social life. Worst of all he may have been *sidelined* from his children.

It's a very different situation from that of the separated mother or the father who has custody of the children. Many of the problems, hurt and angst are the same, yes, but there are marked differences. The principal one, of course, is that the non-custodial parent is without the children and, in most cases, without the family home.

This book is written principally for separated, non-custodial fathers. It is this group of men that has been the least successful in coping with separation and divorce. There is plenty of evidence that the separated man, without his wife and without his children, is not managing too well – as I discovered in researching this book.

Effects of separation

In an Australian study by Peter Jordan of men separated for one to two years, most men spoke about how stressful the separation was.[7] They reported having problems with sleeping, eating, crying and headaches, as well as feeling tense and very tired and having hardly any energy. These are the signs of depression and if not dealt with they can have a significant effect on a man's ability to work and cope with everyday living.

Some of the men sought help from family and friends, while others used professional counselling or psychotherapy. But many just did the 'manly' thing and tried to forget the pain by using escapist strategies such as burying themselves in work, sport, sex, religion or alcohol.

The same researcher later followed up a group of men who had been separated for around 11 or 12 years and found that the majority of them had still not resolved their grief and sense of loss after all those years – many were still showing antipathy towards their ex-spouses whom they saw as having wrecked their lives. The men felt they had been dumped and would never get over the loss of their wife and children.[8]

US studies report that separated men are more prone than women to depression, psychological illness, eating and sleep disorders, disease, accident, suicide and death from other causes.[9]

The problem

My research and interviews with men reveal that the problem for separated men is a manifold one.

Firstly, such a man is often a dependent creature, more dependent than the female of the species. His wife and children may mean everything to him. He has invested so much of himself in the marriage.[10] He takes his identity from his family and his job. When either of these is removed from him he flounders. One of the goals of this book is to help the separated man develop a sense of his own self-worth as a man.

Moreover, many men fail to realise just how *emotionally*

dependent they are on their partners. Although just as naturally vulnerable as women, men are taught to hide their fragilities by concentrating on strength, competition and independence. They end up with no established emotional support network and this leaves them desperately unprepared for a major emotional crisis such as separation.

Secondly, the manner in which separation and divorce are handled in our society is basically flawed. When partners separate they reach immediately for lawyers and the Family Court. But that system is depressing, divisive, hostile and costly.

Although divorce is framed in terms of 'no-fault' law, the court normally elevates the mother to the role of *primary parent* and the father is relegated to *contact parent* status. He is seen as the *disposable* parent. This inexorably results in a savage sense of loss and low self-esteem. Usually, after separation, the children live with their mother and the father is allowed little more than fortnightly contact with them. This often sidelines him and reduces him to a pale and distant figure in their lives.

Thirdly, the above factors plus a good measure of prejudice cause a large part of society to see the separated father as a failure, and sometimes he sees himself that way. However the concept that divorce is not bad but can be *good* figures prominently in this book.

In our concentration on husbands and wives we must not forget the *children*. In spite of all the talk about the welfare of the children of separated parents, the children's real needs are often forgotten. In the stresses and strains of separation, in the couple's efforts to re-establish their lives in what often becomes a fight for parental superiority, the children's needs are lost in all the hostility. Yet they, too, go through sadness and suffering and desperately need healthy support from both parents.

A new divorce culture

What is now required is a new *divorce culture*. This is not the culture of promoting divorce as an easy solution to marital problems. It is rather a culture that, among other things, embodies the following:

★ **recognition that some marriages fail**
★ **acceptance that this is not disastrous**
★ **a conviction in parents that though their relationship is over their parenthood is not**
★ **willingness to put the welfare of children before adult needs**
★ **a strong desire to reach agreement about healthy parenting arrangements and to avoid the stresses of litigation**
★ **recognition that fathers as well as mothers are important in children's lives**

The last point is crucial and is starting to happen. What is taking place is, in Steve Biddulph's words, 'an outbreak of common sense',[12] an acknowledgement in our communities that fathers are just as important as mothers in the lives of their children. It is now vital that this 'outbreak' spreads into all areas of society, particularly to government policy-makers, to the judges and professionals of the family law system, and into the minds and hearts of men and women.

The children have been trying to tell them for a long time.

The book

This book does not pretend to solve the problems of all separated parents and families. That subject is too vast for one book. I trust that it might be read with profit by all kinds of separated mothers and fathers. But you will quickly see that it has been written with one type of separated male in mind: the lone father (possibly divorced) whose ex-wife has custody of the children.[11]

I hope the book will assist other people, too: separated men who have custody of their children, wives who do and don't, relatives and friends. Perhaps it would make a good gift from a reasonable ex-wife to an unreasonable ex-husband!

What I want *you* to get out of this book is the capacity to ask yourself questions, to identify **negative thoughts**, and to find the determination to replace them with **positive attitudes and resolutions**. Negative thoughts are the things that lead you and others to see you as a failure. Positive attitudes and resolutions will assist you to see yourself as a good and useful human being and, very importantly, as a good and useful father.

I will conclude each chapter with two lists: **questions** to ask yourself and **positive thoughts and resolutions**. Even after you've finished the book, you may like to come back to these from time to time. I hope they will serve to refresh your mind and stiffen your resolution to be a positive and successful person. You may even find it helpful to write out a thought or resolution and stick it on your mirror or in some place where you will see it every day. Mental reinforcement works!

There is also a lot in the book about **talking to yourself**. Encouragement is the word that springs to mind here. The value of talking positively to yourself is manifold: it helps overcome depression; it counters fear and negative thoughts; it leads to changed attitudes (that is no idle boast, it works!); it stops you from becoming discouraged and encourages you to go on with your life. We all need encouragement, not just from others but also from ourselves. We need to *hang on to hope*: that is, the hope that all is not lost and that our lives – though changed – can still be worthwhile.

The 'Notes' section at the back of the book contains extensive references to facts and people quoted in the text.

No apologies are offered for the trenchant criticism made in the book of the present family law system and the negative attitudes towards divorce in various sections of society. The evidence of such failures and shortcomings is overwhelming. I hope that the book will stimulate debate in these areas and contribute to positive steps towards reform.

1

Separation: What it Means for Men

I had no warning. She simply announced one day that she was leaving. I was shattered. I was too embarrassed to tell my friends and workmates and for a time I lived a lie. I finally realised that this was stupid. When I started to think clearly I could see that we had drifted apart and had little in common. We both had the resources to start again. I saw that separation was not the end of the world. When I got around to talking about it at work most people were really good. Everyone had experienced divorce either personally or through a family member or friend. It was nothing to be ashamed of.

Greg

Separation and divorce are not easy times for anyone. Experience tells us that it is often the wife's idea, and certainly statistics from the Family Court indicate that more women than men initiate applications for dissolution of marriage. Accepting that people do not do things like this on the spur of the moment, this suggests that wives are more prepared for the break than their husbands are.

In that small proportion of cases in which the separation is instigated by the husband, although he may have prepared himself for it mentally and physically he simply cannot anticipate all the problems, heartache and pain that the change in status will cause – for himself, his ex-wife and his children.

In many cases one of the parties does not expect it at all. Often this is the husband. Janne Gibson's study revealed that 61 percent of the men reported that it was their wives who had initiated the separation. In only 24 percent of cases did the husband consider that he had caused or initiated the separation. Another 15 percent of men regarded it as a joint decision.[13] Overall, some 65 percent of men did not want the divorce.

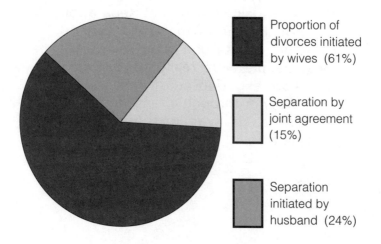

Proportion of divorces initiated by wives (61%)

Separation by joint agreement (15%)

Separation initiated by husband (24%)

Jumped or dumped?

Research by Peter Jordan reveals that most men react with total shock to their wives' announcement of separation. The small percentage of men who initiate it are often riddled with guilt or anger.[14] Others, while having their suspicions over the years, have developed coping mechanisms, turned a blind eye, and trusted that time would look after the problems. They never anticipated that the relationship would end in divorce.

Even where the serious problems in the marriage are acknowledged by both husband and wife, and the decision to separate is a joint one, the process ahead is laden with painful difficulties, emotional, financial and legal. As we've seen, there are good reasons to believe that men cope with these hurdles less satisfactorily than women. Indeed, many men simply do not get over separation and divorce.

The reports given by a group of men 11 or 12 years after their separation provided some surprises.[15]. Although most of the 63 men appeared to be coping well with their lives, a substantial number still felt angry about the separation and carried hurt memories and feelings. Almost two-thirds continued to feel *dumped*. One-third claimed that they would never get over the divorce and that it had all been a terrible mistake. About 60 percent blamed their wives for the end of the marriage.

Contrary to popular belief, men appear to 'get more' from marriage than women do and are more attached to marriage.[16] They depend on the relationship for comfort, safety and emotional security. They are able to deal with separation and divorce *legally* but not *emotionally*. In other words they accept the reality of their divorce but tend to avoid or push away their feelings of hurt and grief without dealing with them.

> I did not expect the separation. I was devastated. Suddenly I had no wife, no children, no home and very little money. I do not think it has been for the best. I have lost everything: the love of my wife and the life of my son. I am unable to be the father I wanted to be.
>
> *Warwick*

Studies have shown that in the early years of men's separation little more than half accept what has happened to them. The other half remain bitter, feeling sad and hurt.[17] Even after some years of separation, few men describe themselves as 'well adjusted'.[18]

> **The separation was a relief as the marriage had deteriorated over the years. However, at the same time I felt fearful – I did not know what lay ahead. There was a real fear of the unknown.**
>
> *Graham*

Loss of control

An overwhelming feeling experienced by most men in the process of separation is one of lack of control. They feel that a lot is happening over which they have no influence. They feel powerless, especially in the court system. Their experiences there can set off *victim*-type thinking which further alienates them from their children and leads to desperate actions to regain some sense of control and respect.

This sense of *disempowerment* can have serious consequences. It can lead a man into depression, victim-thinking and suicide. It can cause him to withdraw from contact with his children. It can also release powerful emotions in the abandoned male, including anger. These emotions need to be addressed, otherwise his approaches to negotiation, counselling and relationships with his children and ex-wife may be pathetic and futile.

> **I'll never forget the morning she left. The boys were only two and four years old. She simply put them in the car and drove off. She told me she was going back to an old boyfriend who lived in another State. I was devastated. She would not give me an address and I have not been able to catch up with them. I have never**

seen my sons in fifteen years. I don't think that I have recovered from what happened.

Noel

Loss of identity

What makes things particularly painful for the separated, non-custodial father is that at this time he will be experiencing the full force of the loss of his family life. I have already mentioned the devastating effect that this has on most men, no matter how the separation occurred. It's largely a matter of *identity*. Before the separation the father was 'kingpin', a central figure in a family unit, recognised as such by his wife, children and community. Now all has changed. The identifying framework, the safety net, in which he had felt so comfortable, has been whipped away from him.

For most men it's a composite loss. It's not only the wife, children and home but the *trappings* of marriage, too. Men should minimise that loss by setting up a strong position right from the start of the marriage: being an equal parent and really involved with the children, not being the sole breadwinner, and on separation being well informed of their rights.

Nicki

Daily problems

Quite apart from the bigger picture is the clutch of daily problems that separated life throws up for the typical man. He has to find a home and set himself up. He has to structure each day differently from what it was before. His daily routine has been upset and has to be re-established. Routine is important to everyone. Few people enjoy change. Whereas, when he was at home, his day began with breakfast and the flurry of contact with his wife and children, now he breakfasts alone, sometimes with only the radio for company. He lives in a different area, travels to work by a different route and means of transport, goes through each day without speaking to his children, and often returns home to an empty house or flat.

Many fathers say that the thing they have missed most is the everyday world of their children's growing up.[19]

These things are not trivial.

ONE MAN'S STORY
It would have been all right if she had cooperated. But she didn't. The hardest part was going back home to pick up the kids. She had created an atmosphere of hostility and it was very unpleasant. It was demoralising. This unsettled the kids and I found that I could not relate to them easily. I found it difficult to be a part-time father. It was a miserable time. Perhaps I could have handled it better.

Hope and inspiration

Are you going through this at present? Have you been through it and are still hurting? Are you some years down the track and still finding your separation and divorce a big, black hole in your life? Is there no hope that things can get better, that you can be happy again?

You need a lot of strength to get out of this hole. Hope and inspiration can give you the *energy* you need to overcome grief and depression and to make decisions that will enhance your health and wellbeing. They will persuade you to think about your manhood and how important you are to your children and to others around you.

Sources of hope and inspiration:

★   the example of other men who have suffered and survived and been successful
★   your own strength and capacity to adapt
★   your realisation that you can be different
★   your awareness of your importance as a father

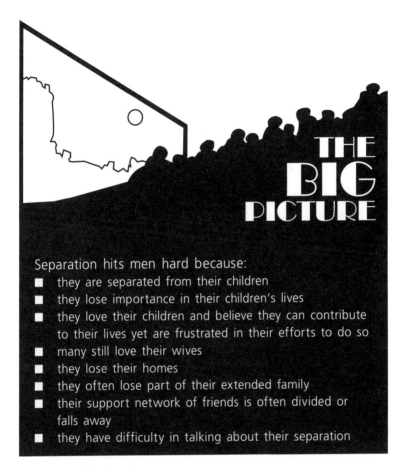

THE BIG PICTURE

Separation hits men hard because:

- they are separated from their children
- they lose importance in their children's lives
- they love their children and believe they can contribute to their lives yet are frustrated in their efforts to do so
- many still love their wives
- they lose their homes
- they often lose part of their extended family
- their support network of friends is often divided or falls away
- they have difficulty in talking about their separation

★ **meditation, prayer, spirituality**
★ **support, therapy**

Grief

For most men, separation brings with it hurt and grief. It is harmful to push these emotions away without dealing with them. It is dangerous to deny them. They can fester away for years and destroy your chances of peace and happiness. It's vitally important that you allow yourself to experience these feelings. It's the most natural thing in the world for you to have them. There's nothing wrong with you. You are in a state of shock, of pain and loss.

Unresolved grief tends to leave people preoccupied with their own pain and loss and renders them unavailable to others – their children, relatives, friends and workmates. It disturbs their thought processes and judgement. How you feel will often determine how you think and act.

Dealing with grief involves:

★ acknowledging what has happened
★ accepting your pain and loss
★ allowing yourself to feel angry and hurt, and channelling this into talking with someone or writing a diary
★ talking to a friend or counsellor who will allow you to manage your anger safely and who will help you not to remain stuck there
★ giving yourself time to heal

Time alone does not heal wounds. They also require proper management. It is time for you to move on. You need time and thought, but you also need someone to talk to and a load of support.

The example of others

How do men cope successfully with separation? The men that have come through divorce and are living happy lives, have they got things to teach the rest of us? What have they done? What *haven't* they done?

Those who are coping with separation have:

★ been willing to talk about it
★ brought themselves to accept the changes in their lives
★ worked on re-establishing a network of support
★ set up a decent home and routine for themselves
★ stayed as close as possible to their children
★ accepted some responsibility for what has happened

They have not:

★ denied that things are now different
★ refused to accept their change in status
★ stayed angry for too long
★ persisted in blaming their wives
★ turned away from their children
★ pretended that they were coping brilliantly

Support for men in crisis

There has been a real lack of support services for men. For years women have been offered specialist doctors, health and psychiatric services, community social work centres, refuges and the like. A lot of money, research and publicity have been given to women's issues. This has been good for women. Until recently it appears to have been the accepted wisdom that men needed no such thing. We have realised now that such an assumption is based on myth. In times of great need such as separation, job loss, personal grief and the like, men need support.

So many reports point to the need for specialised medical, psychiatric and counselling services for men. Men are less healthy than women are and do not live as long. They are three times as likely to be injured and four times as likely to commit suicide. Men have a higher incidence of hypertension than women have but are far less likely to have it diagnosed and treated. They are heavier smokers and drinkers, are more overweight and lead less healthy lifestyles.

As for emotional problems, depression, grief and the like, men are traditionally unaccustomed to discussing such issues. Unlike women, they have been brought up to be *tough*, not to display emotions and certainly not reveal weakness. They therefore find it difficult to expose their feelings to friends or therapists.

Women benefit from some other advantages. When a woman suffers a crisis such as separation she often has the support and attention of an extended family and a circle of close friends. If she has children, she attracts sympathy and understanding. Also, she is usually more at ease with self-expression: she does not mind talking about her problems, exposing her vulnerabilities. She is naturally open to a host of friends and also to specialist support services.

Not so the man. He has generally done what he feels he is best at: earning a living and supporting his family. He has left much of the parenting to his wife and this has suited each of them. He may have let go close friends and, if not, is usually unaccustomed to sharing intimate matters with them. This, he thinks, would tend to show himself as weak or, worse still, a failure.

Many men are simply too shy or lacking in confidence to talk to even a close friend about their feelings, let alone to a psychiatrist or counsellor. But, because of their 'hands-on' parenting experience, women tend to be more articulate about relationship issues. This gives them a powerful advantage in their dealings with the Family Court, whose judges and counsellors rely heavily on subjective impression and verbal fluency rather than on hard evidence. Worse still, most fathers feel powerless in a system which appears to regard them as less important than mothers and which relies on a level of emotional maturity that – at this point of their personal crisis – is simply beyond them.

> Among all the men I talk to, those who have been the most successful in dealing with separation and divorce – even the bitter ones – are those who have worked through their feelings and reached for help. They have made themselves open to support from friends and men's groups, together with counselling or therapy.

If there is ever a time when a person needs help it's when he or she goes through separation and divorce. Psychological research tells us that these events, together with changing home and losing a job, can constitute the most critical and traumatic episodes in a person's life.[20] Little wonder then that separated men go though a tough time: most experience two of these changes at the same time, and a proportion lose their jobs shortly after the main event!

Support at work

You will find it better in the long run to tell your colleagues – management and fellow workers – about your change in circumstances, rather than hide it from them. You may be pleasantly surprised to find how supportive some people can be. And it may also have the effect of enabling management to be understanding if your performance flags and to be sympathetic to requests for time off. Of course, in performance-oriented industries, any slackening in output and results may not be so kindly regarded. This puts enormous pressure on you if you are caught up in the turmoil of divorce and court proceedings. You may need special help, not only from your colleagues but from on-the-job counselling. Some companies have employee assistance programs which provide counselling for staff.

Negotiations between the lawyers dragged on for months. There were arguments about money and contact. I found that I could not concentrate on my work and my performance showed it. My supervisor counselled me on two separate occasions, and though I tried I could not keep up. After about twelve months they terminated my employment. Given the nature of the business, it was probably fair enough.

Vince

Support from friends

You will probably find that you need help with the children, too. What happens if you have to pick them up at 5.30 on Friday afternoon and you can't get away from work? Or if you are called into work during your holiday with the children? You can see the need for someone to rely on in these situations.

So, consider what support you can call on – some relative, friend or neighbour who will step temporarily into your shoes and look after the children. It is much better to make alternative arrangements than simply to ring up and tell your ex-wife that you can't make it!

To have these resources available you need to have cultivated them. That is, after separation you have to rebuild your support network or create a new one. There *are* good people out there. If you do not abuse their generosity, and as long as you reciprocate it, they will stand by you and enable you to achieve things that you simply cannot do alone. But you have to be willing to share your life and needs and worries with them and not remain isolated. Being *independent* is a luxury that separated fathers can't afford!

Support from men's groups

Many men have told me that their most valuable support came when they joined a group. There are associations for separated men and women, family law reform movements, and men's groups. You will find a list of some of these at the back of this book.

The benefits of talking to other men and women who have gone through the process of separation and divorce are obvious. You will discover that their experiences are not very different from your own. They will suggest strategies for dealing with difficulties with your children, with child support, the Family Court and others.

The focus of men's groups is on personal development. Meeting and talking with a small number of men offers you the chance to talk without fear of judgement and the opportunity to share what you are feeling. It can help you rise above day-to-day problems and explore the possibilities of personal growth.

The support I got from the group was wonderful. I soon realised that I wasn't the only one with problems, and

many were worse off than I was. I learnt about the Family Court and the Child Support Agency and how to handle them. One of the blokes helped me with my affidavits and came to court with me. Every time I went I heard a new story, but underneath it was always the same: men struggling with separated life.

Tom

Professional support

Reactions to counselling differ markedly, but many men have found it to be of great value. At times of crisis in a relationship it's almost impossible to think things through clearly without help. There are so many harsh things said; you may feel desperate; everything is emotionally highly charged.

So, who is helping *you*? Are you in a position to consider clearly all the issues and emotions involved? There are so many painful areas – children, partner, lover, relatives and friends.

My local doctor was also a counsellor and he was terrific. A lot of my problems were personal ones, not just marriage related, and I wasn't facing them. In a way I was quite crazy. Through talking to him – and medication for a while – I learnt to get my head into shape.

Greg

While Family Court counselling can be useful in assisting you and your ex-wife to resolve issues that arise after separation, it could be that what you need is personal counselling from a professional who will focus on you as an individual man and with whom you can share your thoughts and worries. Take some trouble to find a really good counsellor, and if you experience bias or lack of competence, don't hesitate to find another one.

There is an abundance of professional counselling services.[21] Some of them cost nothing. Others cost money, but you may find that it is money well spent.

Being able to share your feelings and hurt with a good friend or a wise counsellor is a habit worth cultivating. It may lead you to insights and possibilities that you would not otherwise have discovered. Remember that women have the advantage here. Generally they are further along the track in the process of separation. They have thought it through, they have discussed it endlessly with friends and relations, they have talked to other women with similar experience, they have read about it in women's magazines.

It's often the case that we men have to catch up! There's nothing wrong with this. It just happens that way in the present scheme of things, and will continue to happen until men and women learn to talk honestly with one another and men learn that it's not weakness to talk about feelings and emotions.

We will be looking at all these matters in later chapters.

✔ Face facts and make changes.
✔ Talk to someone.
✔ Learn to listen.
✔ Join a support group.
✔ Tell your workmates.
✔ Hang on to hope – and keep your sense of humour.

QUESTIONS	POSITIVE THOUGHTS AND RESOLUTIONS
★	★
What things should I do to handle the shock of my separation?	I will accept that I have been separated.
★	★
How should I go about getting support?	I will work to become a different kind of father.
★	★
What are the issues that I need to discuss?	I will be willing to get help.
★	★
How do I begin to talk about my feelings?	I will talk to other men.
★	★
How do I best manage the changes in my role as a father?	I will maintain my sense of humour, if it kills me!
★	★
What should I do to *move on*?	I will learn from this experience and look to the future with hope.

You are a child of the universe, no less than the trees and the stars; you have a right to be here.

Desiderata

2

Facing up to Separation

The worst thing is being confronted with your incapacities, your weaknesses. But these made me resolute. I faced up to them. I had to do things. Being able to buy my own home was symbolically very important: I had re-established my territory.

James

There's a lot to be faced in the early stages of separation. Some are purely physical things, like setting up a home, sorting out finances and telling people what has happened. Others are more than physical because they involve personal and relationship issues such as working out arrangements for contact with the children, and dealing with the emotional upheavals that the separation will cause for husband, wife and children.

> **The hardest part of leaving home is leaving your territory, your wife and family, your identity. You feel like you've got nothing. There's a terrible emptiness. Looking for a place to live I felt different, a loser, impoverished.**

Tim

Who goes, who stays? In some cases this is not an easy question. It depends not only on personal circumstances but also on individual temperaments.

Some men are established in strong parenting positions in their families. They have been heavily involved in their children's lives. Perhaps they have been the primary nurturer. They have encouraged their wives to work. They are competent home managers.

> **My work kept me at home most of the time and I was more involved with the children than my wife, who had a busy job in town. When she announced that she did not want to live with me any more she knew that I would never surrender my position by abandoning my home and children. So she moved out, and the children move between our houses on a shared-week basis. It is working well.**

Dennis

Such a stand will only work in certain circumstances, and perhaps also when the wife's willingness to cooperate is apparent. But it will not work if she decides to dig her heels in and wants you out of the house. If no agreement is reached and she takes the dispute to court, the court will do it for her. In our present system of family law, in any dispute about home and children, a mother normally wins, notwithstanding the merits of the father's case.

So, if it comes to that, the question you really have to ask yourself is: For my own sake and for the sake of the children, is it worth the trauma and expense? I suspect that it's on the basis of the answer to this question that many men leave home as peacefully as possible.

Common sense

Rather than allowing this to degenerate into a fight about the matrimonial home, surely the one question that sensible separating parents should ask themselves is: what will be the best living arrangements for our children?

The possible answers to this question are:

- ★ **Father moves out and lives close by.**
- ★ **Mother moves out and lives close by.**
- ★ **Children stay in the home and the parents take turns to live with them.**

Parents who love their children more than themselves will make sure that, whatever solution is decided on, it will promote the children's relationships with both parents and maintain their contacts with relatives, friends and schools.

A good start – telling the children

It is important to get off to a good start in your relationships with your ex-wife and children. Ideally parents will sort out living arrangements privately and then together break the news of the separation to the children. They will jointly give them all the reassurances that this major dislocation demands.

It's not good to keep children in the dark. How and when

this explanation is done depends on you and your circumstances. For most people, talking about separation with their
children is the hardest part of all. It demands great courage,
firmness and sensitivity.

But it's essential that your children be told what has
happened, what has been decided and what will happen in
future. It's their opportunity to ask questions, to express their
ideas and fears. It's your chance to answer them and to soothe
them. This has the enormous advantage of allowing the children to see that their parents are reasonable people, that they
still love their children and will have solid relationships with
them. In particular, it is an opportunity to assure them that
they (the children) *are in no way to blame for what is occurring*.

This last point is particularly important. Often children will
already know that things are not good. They will want to know
what is going to happen. They sometimes blame themselves
for the problems in a relationship – even the break-up itself.
Any such notion needs to be quickly and firmly laid to rest. It
is crucial that right from the beginning you and your ex-wife
clearly distinguish between the end of your marital relationship
and the continuation of your loving relationships with your
children.

ONE MAN'S STORY

After she decided to go we talked about what we
would say to the girls. I wanted her to tell them the
whole truth: that she had fallen out of love with me
and into love with another man. But she wouldn't be in that.
Finally we compromised and worked out a pretty lame
formula. We called them in and told them that Mummy and
Daddy were not going to live together any more and that
Mummy would be moving to another address. I will never
forget the look of shock and hurt on my six-year-old
daughter's face. When she recovered she said: 'Well, Mummy,
why can't you live next door?'

Avoiding blame

Regrettably, the ideal approach is all too rare. More often than not the conflict between the parties prevents it from happening. The children get the story from one party at a time, with all the contradictions and ambiguities which that inevitably involves. One parent is often blamed for the separation and is presented to the children as a *traitor* to the family. This immediately presents them with a dilemma: this person whom they have loved, and even been close to, is now a villain. They are confused and hurt, and the whole process gets off to a very bad start.

This lamentable situation makes things very difficult for you as a separated father. It can leave you with the unenviable and hazardous task of justifying yourself, or at least attempting to explain to the children what has gone wrong, while all the time you are being 'shot down' in their eyes by their mother.

Whatever lies behind the separation, such a presentation is very harmful for the children. They will be left to their own devices to sort out in their minds just what is going on. This is an unnecessary burden on them and can cause harm and grief.

> **Our relationship just wasted away. In the end we avoided one another and our health deteriorated. Someone had to leave and I did. But then she refused to take any responsibility for the separation and told the kids that I had deserted the family. The kids grew up with the idea that I was the bad man who had left them.**
>
> *Dennis*

The 'blame your father' way of handling separation adopted by some mothers can continue for years. Separated fathers must be careful not to make the same mistake. The experience of many men is that if they refuse to blame or criticise the mother, answer their children's questions honestly and calmly, and show themselves to be good and caring fathers, the children eventually wake up to the nonsense and reject it.

Your children's right to know

Overseas studies show that separating parents are quite dishonest with their children, giving them inadequate, conflicting or no information at all about what is happening.[22] This is simply not fair to the children and causes confusion, resentment and anger. They want to know what has happened to their family and they have a right to know. As painful as it may be, they are capable of absorbing and coping with more than we imagine.

How do you tell your children?

★   make allowances for different ages
★   answer their questions honestly
★   be patient with objections and complaints, even outbursts of anger and disapproval
★   let them express their hurt and anger
★   console and encourage them
★   tell them they are still loved by you both
★   assure them that what has happened is between their mother and father and is in no way their fault
★   acknowledge that there will be some changes but promise that their daily routines will not be interfered with
★   guarantee that they will remain part of your lives

Spreading the news

Besides announcing it to your children, it is only reasonable that you inform the people who have to know: your relatives, friends, associates and people at work. This procedure can be difficult and upsetting. Make it a bit easier for yourself by getting it over as quickly as possible. Make a list of those who need to know and set about it in a businesslike fashion. Most men find it helps if you tell each of them – in person or by telephone – in the briefest possible terms, without too much elaboration or detail, and without apology. Whether you give them a reason for the separation or not is a personal decision, but it's better to avoid assigning blame and picking faults.

The difficult calls are those to *her* relatives and to mutual friends. With these people you will be particularly careful to avoid assigning blame or fault. Talk to them in decent and objective terms. It's important that they hear it from you in order that they can see that you are being sensible about your separation and so that you can assure them that you and your children want to stay in touch with them. This is especially true for both sets of grandparents.

> **The signs of failure were there even before we got married. I eventually left my wife. I was depressed and sick and I realised that we could not go on. I felt such a failure and I was reluctant to tell people about it; I only told my sister and a couple of friends. But after two months I burst out and told everyone.**
>
> *Nico*

Appreciating your supporters

The good news is that your true friends will rally around you. They will give you the unqualified and unselfish support that we all need in times like this. In time, some of your old friends and relatives will also come back to you because they have become used to your new life and the success you have made of it. Soon you will have made new friends, including people who are in the same situation as you, or just good, open-minded people who accept others as they find them.

Practical arrangements

Getting off to a good start also involves parents coming to sensible agreements on such matters as contact with the children, where everyone is to live, and the financial measures that will have to be put in place to support two households. There is no doubt that the easiest, most successful and least costly way to achieve this is for husband and wife to talk about it themselves and to come to generous and practical arrangements. Central to achieving this is that they consider the needs of their children over and above their own.

Experience has taught us that *the first two or three months of separation are a critical time.* The early stages of separated life are vitally important not just for the man but for his ex-wife and children. It seems pretty clear that the sooner the separated father gets himself on track the better he's going to feel about himself. If unsatisfactory arrangements go on for too long, they will cause problems which are difficult to correct. Bad habits can be changed but it takes time and is painful.

Parenting

Most separated men are at a disadvantage when it comes to parenting their children. In most families this is the women's domain. It is the mother who has traditionally taken on the principal nurturing role. She it is who has taken on the task of *hands-on care* of the children. She cooks their food, washes their clothes, shops for them, runs errands for them, listens to them and supports them. Even when she gets a part-time or full-time job, she remains the principal carer. Their father might love them dearly and spend what time he can with them, but more often than not the responsibilities of his job mean that his physical contact with his children is limited. In many families he is out in the market place earning money to support his wife and children and they know it and appreciate it.

Your new life as a separated father

What happens to parenting after separation? In most cases the mother's role stays much the same. Normally the children live with her and she continues to do the same things for them.

But your role as a separated father undergoes a cataclysmic change.

You become the absent parent, the 'contact parent'. This often presents two areas of difficulty.

Firstly, if you have been the 'traditional' dad that I mentioned, then you may not know a lot about 'hands-on' caring for children. You may have to learn to cook and clean and manage a household. Above all, you may have to learn how to talk to and listen to your children, and to do that you have to create time for them. In other words, at least for the times when the children are with you, you must be the *principal carer*.

Secondly, you have to set up a home.

So, the separated father:

* ★ **loses his traditional role**
* ★ **has to learn to be a carer**
* ★ **suffers from lack of support**
* ★ **has to become a hands-on parent**
* ★ **has to set up home**

Setting up home

For non-custodial fathers, separation brings with it the necessity to find a new home. The experience of most men is that having a decent place to live in helps them to feel better about themselves and assists their readjustment in life.

> **After the separation I was hopelessly adrift. I felt intense pain. I almost had a breakdown. I lived first with my mother and then with a mate. Gradually I sorted my life out and I moved into a place of my own.**
>
> *Bernie*

The choice of your new home is a serious and important matter and you should put some careful thought into it. To begin with you may be forced to take temporary accommodation that is not ideal. But as soon as possible move into a place that you will be happy to call your own, and that your children will be happy to call a second home. Remember that children do not like change. It will not assist them to accept your separation if you move around a lot or live in a dump or in a place where they are not comfortable.

It's easy for those who have money, of course. They just buy or rent whatever takes their fancy. For most separated fathers, establishing a new home is an expensive business which takes a lot of effort and some sacrifice. Some may still be paying off the matrimonial home. This, on top of child support, makes life hard for a man on an ordinary wage.

> **For me the hardest part was leaving home and then selling it. I went through a terrible time setting myself up in a one-bedroom apartment, feeling very much alone, and with not much money. To make matters worse I changed jobs at the same time.**
>
> *Matt*

Ideally, you need to buy or rent comfortable accommodation. It will help if it is not too far from your work and not too far from your children. This minimises travelling time for you both. You may even be able to do without a car!

Studies in the United States have shown that the happiest children of separated parents are those who have easy access to both homes.[23] So if you are lucky enough to have a cooperative parenting arrangement (*shared parenting* in the true sense of the term) it will be great if you can set up home within walking or riding distance from the children's first home.

Home sweet home

The important thing is that you create a *true home* for yourself and your children. An American study showed that fathers who created their own households and set up schedules for frequent access successfully re-established themselves in society.

Their feelings of inadequacy, anxiety and depression were gradually replaced by a sense of confidence and achievement.[24]

> I know I have become a better person. I learnt to be independent and to look after myself, to manage a household and to look after the children.
>
> *Greg*

In the same way, if your children have feelings of upset, insecurity and resentment, these should pass when they see you successfully established in your new home and life, especially if they feel that there is a place in it for them.

Hints for setting up home:

- ★ **think and choose carefully**
- ★ **locate it as close to your children as possible**
- ★ **put a bit of yourself into it**
- ★ **hang up photos of the children**
- ★ **encourage your children to have their own photos and pictures, clothes and belongings**
- ★ **have separate bedrooms for them if required**
- ★ **involve them in cooking, cleaning, etc.**

If you cannot afford to buy or rent premises that you feel are adequate, all is not lost. You might consider sharing. If handled with care, this can work out quite well. Scan the 'share accommodation' section of your newspaper or advertise your requirements in the local newspaper. Try a flat-sharing agency: this can give good results and is often well worth the fee charged. You can be clear about your need for a comfortable home for yourself and your children.

Home management

Okay, you've got your home, what's next? You need to *learn to manage it competently*. If you're not experienced, talk to someone who is – your mother, your sister, the woman next

THE BIG PICTURE

It's important for you to get off to a good start in your separated life. You have to announce it sensibly to your children, relatives and friends. You and your ex-wife need to make practical decisions regarding your contact with the children, living arrangements and financial affairs. Finding and creating a decent home for yourself and the children involves serious effort. You learn to cook and to manage your home competently. You start to enjoy your new life.

door. They'll be happy to help with advice on cleaning agents, washing powder, how to iron a shirt and the like. Don't be too proud to ask. Find out where the neighbours do their shopping. It's a good way to get to know them.

Keeping the place clean and tidy shows yourself and your children that you can cope.

If you can't already do so, *learn to cook!* This is critical to your physical, moral and financial survival. Anyone who can read can learn to cook satisfying meals. Men make terrific cooks and get a lot of fun out of it.

On my first night on my own I went to a local restaurant. It was terrible and I was miserable. I resolved on

✔ Make a firm resolution that you will not buy takeaways or eat out more than once a week.

✔ Buy a simple cookbook or two.

✔ Go to cooking classes. Everyone should attend at least one cooking course. The gas and electricity authorities run them, as do adult education centres and evening colleges, and there are others. Most of them are excellent, don't cost much and are a lot of fun. They are also a good way to meet interesting men and women.

✔ Develop a repertoire of six or seven dishes that are tasty and simple to prepare; persevere with them until you can cook them blindfolded.

✔ Cook large amounts so that you can refrigerate or freeze leftovers and have ready-made meals.

the spot that I would not do that again, that I would avoid takeaway foods and that I would not open tins. My mother gave me the 'Common Sense Cookery Book' and I started from there. After a while I started to enjoy getting my own meals. Even after a long day at work it was refreshing, and the kids were really impressed.

George

It is vital for your own self-esteem and for the respect that your children want to give you that you are seen as an independent person, as a person in control of your life, as a good manager of your home, your work, your leisure time. So get yourself into shape! Organise yourself! Take control of your life! Show yourself, your children and the world that you can do it on your own. It will keep you very busy, but you can do it!

Economies

Most men find that separated life reduces their standard of living and creates a big drag on their finances. They learn to economise. They find that they need to watch their financial situation very carefully. Setting up a new home and lifestyle is an expensive business. Indeed, after separation most fathers are really supporting two households.

Once you are settled you will have time to think about your life and see if there are activities that you can do without, the things that waste time or that cost a lot of money. You have a new life now and you need to develop a new list of priorities. Some things that were important before your separation will not be so now. Other facets of your life will assume more importance. With all its drawbacks, life can still be enjoyable, but it's up to you to sort it out.

Legal costs

Legal fees can be one of the big expenses of separation and divorce. A lot of money is wasted by parents on unnecessary legal wrangles, money that could go towards getting them re-established in life. It is in your own and your ex-wife's best interests to settle residence, contact, property and child support matters as quickly as possible and *outside court*. A day in court costs a lot of money and protracted litigation costs a fortune. It may even be less costly to settle for less than your due, rather than to spend it fighting in court. Mediation can help, but if you must enlist a lawyer, shop around and get one who does not charge the earth.

I realised that our relationship had deteriorated over a long period. But at the time neither of us expected the

✔ Watch what you spend on alcohol and eating out.

✔ Keep theatre, movies and concerts to an affordable minimum.

✔ Check the newspaper for cheap or free entertainment for yourself and your children.

✔ Computer games and videos are cheap sources of entertainment.

✔ Are you in a position to do without a car?

✔ Financial advice is available. Don't be afraid or too proud to ask for it. Look up 'Community Advisory Services' or 'Counselling' in the telephone directory, and you will find agencies that will help.

separation. It blew up over a family dispute. I felt a sense of relief at the separation but at the same time there was fear of the unknown. I didn't know what lay ahead. There were difficulties with the children and financial problems. It was hard work. But I stuck at it and learned to be independent. I gained insight and a whole new outlook on life. It's all been worthwhile.

Harry

QUESTIONS	POSITIVE THOUGHTS AND RESOLUTIONS
★	
What things must I do to get off to a good start as a separated father?	★
	I will talk sensibly to my ex-wife about what has to be done.
★	★
How do I go about setting up a good home for me and my children?	I will create a home and take pride in it.
★	★
How do I become a competent home manager?	I will learn to be a good housekeeper.
★	★
What have I listed as my expenses?	I will enjoy my home.
★	★
What measures can I take to cut out unnecessary costs and activities?	I will eliminate unnecessary expenses.

Beyond a wholesome discipline, be gentle with yourself.
Desiderata

3

Separation and Change

It was tough at first but now I know it has been for the best. At separation I was angry and confused but after a couple of months I realised that the marriage was over and that is when I changed. My friends and I feel that I have become a much better person. Instead of trying to save a marriage that my wife did not want and one that at the time I thought I did, I am now able to spend more time with my children and close friends.

Leo

For the separated man – and for his ex-wife and children – life goes on. It does not stop at separation and divorce. Nor, of course, do the effects of the rupture of family life. Even in the unusual case of an amicable separation, an efficient divorce and a proper parenting agreement, it's not all over just because the papers are signed! Life goes on but it's never the same again.

This need not be a bad thing. Indeed it can be a very good thing. The truth, however, appears to be that most men and women feel *bad* about their separation. While this is entirely understandable in the early stages, it is disturbing to see this feeling continue long after the divorce. For many separated men it goes on for years. They simply do not accept what has happened.

If a man does not accept his divorce then everything that follows thereafter he will inevitably see as *bad for him*: court, orders, access, custody, counselling, property settlement, etc. As understandable as this might be initially, if it becomes a mindset it will keep him depressed and bitter for years and, sometimes, for the rest of his life. His journey after divorce will be marked by sadness, regret and bitterness.

Some causes of grief after divorce:

- ★ **continuing conflict with one's ex-spouse**
- ★ **bad experiences in the court system**
- ★ **unhealthy attitudes to divorce**
- ★ **guilt concerning the children**
- ★ **loss of personal identity**

The roots of the problem

The personal reasons why the journey after separation might remain painful were discussed in the first two chapters. Undoubtedly there are also situations where the divorce has been so bitter that there are huge obstacles to personal or family recovery. Many separated men are badly served by the Family Court, lose their homes, are cut out of the lives of their children and are forced to pay amounts of child support that reduce them to poverty. The causes of their bitterness are tragically apparent.

Then there are those who are caught in a never-ending spiral of conflict with their ex-partners. This reduces the possibility of a peaceful life to a minimum. Approaches to dealing with these situations are the subjects of later chapters.

Attitudes to divorce

Despite the increased incidence of divorce, not everyone accepts it. Still less see it as a desirable occurrence. In fact, a large part of society actively makes separated and divorced people feel guilty. Many church people, community leaders, politicians and social commentators lament the 'broken home' and its dire consequences for society. They blame divorce for many problems of youth: delinquency, crime, suicide, drugs and alienation. They claim that the children of divorce suffer serious and long-lasting damage. I believe that these views are based largely on misconceptions, and will examine them in the next chapter.

This attitude that 'divorce is bad' does nothing to assist men and women in their journey after divorce and gets them off to a bad start. Can divorce ever be *good*?

The good divorce

The experience of a great number of men and women is that not only was their divorce necessary but that it has had very positive outcomes for all concerned. In other words, *it has been good!*

They do not claim that it has been painless or without its problems. But they do say that after a time they and their children have adjusted successfully to the change and have gone on to live satisfying lives.

What things have helped them?

★   a willingness to accept the separation
★   being prepared to communicate and compromise

★ putting the children's interests before their own
★ looking after their own lifestyles
★ working through guilt and blame and loss
★ support and advice

Divorce is good in the sense that it is a good thing that we have it, and in the sense that it *can* be good for husband, wife and children. There *is* such a thing as a 'good divorce'.[25]

Divorce is good when:

★ it forces you to look at yourself and to develop as a person
★ it forces you to examine your lifestyle
★ it gives you the opportunity to become a better father
★ it gives you time for reflection and planning
★ it gives you the chance to create new relationships

Ideally, of course, a good divorce is one where the couple parts without destroying their own or their children's lives. They communicate and their children continue to have two parents and to have good relationships with each. They all continue to be a family.

Even divorces that are less than ideal can still be good. You can have all kinds of problems. Your ex-wife may be making things difficult for you or you may be finding it hard to adjust. But there are ways of managing these stresses that will enable you to make the most of your separated life. These will be treated in detail throughout this book.

> If anyone had said to me in the first few months, 'Everything will be fine; you'll come to like separated life', I think I would have exploded. But, after we got over the legal hurdles and sorted the children out, things did improve. We settled into a routine. The kids were great. I think we had better times together than before. I also enjoyed the time I had to myself. I started to do things for myself and not just for everyone else.
>
> *Mario*

THE BIG PICTURE

Many of the problems experienced by separated couples can be traced back to their perception that something 'bad' has happened to them. Their acrimony and bitterness often relate directly to their feeling of *failure* – in their own eyes and in the eyes of the community. Even these days some people look on divorce as a necessary evil or, at best, a second-rate existence. This can result in couples feeling that they have to *explain* the reasons for their separation, to *justify* it, and they do this by resorting to blame, by finding real or imagined fault in the other party. And so the season of conflict begins.

Change of culture

Understood in this sense, the concept of divorce being good is really important. And a change of culture is taking place which is diminishing the negative attitudes to divorce by recognising that it can indeed be a good thing. This hopefully will have the result that one source of bitterness between ex-spouses disappears. They will not see themselves as *failing*, but as *changing*.

This change of culture is not the disaster described by its detractors. It is not an attack on the family. It is not a product of selfishness or of whimsical solutions to marital problems. To present it in that way is an insult to separating couples who come to divorce after much heartache and anguish.

It has been said that divorce is an essential component of democracy.[26] It occurs now in the lives of an increasing number of men, women and children.[27] There is no indication that the tide will turn: in 1997 in Australia there was one divorce for every two marriages. To present it as an unfortunate aberration that can be corrected by policies that provide greater support for married couples is to fly in the face of reality.

Facing facts

It's a rare man who in the early stages of his separation can say to himself that his situation is good! Still less will he be telling everyone that he is glad that it happened! However, there is something to be gained by recognising that it *has* happened and that there's no turning back. There is also a lot to be gained by realising that the essential question is not *'What went wrong?'*, but rather *'Where do I go from here?'*.

Before we get to that question, however, we must talk more about the early stages of the personal journey of the separated man.

Working through it

While it's never easy, you eventually come to accept that your separation is a reality. In time you get over the initial shock and set about rearranging your life. You find a home and organise contact with your children. *But you still feel bad!*

Perhaps part of the problem is that you have not really accepted your separation at all. You still do not like what has happened, and you have not embraced your changed life. You have not made the decision to *move on*. What you can do is to work on yourself. You can start by making some decisions.

Five decisions for your new life:

★   **decide that you are going to be happy**
★   **accept that life has changed**
★   **develop a positive spirit**
★   **refuse to be a victim**
★   **cast off guilt**

Deciding to be happy

Unlike your marriage – where you were not in total control –
in your divorced state you *are* in control, not of your ex-wife
and children, but of yourself and your attitudes. Given time
and encouragement, you can decide to be miserable or happy.
This may not change how you feel at the moment, but it is a
good start.

Other decisions will also help. Your decision to remain in
close contact with your children, despite difficulties, gives you
a positive goal and is valued by the children. Your decision to
tell the people close to you about your separation will indicate
that you accept that it has happened and that you are going
on with your life.

Dealing with change

In time, and with help, you will come to see that your separation and divorce mean that things are not worse, they are
different. You are not the same as before. You are a different
father, your ex-wife is a different mother, your children will
have a different relationship with each of you. But you are still
a father and can be a good one. Moreover, you are still your
own man.

It's not easy for men to accept this change. After divorce
some of them want things to stay the same, and of course
that's impossible. For instance, they may want joint custody
and parenting and their wives will not cooperate. They want
to maintain the same influence over their children, the same

control. They want to see them every day. In most cases this is neither practicable nor possible. This hurts them. For these men divorce remains bad forever. They neither forgive nor forget. Their journey is a bitter one.

Acceptance

Acceptance involves appreciating what has gone before, letting go and moving on.

It is reasonable to mourn the end of a marriage. There were many hopes and dreams invested in the relationship, both for yourselves and for your children. But divorce is both an end and a beginning. If you encourage yourself to hope for a better life and actively pursue that life, then the mourning period will be shorter.

No matter what has led to the separation and divorce, a *positive spirit* will eventually turn it to good use. It will help you to recognise and accept the positive and the negative things in the former relationship and the immense possibilities that lie ahead. It will assist you to *let go* of the past and turn your mind to building a satisfying life for you and your children.

In Buddhist literature there is a lovely saying: *'Look back, understand, let go.'* This process is seen as one of the keys to happiness.

'Letting go does not necessarily mean blotting out the past and suppressing its experiences, happy or sad. It means a changed relationship with those past events: assessing them for what they are worth in a positive sense and for what they can add to your present and future life.'[28]

Things could not have been worse. She kicked me out of the house, she made false allegations against me, and kept the kids away from me. I exhausted my savings in legal and court fees. I was miserable for months. Finally I decided that I had to let go of all this and get over it. I wanted to live a happy life. I took control of

how I felt about it all and redirected my life. Things are not easy and I still think the system stinks. But my life is good now and it's getting better.

Andrew

Positive language

The language that you use will demonstrate that you have decided to look on your divorce in a positive spirit. So instead of using expressions such as *'our marriage has failed'* and *'we have broken up'*, you might say *'we have separated'*, or *'we are divorced'*. Instead of talking about a *'broken home'*, tell everyone that your children have **two homes**.

Answering the question

There are two ways of answering the question: *Are you married?*

Negative: I used to have a family but my marriage broke up two years ago. My ex-wife has custody of the children and I have access to them every fortnight.

Positive: I have a family of two children. They live with their mother during the week and come to live with me on weekends and school holidays.

It is not fair to regard your marriage as a failure, because the **whole** of the marriage has **not** been a failure at all. Indeed, some parts of it may have been remarkably successful. You have had children, you have acquired a home and material possessions. You have shared valuable and enriching experiences. You probably have a photo album testifying to the happy events in your lives, to your achievements and your experiences. Don't throw these away! (Neither the experiences nor the album!)

The victim mindset

One of the traps for both separated men and women after divorce is to sink into the *victim role*.

Many men and women feel betrayed by their divorce, particularly when they see themselves as the innocent parties. *'The marriage was fine. We had no major blues. The kids were happy. We had a nice home and lifestyle. I came home every night and I didn't play up. We both worked hard. Then she left me. I did nothing to deserve this. Why should I be penalised?'* Some ex-partners see a solution to this hurt in laws that would make it harder for people to separate and divorce and that would penalise the *'guilty'* party. They even suggest compensation for *'marital misconduct'*.[29]

Such thinking is shortsighted and dangerous. It would take us back to the dark days of fault-based divorce. It would drag people through the courts in tortuous contests. It would create disharmony and bitterness, besides providing another fertile field for lawyers and judges. It promotes the *victim complex*.

Guilt

Don't be surprised at feelings of failure and guilt. There's nothing wrong with them. It is the common experience of most men that, after separation and divorce, they feel like this. Indeed, research indicates that men suffer these feelings more acutely than women do, or that at least they tend to cope with them less effectively than their ex-wives do.[30]

> I had a real sense that the relationship had reached its end and that we had to move on. I felt guilt because that's what is put on us by our parents and peers, but no shame because I knew it was the right thing to do.
>
> *Tom*

The nature of the guilt-feeling varies according to the nature of the separation and your personality. Where you have

tips

We can avoid victim-thinking by:
- ✔ Making decisions.
- ✔ Developing positive attitudes to divorce.
- ✔ Mixing with positive and supportive people.
- ✔ Taking steps to re-establish our life.
- ✔ Refusing to give up.

initiated the separation, you might well feel that you have *'let down'* your wife, children and family. Where your wife has been the moving party, you may tend to see yourself as the let-down one; although feeling shocked and betrayed, you might also be inclined to examine yourself guiltily to see where you *'went wrong'* or where you did not *'measure up'*. Where the parting has been by mutual agreement, you may be tortured by thoughts of *'perhaps I could have tried harder'* or *'perhaps I should have given it another few months'*. You will worry about the children's future.

> **The best part has been the children's pure acceptance of me as a person and a father. The worst thing is my feeling of guilt at having abandoned them.**
>
> *Barry*

Depression

Guilt aggravates depression and undermines hope. If you are not careful, your days and nights may become so filled with negative thoughts that you become stuck in sadness and depression. If you find that happening you will find it worthwhile to talk to a close friend or a doctor or a counsellor. Try to be open about what you are thinking and how you are feeling. Once you have spoken about guilt then you can begin to overcome it.

The key to overcoming guilt is **problem-ownership**. That means being willing to take responsibility for the problems you have caused, but not for those that belong to others.

One practical application of this relates to how you deal with your children's expressions of disappointment at your separation. If you are the one who left home, they may be angry. Allow them to express their anger. Don't stifle it. Talk it through with them and respond with care. *'I understand how you feel and I'm really sorry that I have upset you in that way. However, I cannot be responsible for what your mother has said to you.'*

Do your best to counter negative thoughts with positive ones. Talk gently to yourself. When a guilty feeling comes over you, push it away with a positive chat to yourself. For instance, from time to time you may become depressed at not being near your children, at not being around when they need you.

Talk to yourself: 'I will stay in close contact with the children. I will be with them as often as I can. I will listen to them and talk to them. They have my telephone number. I will keep open the lines of communication. I will make sure they know that I care.'

ONE MAN'S STORY
Looking back now I can see that our divorce has definitely been for the best for all of us. My ex-wife and I went to a course on Co-parenting After Separation run by the Family Court. It was good. We listened to what was said. We made a start. It took us a lot of time and effort to get it right. We stopped blaming one another and being angry and adjusted our parenting styles. The really important thing is that my ex-wife and I and our daughter now feel that we have a loving and caring relationship. We are a good family. We've been lucky but it also took a lot of work.

Moving on

In her marvellous book *Intimacy and Solitude* Stephanie Dowrick says: '*You have a right to be alive in your own way.*' She talks about developing '*a sense of self*'. Leaving a marriage can be the opportunity to find yourself, to discover just who you are.[31]

Having a successful divorce is as difficult as having a successful marriage. It's hard work and you have to keep at it. You have to work out a new pattern of living, new relationships with your ex-wife and children, a new lifestyle. You have to keep moving on. If you can become confident about this your confidence will rub off on to others, including your children. Your confidence will become *their* confidence.

> It was a tough time. I had a lot of deeply rooted anger and frustration which I had suppressed. Men are too controlled. It came out in the form of anger with my new partner. Gradually I got myself into shape. I reasoned with myself. I started training at the gym. I made plans, I studied, I worked hard. My real supports have been my fiancee and friends at work. Life is pretty good now.
>
> *Arthur*

QUESTIONS	POSITIVE THOUGHTS AND RESOLUTIONS
★	★
What decisions must I make to begin my recovery?	I will be courageous in handling my separation.
★	★
What can I do to overcome anger and negative attitudes?	I will accept my present situation and change what I can.
★	★
What steps do I take to manage feelings of guilt?	I will take responsibility for what I have done.
★	★
What are some issues that I'd like to discuss with a counsellor?	I will not be a victim or a blamer.
★	★
What can I do in times when I feel sorry for myself?	I will develop a positive attitude to divorce and separation.
★	★
How can I change my attitude to divorce?	I will move ahead with hope and confidence.

With all its sham, drudgery and broken dreams, it is still a beautiful world. Be careful. Strive to be happy.

Desiderata

4

Separation and Children

I was in constant agony over the children. I really feared what would happen to them. We had close bonds but these started to be strained after the separation. I could see their hurt and disappointment. They begged me to come home. I tried to be as loving and supportive as I could, but it wasn't enough: they were getting the wrong messages and hated the whole situation. I worried how they would turn out.

Charles

One of the greatest fears of separated fathers and mothers is that their divorce will injure the children, cause them irreparable harm, and disadvantage them in life. They are not assisted by the purveyors of doom in the media and pulpits and on soapboxes across the country.

'What will this do to my children?' This is the question that torments many caring men and women. They know that the children are upset over the separation, and they are tortured by thoughts that what they have done will inevitably cause the children everlasting harm. Are these thoughts justified?

The simple answer is *no*.[32] However, separating parents will do well to be concerned, because divorce *does* pose definite risks for their children. If parents really care they will take steps to minimise these risks.

Different views on the effects of divorce

The effect of divorce on children remains a controversial subject. The conservative view blames divorce for most of our social ills: family break-up, crime, delinquency, suicide, poverty, substance abuse (and, some comics add, the El Nino Effect!).[33] They see 'no-fault' divorce as too easy and suggest the solution lies in a return to some form of marriage contract with penalties for breaking the contract.[34] They consider the suggestion that there is such a thing as a 'good divorce' to be ridiculous, against the weight of evidence, and an attack on the traditional family system.[35]

Others argue that the evidence of divorce's traumatic effects on children is so overwhelming that we must reassess our attitudes to divorce and increase the level of our commitment to traditional marriage. Couples in low-conflict marriages should work harder to resolve their difficulties for the sake of the children. Except in situations of high conflict, children are usually better off in intact marriages even when their parents are unhappy.[36]

The 'modernists' (for want of a better term) strongly disagree. They argue that adults as well as children have the right to happy and satisfying lives. Rejecting the concept that divorce is easy (from an emotional point of view), they hold that separation is better than a bad marriage. Children are resilient and after some trauma recover and adjust to their new family arrangements.[37]

Research results

Contrasting results have emerged from studies both in Australia and overseas. A review of Australian research concluded that there is evidence that the children of divorce suffer '*a wide range of adverse social and psychological outcomes*'.[38] However, the author conceded that the research is patchy. He was also careful to point out that the problems experienced by these children stemmed '*from family circumstances before, during and after the process of marital dissolution, rather than from loss or absence of a particular parent . . .*' This conclusion is supported by research in the United Kingdom and the United States where it was found that many problems existed *before* separation and divorce.[39]

Some Australian research has shown that there is no evidence that, **in the long term**, children from divorced families are less well adjusted than those from intact families.[40] Overseas, it has been found that not all children suffer adverse consequences and that generally where differences exist between divorced and intact groups these differences are small. Importantly, the effect of divorce on children has been shown to be less significant than other factors such as parent–child relationships, economic stability, parental conflict, father's occupation and gender.[41] In one study, in terms of self-image, depression and anxiety there was little to distinguish the children of separated families from those of intact families.[42]

Different patterns emerged in the United States in a recent longitudinal survey (a study that follows up people over a period of years). While divorce was seen to have some benefits for children, it was detrimental in terms of educational and professional achievement. Problems were also seen in the children's relationships with their parents and in their own tendency to divorce. In terms of happiness, wellbeing and social integration, however, there was little difference between the children of divorced and intact families. It was found that, while children in **high-conflict** marriages were better off after divorce, many children from **low-conflict** marriages experienced adverse effects far into adulthood.[43]

It is important to distinguish between **short-term** and **long-term** effects. In one Australian study about one-third of separated parents thought that their children had been badly affected at first by the separation. However, the vast majority (87 percent) felt that the children had eventually adjusted to the situation, and three-quarters believed that the children were emotionally better off than they would have been had the marriage continued.[44]

ONE WOMAN'S STORY

After the separation the children stayed sad and upset for some months. Little by little, however, as they realised that both parents still loved them and cared for them, they settled into their new lifestyle. We agreed on a form of shared parenting and they spend lots of time with both me and their father. They have now met our new partners and their children. This has opened up a whole new world of relationships and experiences for them, things that they would not have otherwise seen. Their new lives are busy but very rich.

A balanced view

Paul Amato argued that both the conservatives and the modernists are wrong and that the truth in this debate *'lies somewhere between these pessimistic and optimistic scenarios.'* Divorce is not a trivial occurrence for children and the statistics indicate that, compared with children from intact homes, they are disadvantaged in a number of areas. However the differences *'though statistically significant, are modest rather than strong'*.

It seems to me that Dr Amato's conclusion is not only good science but also good sense:

'Many children from divorced families graduate from college, have successful careers, are happily married, and have close ties with mothers and fathers. Correspondingly, many children from two-parent families fail to achieve these goals. Although divorce increases the risk of a variety of negative outcomes, most children from divorced families reach adulthood as competent, well-adjusted citizens. This suggests that divorce and single-parenthood, although problematic, cannot be the root cause of most of our social problems. The differences are simply not big enough.'[45]

Sure, the kids were upset, but not for long. The separation brought an end to the conflict and everyone was able to relax. In the long term we were all better off and the two girls definitely happier. They've turned into wonderful young women, one a teacher and the other a senior professional assistant. They don't have chips on their shoulders and they have a good outlook on life.

Jill

Awareness

We should be aware that most children go through a time of crisis immediately after the separation of their parents. We should also be sensitive in seeing that reactions can vary between children in the same family. We must acknowledge that separation and divorce pose real risks for children in all sorts of ways. These risks can turn into serious harm if the separation is accompanied by constant conflict, crazy attitudes and actions on the part of one or both parents, lack of emotional and financial support for the children, disruption of relationships with either parent, relatives and friends, and long-running legal disputes.

Whether the children of divorce suffer *long-term* consequences is very much in the hands of their parents. The
disadvantages can be minimised if both parents cooperate to
provide them with decent living standards, a good education
and abundant emotional support. If they do not, it is an
abdication of their parental responsibility.

Conflict

We've known about the effects of parental hostility for over
twenty years. United States researchers studied the children of
separated parents some fifteen months after separation and
compared them with children from intact families.[46] They found
no significant differences in behavioural problems between the
two groups. What they *did* find was that the problems in the
children from separated families related to conflict between
the parents, little involvement of the absent parent and little
contact with the absent parent. This finding is reflected in more
recent research both in Australia[47] and overseas.[48]

In other words, children's problems often stem not from
the separation itself but from lots of nasty things that happen
between their parents before and after separation.

> **It was the nonsense that went on after separation that
> did the damage. Children can see the games parents
> play. They are not silly. False sexual allegations, Appre-
> hended Violence Orders, lengthy court hearings,
> doctors' reports – all impact on the children directly or
> indirectly. They feel something has come between them
> and their dad. They hear the things their mother says
> about their dad, they see the involvement of police,
> lawyers, doctors. In the end they think there must be
> something wrong with their dad. And so the process of
> alienation is begun. How can a young child handle this?
> It sets them up for long-term problems.**
>
> *Barry*

Points of conflict affecting children:

★ arguments at contact handover times
★ telephone bickering within children's hearing
★ negative and demeaning criticism of the other parent
★ asking a child to carry barbed messages
★ using children as a 'weapon' or a means of blackmail
★ involving children in legal disputes
★ parents being consumed by lengthy court hearings
★ refusal to allow children to have easy relationships with the absent parent
★ refusal to provide adequate financial support for the children

Being honest with children

In all surveys the message from the children is clear: they want to know what's going on! There is nothing to be gained from hiding things from children in a vain attempt to spare them hurt and disappointment. Better to come clean, answer questions, console and allay fears.

A 1994 survey of 4000 Victorian children indicated that children are not as concerned about divorce as they used to be ten years ago. There is anecdotal evidence that children these days are coping much better with the separation of their parents. As divorce becomes more prevalent and attitudes to it become more positive, its effects on children may be less pronounced.[49] What will become more widespread is the acceptance that marriage is not the only way, that many marriages are not for ever, that there are other lifestyles which are equally useful and satisfying.

Reflection

I believe that there is no evidence that separation *in itself* leads children to delinquency, crime, substance abuse, suicide and failure in relationships and occupation. There are studies, how-

ONE MOTHER'S STORY

It's been a tough two years because of the ongoing court proceedings and the tension that has caused. But despite that the children have coped well in their different ways. The youngest was given to bouts of anger and insecurity but he seems to be over that. The older ones have been forced to grow up and to take on too much responsibility, and I feel guilty about that. Sometimes it's hard to strike a balance between telling them what's going on and not putting too many burdens on them. They seem to be performing well at school and I don't have great fears for their future. They are not cynical and appear to be maturing nicely with an increased understanding of human nature. Throughout all of this their father and I have been at pains to show them that, despite our differences, we both love them and that they are the most important people in the world.

ever, that point to significant risks and disadvantages for children of separated parents, especially in the short term.

Statistics do not tell the whole truth. While it is important not to exaggerate the effects of divorce on children,[50] we should be careful not to underestimate the real suffering that can be inflicted on them at the time of separation and beyond. They can go through times of intense sadness and depression, particularly if there is hostility between their parents and if their contact with one parent is disturbed. Often the adults are so preoccupied with their own practical and emotional survival that there is little energy left for the children and *their* grief. Some parents lean too heavily for support on their children. Long-running legal disputes add to their insecurity. If this pattern is allowed to continue, there are real dangers for a child's emotional wellbeing, self-esteem, happiness and trust.

I am convinced of three things. One, bringing up children in a happy stable family is an ideal situation. Two, it is not always possible and sometimes divorce is necessary. Three,

THE BIG PICTURE

A conference of twenty experts in Virginia in 1994[51] agreed on the importance for children of the following factors in post-separation adjustment:

- an awareness that there are problems for children after separation but that the majority develop normally
- the psychological health of the child prior to separation and that of both parents
- ongoing conflict between the parents
- the attitudes of the parents to their separation and to each other
- economic security
- supporting relationships with both parents and with relatives and friends
- mediated rather than court-driven dispute resolution

The message is: if you cut out the conflict, and support them emotionally and financially your children will survive, adjust and grow up healthy and normal individuals. What affects children most is what they see happening between their parents. So remind yourself that parental tension and conflict will have a damaging effect on them.

Things parents can do for their children to soften the effects of separation:

- ✔ Keep them fully informed about what's going on.
- ✔ Encourage quality contact with both parents.
- ✔ Keep the children in touch with their grandparents, extended family members and others close to them.
- ✔ Recognise your own negative attitudes and behaviour and eliminate these
- ✔ Assure the children by word and action that you love and care for them.
- ✔ Keep disagreements and conflict well away from them.
- ✔ Settle legal and personal disputes as quickly as possible and by counselling and mediation rather than at court.
- ✔ Give the children a decent home with both parents contributing to proper and generous financial support

there *is* such a thing as a good divorce with happy and successful outcomes for both children and parents.

My contacts with children of separated parents indicate that they are not only coping but flourishing. Most divorced parents and their children are getting on with their lives and living happily and successfully. Children can survive separation. It's not an easy time for them, but growing up is not an easy time for any child, and for some – even in stable families – it is especially difficult.

The message from all this is not to urge parents to hang on to a barren and sterile marriage, nor to put up with violence or abuse, even for the sake of the children. The message is that parents should recognise that sometimes divorce is inevitable and that it is not bad, nor a failure, but can be good. I do not agree that 'no-fault' divorce makes things too easy. The vast majority of couples come to it after a long period of soul-searching and agonising worry. It is not a lighthearted or trivial decision.[52] It is no indication that separated parents care more about themselves than about their children. In all parenting, surely there must be a balance between two extremes: *overparenting* (family life revolves around the children and the parents have no individual lives) and *parental selfishness* (the children fit in with the adults). Men and women, as well as children, are entitled to happy and fulfilling lives. They ought not be expected to live in miserable relationships.

QUESTIONS	POSITIVE THOUGHTS AND RESOLUTIONS
What are the stresses I should look for in my children?	I will not brush lightly over the pain in my children.
What can I do to lessen the impact of divorce on them?	I will be sensitive to their concerns.
How can I assure them of my love and support?	I will be honest with them and encourage their mother to be the same.
What steps can I take to soften their worries?	I will not cause conflict.
How can I reduce conflict between their mother and me?	I will strive to be involved in their lives.
	How can I increase my involvement in their lives?
	I will do everything in my power to stay in touch.
	I will be generous in my support of them.

If you compare yourself with others, you may become vain and bitter; for always there will be greater and lesser persons than yourself.

Desiderata

5

Residence and Contact

I had everything going for me. We both worked but I had an easier job and I had definitely been the principal carer. When she left home to live with her boyfriend I had sole custody for two years. The kids were happy to live with me and to visit her. It was all working really well. Then she decided she wanted custody and went to court. My barrister was confident and the case went well. The shock came in the judge's decision: against all the evidence he simply decided that their mother was the natural carer and that the kids would be better off with her. I had to hand them over. They were four and six at the time. They were confused and upset. I was devastated.

David

It has been said that children can survive with the support of one significant person. That's as useful as saying a person can get by with one arm! But children can *thrive* if they have the support of both parents. There is no doubt that the loss of a parent can damage a child. This is especially true if the relationship has been strong prior to separation.

The fact is that, along with their strong bonds with their mothers, *children love their dads!* In the wash-up of divorce and separation this truth tends to be forgotten or obscured. Children are desperate to hang on to a strong and healthy relationship with each of their parents.[53] The present system of sorting out parenting arrangements after separation makes that difficult and often destines it to failure.

> **It was heartbreaking. I could feel the boys drifting away from me. With all the trauma of the court proceedings, psychiatric reports, breakdown in contact arrangements, they were not comfortable with me any more. She was obviously saying lots of negative things about me and these would tumble out from time to time.**

Terry

Loss of the link

The most serious problem for separated men and their children is the loss or diminishment of a meaningful relationship. To some degree, the extent of the problem for both fathers and children can be seen in the statistics. They reveal that up to half of Australian non-custodial fathers have no contact with their children.

Research results

A 1993 report by the Australian Institute of Family Studies revealed some alarming figures.[54] Only one-quarter of the men registered with the Child Support Agency were happy with the custody and access orders to which they were subject. Some 30 percent of fathers wanted custody of their children, 42 percent wanted more access, and a staggering 50 percent were not in contact with their children! The Institute's conclusion: the unfortunate reality is that the non-custodial parent often withdraws from the life of the child.

In another Australian study, published in 1992, while 64 percent had 'regular' access to their children, only 48 percent had overnight access. About 13 percent had 'holiday' access, i.e. one long visit every three months. Another 8 percent had little access, and 15 percent had no access at all.

Only 30 percent of fathers were satisfied with their access arrangements. 53 percent were not satisfied. Some 73 percent wanted more access to their children, but 32 percent of men claimed that there was nothing rewarding about being a non-custodial father and some found it 'devastating'.

Also, 76 percent of the separated men surveyed rated their relationships with their ex-spouses as poor, and reported situations of conflict, anger and arguments.[55]

A report in 1992[56] revealed that about half the children surveyed saw their fathers less than six times per year or not at all. The most recent figures show that 30 percent of children under 17 see their absent fathers only once a year or never. This means that about 300,000 children have no real relationship with their fathers.[57]

Let's look briefly at the US scene. Earlier research in the United States was not encouraging. It showed that 30 percent of children from separated families never saw their fathers. Around 60 percent saw them several times a year or less. Only 25 percent were seeing their fathers weekly or more often. But more recent US research showed a marked improvement over a ten year period, with two-thirds of American fathers in fairly regular contact (at least fortnightly) with their children, and an increase in joint parenting arrangements. This reflected the US trend towards joint custody, also evident in most American family legislation.[58]

Involvement

Contact is one thing, real involvement is another. Research has revealed how fathers' level of involvement with their children falls in the years after separation.[59]

Level of involvement:

★ only one-third of fathers were still involved in the major issues of their children's lives (discipline, health, holidays and the like)
★ only half were still involved in events that were significant in their lives (Christmas, birthdays, school, sports, etc.)
★ about two-thirds of contact fathers talked to their children, cuddled them, played games with them and watched television with them
★ only 55 percent reported good communication with their children

This means that – for whatever reasons – fathers and children are missing out on knowing one another. Research here and overseas demonstrates loss and maladjustment in children who lose contact with the absent parent.[60] More positively, a recent study has demonstrated the real benefit for children of 'authoritative parenting' by their non-custodial fathers.[61]

Why contact is lost

The truth is that after separation a substantial number of fathers go away, stay away or are forced away from their children. In some cases it must be their own fault. In many cases it isn't. Regardless, I believe a good proportion of these cases are preventable. Problems in access almost inevitably occur immediately or very soon after separation. I am sure that a more enlightened family law system, better educated parents and more resources for early intervention would result in keeping more fathers and children together.

There has been little research into the reasons why many fathers after divorce lose contact with their children.

Some reasons why fathers lose contact:

★ the separated man feels *marginalised* as a father when the court, counsellors and his ex-wife minimise his worth for his children

★ he does not care, won't pay maintenance, takes no interest

★ he is poor, unable to pay and withdraws

★ he meets rejection, is unable to cope and stays away

★ he finds contact difficult, receives no support and gives up

★ he feels incompetent as a *hands-on* parent

★ one of the parents moves to a distant town or State

★ one or both parents repartner and create new families which absorb their attention and energies

★ the custodial parent obstructs or destroys the relationship

A study of divorced fathers in Scotland and Canada revealed that all the *disengaged* fathers actually wanted contact with their children. They had been discouraged from contact by a variety of factors including obstructive ex-wives, antagonism and tension created by the adversarial legal system, and a perception that the little contact they had with their children was superficial and meaningless. Many fathers believed that shared parenting was the only custodial arrangement that would allow them to maintain a meaningful relationship with their children.[62]

US research indicates that the frequency of access diminishes through time, distance, remarriage and age of children. The same study shows clearly that conflict between parents always spills over into the parent–child relationship in ways that are detrimental to the child.[63]

All these studies present a sad picture.

My ex-wife and I tried to tell the children why we were separating. But they didn't understand and were terribly

> upset. Then we took them to my apartment and showed
> them where I was going to live, and explained the new
> arrangements to them. This seemed to take away the
> mystery and they settled down pretty quickly after
> that.
>
> *Lance*

The importance of contact

It is critical that separated men and women realise just how important it is for their children to maintain contact with each parent, in particular the absent one.[64] Studies have shown that up to a third of custodial parents do not consider it necessary or worthwhile.[65] There is little doubt that a custodial mother's attitude can make or break it.[66]

However, it is not always the mother's fault. Many men simply do not adjust to their new lives and the changes in their relationships with their children.[67]

What about the children?

Many children are extremely confused about the separation and divorce of their parents and are unable to make sense of what is going on. Their parents may not be honest with them or may give them conflicting explanations. Some parents have no idea of what is going on in the minds of their children. They fail to see and understand their needs.

Children want to stay on good terms with both parents. They also want to hang on to *all* the other relationships that have been important to them – grandparents, uncles and aunts, friends, etc. There is overwhelming evidence that free or regular contact is the access arrangement most favoured by children.[68]

They want to see that both parents care enough about them to put aside their differences and make contacts work.

THE BIG PICTURE

Contact with both parents is vital for stable and happy children. In one study, 60 percent of children said that although they were seeing their absent parents, they would like more contact. The overwhelming majority in healthy access situations said that what they liked most about their separated parents was that each was loving and caring – that is, each displayed positive personal characteristics.[69]

American research has shown that children who have contact with the absent parent are more likely to have happy, balanced and positive outlooks. A meaningful relationship between children and the separated father is not only good for the children but also has a positive effect on the father's adjustment to his divorce.[70]

Another US study revealed that while none of the children in their study welcomed the separation they all wanted to maintain contact with the absent parent, and *the happiest were those who could bicycle between the two homes.*[71]

Surprisingly, recent surveys have shown that children are more concerned about *contact* than about where they live.

Both my ex-wife and I went through a lot of grieving. We saw the separation as a loss. There was a sense of things gone wrong. My father's death at the same time compounded the grief. My wife and I continued to communicate very honestly. We shared the experience and pain with the children. We did not hide things and emotions from them. They were ten and thirteen at the time. They were great. I am convinced that it gave them a healthy attitude to the separation and to our relationships.

Frank

The absent father

Most children of separated parents complain that they do not see their absent fathers often enough.[72] They resent their mothers' attempts to weaken the relationship. They are deeply saddened by the failure of their fathers to keep appointments or to turn up on time.

Many custodial mothers do not see the value of maintaining a relationship between father and children. However, there are also complaints from custodial mothers that fathers are not bothering to see their children on a regular basis. Indeed many mothers who believe that their children have not adjusted to the separation blame this on the fact that they are seeing little of their fathers.[73]

The situation most commonly reported by mothers was the husband who had left home to live with another woman and whose visits to his children were infrequent, irregular, cancelled or postponed.

Do such men appreciate what this neglect means to their children?

The removal of fathers

For the separated man it is often a battle against being *sidelined*, or cut out of his children's lives and they from his life.

In the current climate it is just too easy for this to happen. He is prevented from joining in their activities, from being involved in decisions that affect their lives, from having any influence on their development, from knowing about their welfare. Often he is seen as unimportant to them. In most cases there is little chance that his children will live with him.

Residence

The extent of his involvement will depend in large measure on where the children live. Strictly speaking *residence* is not the same as *custody*. Under the old law, custody carried with it the care and control of the children. Under the amended *Family Law Act 1975* (Cwlth) a *residence order* simply spells out where the children will live. Anything more about their management ought to be the subject of separate orders[74] which encourage some form of shared parenting. In the great majority of cases, however, the reality remains that the custodial parent exerts the major influence on the children.

The Family Court

Fathers, even those with meritorious cases, have not been hugely successful in gaining the 'residence' of their children. The traditional pro-mother bias in the Family Court and its judges is alive and well. Don't believe anybody who trots out the hoary old chestnut that 30–40 percent of men gain custody of their children. It's nonsense! The truth is that in **contested** custody hearings – they are the ones that go down to the wire and are decided by a judge – less than 40 percent of men win. If you think about it, that is not a good result. That figure encompasses men who not only had an extremely strong case but who also had the nerve, tenacity, courage and money to take the fight to its end. You would therefore expect a much higher success rate.

The figure that really brings home men's lack of success in the custody stakes is that only about *one in six* men who apply for custody of their children eventually gains it. That means that most simply give up, either by settling the case in favour of their ex-wives or through lack of money to pursue it.

We cannot expect a big change in attitude to happen quickly. After all, the judges are simply reflecting the traditional prejudice in society that women are the natural carers and nurturers of children. Given generations of men at work and women at home, this has not been surprising in the past. However, things have changed dramatically. Society and the courts have yet to recognise this change.

 ONE MAN'S STORY
When my ex-wife announced that our marriage was over, she expected me to leave the house and the children with her. This expectation reflected a belief which I feel is commonly held: the belief that mothers are sacred . . .

What underpins this belief is the view that a father couldn't possibly love his children as much as a mother and that he should be able to go for long periods of time without seeing his children, particularly after separation. It also asserts that a father couldn't possibly provide the same level of care for children as a mother – it is the primary role of a mother to raise children . . . It is as though the act of childbirth has magically endowed a mother with knowledge and emotions that a father could not possibly hold or attain. Thus children should reside with their mother.[75]

*   *   *

If gender equality means anything, then under normal circumstances children of a divorce have a right to a relationship with both their parents, not to a relationship with one and a visit from the other.[76]

It is time for a challenge to the usual court orders – residence of the children to the mother and fortnightly access to the father – and the *Family Law Reform Act 1995* provides a springboard for this challenge. *Arrangements for shared custody and joint parenting should be installed as the norm.*

Benefits of joint custody:

★   it involves the children spending large slabs of time in each home

★   the parents share authority and involvement in the children's lives

★   it can be made to work even in situations that are not conflict-free

★   it empowers children – to be free to grow in healthy relationships with both parents and with others important to them

★   it empowers mothers – to develop social and financial independence and to avoid the *victim mindset*

★   it empowers fathers – to create more meaningful relationships with their children and to remain responsible parents

★   it gives everyone time to do their own thing and grow as individuals

★   it shows children that their parents are decent, caring people

---

An American approach

In the United States educational workshops are run for separated parents assisting them to set up a 'two-home' system of joint custody.[77]

The system has been made to work even for parents who have little communication. It has been found that younger children always prefer the two-home alternative.

One child who was asked what he saw as the ideal situation for children of separated parents replied: *'Two homes with no fighting.'*

After divorce 'the traditional one-home settlement with one parent consigned to the sidelines'[78] must be laid to rest. But in Australia this sidelining of the non-custodial parent is entrenched. Consequently many fathers are crying out for recognition as *parents* and not as *visitors*. And their children are crying out for a meaningful relationship with their fathers. One wonders if the critics of joint custody have ever bothered to ask children about it – or indeed the many parents for whom it is working well.

> **About a year ago, my daughter told me that she had a friend whose parents were also divorced. This child used to live one week with her mother and the other week with her father. Both of my children thought this would be a good idea. So I filed an application in the Family Court. My ex-wife strongly opposed it. The counsellor's report stated that it could not work as there was too much conflict in the relationship. I don't know where this came from because my wife and I hardly saw or spoke to each other.**
>
> **I then obtained separate representation for the children. Their lawyer reported that both children were in favour of the idea and reported no conflict. However the court-appointed psychologist (a female) recommended that there be no change in the contact arrangements. The judicial registrar spoke to us both about the 'psychological damage our continuing conflict was having on the children'. The only real conflict was in court and my wife's opposition to shared parenting. I am convinced that she was against it because she did not want to lose out on child support. I had no legal representation and I felt completely out of my depth. So I simply gave up.**
>
> *Allan*

Allan's lack of faith in the court is well supported by other cases, all of which turned on the judge's (and counsellor's) easy acceptance of mothers as the *natural carers* of children, despite clear evidence in favour of the fathers.

My case was difficult for the court to decide – there had been no violence, in fact we were both complimented by the judge on our parenting and at no time did my wife hold that I was an unfit father. The court had made interim orders for joint custody and we had shared the children on a week-about basis for the 13 months before the final hearing. Apart from the occasional hiccup, the children were coping well. But this arrangement did not suit my ex-wife. Spurred on by her lawyers she asked the court to give her primary care and residence. She won, I lost. Now I'm making do with three weekends a month. That's better than most but not as good as it could be.

Carlos

Attitudes to joint custody

Despite the emphasis on joint parenting in the Family Law Reform Act, true joint custody is still regarded with suspicion by many judges, counsellors and parents. The problem is that judges and counsellors do not see or hear of the success stories: they only come into contact with failed arrangements. Most mothers have never seen true shared parenting in action.

Some argue that this type of flexibility is not in the best interests of the children, that they need stability and that frequent changes of homes will upset them. In any case, they say, it could only work in totally cooperative parenting situations. I do not agree. I believe that the majority of children from separated families will always prefer some form of shared parenting and that it can work so long as parents agree to follow some basic rules.

The usual court orders of sole custody to the mother and visiting rights to the father, no matter in what terms they are now dressed up, do not benefit mothers, fathers and children. Sole custody limits women socially and in the workplace. It disadvantages them financially, intellectually and emotionally. It places too heavy a burden on them. It does not involve men sufficiently in family responsibilities, nor allow them to share the burden.[79]

The American experience

Most American family legislation introduced provisions for joint parental responsibility in the late 1980s and early 1990s. Lawyers, social workers and parents have been involved, and over the last decade there has been a definite movement towards cooperative parenting arrangements. Programs of counselling and mediation have been designed which have resulted in separated parents signing parenting agreements that involve various forms of joint custody. These have been shown to work even in cases where the parents had been in conflict and there were serious difficulties in access.[80]

The results:

★   many American children now spend roughly equal periods with the two separated parents

★   the parents agree to make joint decisions about the major issues in their children's lives

★   in situations of conflict the parents agree to abide by a set of rules which provide for dispute-resolving mechanisms

★   surveys point to a high success rate[81]

★   most children prefer substantial contact with both parents

★   many professionals are now convinced that joint parenting is the fairest option for all parties and that the old system of sole mother custody is shortsighted[82]

Reassessing joint custody

The Family Law Reform Act separates *parenting orders* from *residence orders* and emphasises *parenting plans*. It thus provides a framework for joint custody. It offers hope to fathers who desperately wish to be more involved in the upbringing of their children because it insists that both parents have parental responsibility for children under eighteen.

A Father's Plea

I know my children need me more than I need them. They love me and I love them. I may not be able to express this in convincing ways, but I know that I can show them. I am convinced that, with all my faults, I have a lot to offer them. I do not want to prise them away from their mother or diminish her in their eyes. I simply want them to know that they have two parents who care for them. This means two parents who share responsibility for them and who both make the decisions that affect their lives. This cannot be achieved in a couple of days every fortnight. It needs time.

Children need security. But security ought not be confused with stability and inflexibility. The security that children need is the security of knowing that they are loved by **both** parents. This can be effected in both homes and in different ways.

It is to be hoped that professionals in this field will move away from negative attitudes such as 'It won't work' or 'It's too difficult' or 'It's no good for the children'. The fact is that it has not been tried on a large scale. What needs to be developed is a pilot program of education, counselling and mediation through which a group of parents will be encouraged and assisted to work out a plan for the continued parenting of their children. This plan will involve the children spending large periods of time with each parent. This program should be conducted by a team of professionals over a period of several years, with appropriate review.

Fathers who are applying to the court for a form of shared parenting should present evidence from a psychiatrist or counsellor who supports joint custody, and from a mother and father for whom it is working successfully. These people exist!

- ✔ Get some help and work out a parenting plan
- ✔ Make sure it provides for real involvement in your children's lives
- ✔ Be interested in your children at home, at school and elsewhere
- ✔ Be as cooperative as you can
- ✔ Let your ex-wife know that you want to help her
- ✔ If difficulties arise, read chapter 13 or get help
- ✔ Call it joint or shared parenting
- ✔ It should always mean more than fortnightly contact
- ✔ If in court, call evidence to support your case

Creating better arrangements for the children

Mind you, it's happening already to a limited extent. Many couples have avoided the lawyers, counsellors and court and have simply worked out for themselves practical and workable plans for the parenting of their children.

> As for custody of the children (ten and thirteen at the time of separation) we retained the family home and one of us moved out, rotating according to a prearranged schedule. This worked well for a year and a half. Then, because of financial problems, we sold the house and each of us established a new home. The children then rotated between homes. At times this has not

been easy for the children but they adjusted and overall it has worked out well.

Paolo

My new wife and I each had children from our first marriages. Thankfully we both had amicable relations with our ex-partners. The children spent a week or a month at each home – normally we did not mix the families. This worked pretty well until they got older and other involvements complicated arrangements. So changes were made. However, they all know they have this home to come to if they wish, and they do come.

Jeremy

The Family Court and contact

The court's attitude to access or contact is disadvantaging children and their fathers. The usual orders in the Family Court of Australia are that the children reside with their mother and have contact with their father every fortnight and for half the school holidays. These orders are often made without any real examination of the needs of the parties, without exploring alternatives, without any mediation and without consulting the children.

Such orders can be a giant cop-out by lawyers, counsellors and judges. Plans involving more generous contact between children and fathers are generally not presented as viable alternatives. It is disturbing to see some parenting plans providing only for fortnightly access.

As the kids were being neglected and allowed to run wild, I fought for custody. They told the counsellor that they wanted to live with me but she wrote in her report that this was 'through pressure from the father'. Despite the fact that my ex-wife said in evidence that if she had her way I'd only see the kids once a month, the judge found that she was the parent more likely to promote access! I was reduced to fortnightly access.

Lionel

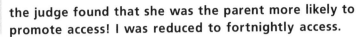

The fortnightly father

A fortnight is a long time, especially in the lives of very young children. A weekend is such a short time. It is simply not sufficient for them to build a continuous relationship, particularly if the children have no other contact with their father. Not only is he not involved realistically in their lives, he feels totally removed from his children's lives. He is effectively sidelined. This pattern of access is accepted in Australia as the norm.

It ought not be. It is not *positive* parenting at all. It equates the welfare of the children with routine and predictability.

'It's ridiculous to think that a man can be an adequate father given such restrictive access arrangements.'[83]

Why should this arrangement be considered desirable in all cases? Why should a father see his children only once per fortnight? Why not add a couple of hours in the 'off' week? One couple, without any assistance from the Family Court, did just this: the father has his daughter from Friday evening to Monday morning every fortnight, and for three hours after school every Monday of the 'off' week.

Another separated couple negotiated it this way: the father picked up the children after school on Fridays and returned them to school on Monday mornings. This avoided confrontation with his ex-wife, provided her with a whole weekend to herself, and came at a logical break-point in everybody's week. It also avoided the sad, empty feeling experienced by some fathers after the Sunday evening 'drop-off'.

Many separated fathers that I talk to are no longer content to accept being sidelined. They are insisting that they have more to do with their children and a lot of them are being successful. Whether by personal negotiation with their ex-wives or through mediation or even in the Family Court, they are breaking out of the traditional *fortnightly* mould. It is encouraging to hear of some judges making more enlightened contact orders.

> I had been a really involved father and when we separated there was no way in the world that I was going to cop the once-a-fortnight nonsense. I mean, the kids are only six and seven: what kind of relationship would we have if I saw them once every two weeks? She wouldn't agree, so I took this and other things to court. After a lot of hassles the lawyers sorted out a plan whereby I could have the children every weekend. While she is not working this is okay for her. If she gets a job we'll have to have another look at it. But whatever happens I'll never agree to being just a fortnightly father!
>
> *Shane*

There should be much more flexibility, more imagination and more courage in working out patterns of contact that suit parents and children. Children are much more tolerant and adaptable than professionals like to imagine. They can take a certain amount of disturbance, particularly when it means that they are staying in touch with the two most important people in their lives.

Schools and the non-custodial parent

Nowhere is the sidelining of the father more obvious than in the attitude of schools to non-custodial parents. They have been excluded from school functions, prevented from involvement in their children's class activities and refused school notices. Up till recently it has been all too easy for a custodial mother (with or without the help of the Family Court) to persuade a school principal that a father has no right of contact with his children on school premises.

It is time that the Family Court dealt firmly with this

manipulation and that schools developed acceptable protocols that allow both parents to have reasonable involvement in their children's schooling.[84]

Bettina Arndt, the well-known author and commentator, says:

> The shoddy treatment of many non-custodial fathers by the schools is a disgrace, an indictment of a society which lost sight of the very obvious emotional and economic benefits for children of maintaining relations with both parents. Instead the court and the schools have been led astray – by two decades of misguided social policies based on distrust and suspicion of men and excessive promotion of the rights and virtues of mothers.[85]

Authoritative parenting

The moral of all this is that separated fathers must do their best to sort out with their ex-wives a pattern of residence and contact which ensures that they remain part of their children's lives and which fosters good relationships.

They must then develop an 'authoritative parenting' style. It is this form of parenting that Dr Paul Amato has found to result in positive outcomes for the children of separated families. His research indicates that frequent contact and good fun are not enough. Emotional bonding and positive parenting are what counts. When children feel close to their fathers, they do better at school and have less behavioural problems. They continue to need their fathers as they grow and develop.

'Authoritative parents provide a high level of support to their children, as reflected in warmth, responsiveness, everyday assistance, and instruction. These behaviours facilitate children's development by conveying a basic sense of trust and security, reinforcing self-concepts of worth and competence, and promoting the learning of practical skills.

'Authoritative parents also provide a moderately high level of control, as reflected in setting rules for children, monitoring their behaviour, and dispensing discipline when children misbehave.

Parental control is harmful, however, if it is enforced with coercive punishment, such as hitting. The combination of high support with a moderately high level of noncoercive control – authoritative parenting – is the parenting style that best predicts children's positive development.'[86]

Some commentators have interpreted Amato's findings to mean that frequent contact between fathers and children is not important. This is simply not true. Indeed Amato comments that traditional contact arrangements are so limited that they allow most separated men only superficial relationships with their children. He suggests that *'shared parenting within the context of a parenting plan may not only provide better opportunities, but also increase men's motivations to be good parents.'*

Both I and my ex-wife are better persons. We've created independent identities. We are two responsible persons and our daughter sees us as such. I have changed as a father and a man. I am less driven by corporate goals. I am driven by what I think is right.

Jack

QUESTIONS	POSITIVE THOUGHTS AND RESOLUTIONS
★	★
What am I doing to be a better father to my children?	I'll fight for real involvement with my children.
★	★
How am I trying to make their time with me more enjoyable?	I'll insist on a practical parenting plan.
★	★
What have I done to get to know them as individuals?	I'll be in contact more than once a fortnight.
★	★
How am I showing that I appreciate their qualities and interests?	I'll try to improve relationships with my ex-wife and children.
★	★
What have I said to show them that I think positively about their mother and about our separation?	I'll remind myself of the value of contact for the children.

Neither be cynical about love; for in the face of all aridity and disenchantment it is perennial as the grass.

Desiderata

6

Making Contact Work

It was a stormy time. There were periods of extreme loneliness and despair. Some pain is still there several years on, but I can manage it. I see men in a lot of pain. We all have a certain amount of emptiness in us. We try to fill it with material things, sex, drugs. We have to learn to live with it. It's okay.

Adrian

The separated male needs to *redefine* himself as a man and as a father. In other words he has to accept that his new situation means that he is going to be a *different* kind of father – still a father, yes, but somewhat different from the father he was before. He has to forge new relationships with his children and discover ways to maintain and deepen those relationships. He also has the opportunity now to think about his manhood in isolation from his family.

Sorting out your place in your children's world after separation does not come easily and takes much effort, trial and error. Many fathers are unsure of their new role and are not confident about how they should go about it.[87]

It is important, after separation, that you do not lose your confidence as a father.

Self-esteem is vital for all parents and this is doubly true for the separated parent. It is essential that a father feel positive about himself in order to bring up his children as competent and confident individuals.

Recipe for success in contact:

★   be confident of your value for your children
★   redefine yourself as a father and accept your new role
★   don't waste time and energy in recriminations
★   accept that your situation has changed
★   be a reliable father
★   be a competent father
★   talk to men with similar experiences

> The separation has been good for me. I've been recon-structed. I have taken a different path and my whole world has changed for the better. At the time of my divorce my father died and I changed jobs. This was a triple crunch. But with effort and counselling and time I coped and came through it. It has all been for the best. I feel confident as a father and I know my children regard me as a good father.
>
> *Simon*

In your role as a separated father, try to throw off the feeling that you are odd or strange. Though separated from your children you can still have a positive relationship with them, as good and as strong as that enjoyed by many fathers at home. It will be different and have its difficulties, but what relationship doesn't! Remember that there are thousands of fathers in a similar position to you.

Recriminations

A reasonable attitude to your children's mother is important. Some separated fathers consider that they have been robbed of daily contact with their children, and spend all their lives blaming their ex-wives. Though understandable in some cases, this is a negative and unfortunate way of looking at their situation.

Recent Australian research has found that almost all the separated men interviewed had strong feelings for their children and wanted to be near them. About 13 percent complained that the loss of their parenting relationship was one of the worst things that had happened to them.[88]

We all sympathise, of course, with the men who have been ordered out by their wives and have to watch other men take their place. There is a double resentment there: not only do they hate losing their full-time parenting role but they suffer the indignity of losing it to, they feel, an impostor. Anger and bitterness in such cases are understandable – but only for a time. It will do them and their children no good at all if they persist in recriminations rather than accepting the new situation and pressing on with redefining their status as a father.

When I heard that the children had been on a holiday with their mother and her new man, I was plunged into depression and anxiety. I guess I was jealous, and I feared it would mean that I would lose the children. But that did not happen. The kids took it more calmly than

I did and told me that he was nice to them. I tried to
tell myself that that was the important thing.

Jamie

Change

The key is being prepared to change. If you can accept the
challenge to change, then recovery from divorce is possible.[89]
     You might begin the process of change by telling yourself
with conviction that you are still your children's father, no
matter how vulnerable you feel and how fragile you consider
your status to be. Don't forget that life will not be a bed of
roses for your ex-wife, either, whether or not she has a new
man. Bringing up the children alone or with another man is
going to prove a very difficult occupation. She will experience
confusion, frustration, anger and exhaustion. Instead of feeling
sorry for yourself feel just a little bit for her!
     Your enforced isolation brings you the luxury – probably
for the first time – of being able to think about your role as
a parent and to identify the changes that are necessary to make
you a good separated father.

It's been two years now. I think I am a better person
but sometimes I wonder. Old patterns seem to surface,
especially when I try to communicate with my ex-wife.
As far as change goes, I've started to look after *me*. The
sense of relief after separation was liberating, but I'm
at a stage now of pondering my future.

Ray

**It's even possible that you can be a better part-time father
than you were a full-time one.** It's a matter of attitude and
organisation. Develop a positive attitude to yourself as a father,
and be willing to organise contact with your children so that
you share worthwhile and enriching experiences. The latter we
will discuss in the next chapter.

It has been for the best. The children are thriving and so are my ex-wife and I.

Leo

Your worth as a man

Do you value yourself as an individual person, as a man? Perhaps working on your sense of manhood will strengthen your confidence in yourself as a father. Remind yourself that you are not just an appendage of a family. You are firstly a man with your own place and purpose in the world. Contact with men's groups is a good way to deepen your awareness of these issues.

Your worth as a father

You need to do more than to convince yourself of the value of your changed role as a separated father. You must try to convince your children and others, particularly your ex-wife if she is open to it. If you and your ex-wife are not getting on well, it is important that you remind one another that reducing your conflict will greatly assist your children to cope with your separation.

Life has been busy since we separated. I wondered how each of us and the children would cope with the shared custody arrangement and the movement between homes. I discovered that looking after the kids was not as bad as I thought it would be. A few months down the track I asked them how it was going. They both said: 'Good. We do more things now.'

Joshua

I do feel involved in the lives of my children, but that did not happen overnight. I kept plugging away. I stayed around through a lot of problems and difficult times. I

✔ When the opportunities present themselves, talk confidently to your children about it.

✔ Tell them that you are intent on being a good father and believe that you can do it.

✔ Tell them that you are going to devote more time to them than you have ever done before.

✔ Defend yourself against attack no matter where it comes from, but do it reasonably and quietly.

✔ Answer the children's questions honestly and tenderly, but don't let them spend too much time in complaint and recrimination.

✔ Don't be mournful: be bright and positive and lighthearted, even if you don't feel like it.

✔ Let your attitude show them that you believe life is to be enjoyed and not wasted!

found ways to show my love and interest in them. I eventually achieved a good relationship with my children and my ex-wife. I gain satisfaction in being generous with them in a number of ways. I now feel confident about the future.

Terry

The competent father

Being competent as a father is part of being successful in your new role. You must turn yourself into a *competent* person. That means you have to get organised and learn how to run a home as well as how to care for your children. This will take effort at first, but after a time it will become second nature and will give you a great deal of satisfaction. After all, balancing all these demands and learning new skills is quite an achievement. On top of that, your children will admire you and will feel secure in having a competent father.

'To be competent non-resident fathers, men must have a strong commitment to the parent role, competent fathering skills, and a sense of fathering self-efficacy (that is, **a belief that what they do can make a difference).**'[90]

Giving them time

The important thing is for you to **be** with your children. You can get a lot of pleasure together out of games and videos at home. If you can, involve them in the cooking and other chores.

> **I found these times really exhilarating. We shared a lot of talk and activities. We used to do things together like cooking and cleaning. There were other times when we did nothing and just hung about.**
>
> *Stephen*

Children enjoy contact:[91]

★ when their regular activities are not disturbed
★ when they can play with other children
★ when they can talk to the access parent about life
★ when their custodial parent has a positive attitude
★ when their access parent is pleased to see them

How much **quality** time do fathers in **intact** families spend with their children? Some spend as little as fifteen minutes a day, while others spend over five hours each week.[92]

Perhaps this will give you confidence as you redefine yourself as a father. Even if you only see your children once a fortnight, you can still be an effective father.

It is handy to have some statements up your sleeve when some well-meaning relative or friend sympathises with you and says: *'You only see your children once a fortnight.'* Try the response: *'Yes, and we have twenty hours of quality time together!'* or *'Yes, and it's great that I spend more time with them now than I used to when I lived with them.'*

If you are a father whose contact is limited to once a fortnight and some part of each school holiday, then you must set aside those weekends almost exclusively for the benefit of your children, especially while they are young. You must 'fit in' with them rather than the reverse. So, things that are essentially personal to you (social life, sport, meetings and so on) should be avoided during those times.

> **I decided right from the start that every second weekend was sacred: that was my time with my son. So my new wife and I planned the year with that in mind. It sometimes caused problems for other family members and I wonder if I could have done it another way. However, given the tough time he was getting from his mother I think it was the only thing to do.**
>
> *Jack*

Time with family

Family parties, gatherings and outings are quite different, of course. They can be very good for the children by keeping them in touch with their relatives and assuring them that they are still part of a large family.

Your children should be encouraged to take their place in your normal home life, to be comfortable there and to regard it as a second home. They must also see enough of your friends and relatives to know that you are living like an ordinary social being.

The important consideration is to give your children your

time and attention and (as far as possible) to limit activities that exclude them. Their time with you is very special. Some fathers treat their children as mere 'attachments' as they do the rounds of their normal activities.

Being with your children

'Fortnightly fathers' should generally avoid using babysitters. If you are intent on leading your usual social life while the children are with you, they will feel that they don't matter a great deal to you. If you are seeing your children once a fortnight, dedicate the whole of that weekend to them.

Moreover, you *need* that time with your children and they with you. There's so much to do and say. There's a lot of listening to be done (by *you*). Depending on their ages, you may want to read them stories, or talk about school, or play games or sport with them. It takes time to cook them good meals. It takes time to watch television or videos with them, or (better still) to play cards or other games. It takes time to get to know each of them better as an individual. Give it to them generously.

You don't have to be always *doing* something. It's important as a father that you simply learn how to *be* with your children.

I had to learn how to be a father. Before separation I was pretty hopeless and really didn't know how to do it. After we separated I found that I had all this time with the kids and I just had to learn how to be involved with them. It was a real learning process and I gave myself to it. I learnt how to talk and listen to them, how to help them, how to be with them. We did not have to go out all the time. The home base was important.

Josh

You should not expect your children to come along and to fit into your life and home without disturbing it or you in any way. It can't work that way. You have to make it a life and a home for them, too, and you do that best by spending **time**.

Of course, there will be times when illness, work commitments, an extraordinary social engagement and the like will force you to cancel or modify contact or to arrange for someone to mind the children. These occasions, however, should be the exception rather than the rule.

Coping with the demands

The other important reason for dedicating contact periods to your children is simply a question of energy. To be with children, to communicate with them, to listen to them, to play with them, all takes a tremendous amount of energy, particularly if they are young. It's an intensive time and they will make big demands on you. Remember, too, that coping with yourself and them in times of trauma and difficulties uses up a lot of emotional energy. So you can't spread yourself too thinly during contact periods. You need your rest and you need to be fit!

> **I found my time with the children exhausting. Perhaps I tried too hard and was not relaxed enough. But they wanted a lot of attention and there was no way that I was going to deny them that. I was living in a suburb where there were no kids their age. TV and early nights helped.**
>
> *Gordon*

The situation may be different for those fathers who have joint custody of their children or who are fortunate enough to have more frequent and extended periods of access. In those cases the children will share their father's ordinary, everyday life to a greater extent. They will see him going to and coming from work, socialising without them, working around the home.

But fathers who have more involved parenting also need

THE BIG PICTURE

Lots of fathers have ongoing battles with contact. Some lose contact or rarely see their children. However, many men find that, if they persevere and are reasonable, the difficulties and conflict they experienced early in their separation settle down. Life is not always perfect but they have managed – through effort and generosity and perseverance – to maintain good relationships with their children. That's what it's all about!

to be careful to reserve special times for doing things exclusively with their children, whether it's going out or playing games or watching a movie or just *being* together.

Alcohol

Apart from sleep, watch your alcohol intake before and during access. A big night out on the evening before you pick up the children is not calculated to make you a kind and agreeable father! You will be like a bear with a sore head and the last thing you'll want to do is play cricket or hide-and-seek.

A sensible approach is that you drink little or no alcohol during periods of contact. You will feel better, have more energy, be more alert and patient.

Finding ways to stay in touch

There are dozens of ways most separated parents can find to stay in touch with a son or a daughter as he or she grows older. It's a matter of being sensitive, caring and unselfish, of keeping the lines of communication open.

Young children take up more of your time and energy than older ones do. As they grow older, your children will become more independent, they will amuse themselves and will seek the company of their peers. The amount of time they will want to spend with you will diminish. This is perfectly normal for older children and happens in all families. Most sixteen-year-olds have other interests and do not want to spend whole weekends with their father (or mother).

But be flexible and keep some time free so that you can be with them if they want you. Take it slowly and thoughtfully: as their needs change so do your responses, and so does the pattern of your contact.

The important thing is to make sure they are welcome at your home at any time and that there is a bed for them if they want it. Ring them weekly and follow their progress at school, university or at work. Attend their functions when you can, make a fuss of birthdays, Christmas and the like. Invite them out to dinner – at your place or at a restaurant. Take them to a movie, a sporting or cultural event, a weekend away or for a holiday.

Don't forget letters, cards and telephone calls. They are personal reminders that you are thinking of your children.

> **I was prevented for many years from seeing my daughter. Her mother had decided that it was okay for my son to see me but not my daughter, no doubt on the strange belief that girls can do without a father but not boys! I found this immensely distressing. In order to stay in some form of contact I wrote her a letter every month or so, sent them to her, and because I believed they were not reaching her I kept copies on my computer. Some years later she started to re-establish**

contact and I was able to deliver these letters to her. She was impressed and reassured.

Joseph

Getting organised

A word about younger children. Good and caring fathers can often be at a loss to know just how to keep them amused. It may be hard to decide where to go and what to do with children during contact periods.[93] The way to overcome this is through planning and organisation.

Make sure that you establish your home as a place where everyone can relax and do their own thing. If you have a comfortable home, you don't have to be a '*zoo father*' and be taking the children out all the time. They – and you – will soon get sick of that.

In the early days of your separation, before you get properly established, particularly if the children are little, the days will seem very long. You quickly exhaust your stock of games and toys and wonder what to do next. Before long they are asking when can they go home. You feel frustrated and angry.

Don't despair and don't dump them on your next-door neighbour. Get organised and use your imagination!

Some ideas:

★ Build up a good store of toys and games appropriate for the ages of your children.
★ If money is a problem, look for secondhand items from other families you know, garage sales and in the 'For Sale' columns of the newspapers.
★ Use your local library: it can be a great source of books and tapes for children of all ages.
★ Search the newspapers for holiday and weekend entertainments for children: cheap movies, special programs for children at museums, picnics, skills courses, theatres and the like.

★ Scrutinise the TV guide for suitable programs. Hire video cassettes (not as babysitters, but to watch with them!).

> We generally talked about what we would do. My daughter would suggest something one week and my son the next. It was a process of negotiation and sorting it out. Kids are often happy with simple things and at times need the company of other kids. Having personal belongings in the house is important.
>
> *Terry*

More ideas:

★ If you have a backyard, fill it with the things that young children love, such as a sandpit, swings and climbing apparatus, bikes, plastic toys, a tent.

★ Television is a great standby. Have a video ready for that time at the end of the day when the children are tired and you need time to prepare the evening meal.

★ Apart from that and their favourite programs, encourage them into other pursuits.

★ A home computer is a wonderful source of entertainment for children. Most children have access to them at school and at home. The programs can be both educational and fun, and you can avoid the undesirable or violent ones by checking them first. In terms of enjoyment and educational value they are an excellent investment.

Contact with other children

It's important for you and your children to have some contact with other families, both separated and intact. Picnics and other outings with friends provide opportunities for you and your children to relax together in normal family situations.

If you have relatives or friends with children of similar ages, your children will enjoy playing with them. But be sensitive about this: make sure it's a time that suits their parents, and don't wear out your welcome. Return the favour when you can. Don't 'sponge' on people by using them as babysitters: occupy your children by using a bit of initiative!

Contact with other children can also be organised through groups such as Parents Without Partners. Such involvement may help the struggling father with family activities for both adults and children. You can find PWOP in the phone book.

Clothes

Create a nice home for your children, with their own rooms if possible and enough of their things, games and clothes to make them feel that they are at home. This is especially important to younger children. If your ex-wife never seems to send adequate clothing with the children, don't despair and don't let it beat you! With the help of your mother, sister, partner or friend, assemble a modest wardrobe of nice clothes for each of your children. You don't need a lot and you don't have to spend enormous amounts of money, particularly if the children are young. Look for the sales and discount shops, and don't be afraid of good secondhand stuff for younger children.

When your children become interested in clothes, use birthdays and Christmas to buy them things that they will like. If they are fussy, take them with you when you buy the item. They may agree to leave these clothes at your place, but don't be silly about this! They may wish to show off to their friends at home.

Ideally there should not have to be rigid rules about what items stay at your place and what go back to Mum's. Most children like to have their clothes/books/toys near them all the time, and it saves trouble and expense if they are allowed or encouraged to move these things between homes.

Initially I found organising their clothes to be a real drag. They were always leaving things here – and I would cop a blast – or they would leave things at their mother's that they would need for the weekend. I solved it by drawing up a list and training them

to check it every time they left home. They became
very good at it.

Jeremy

Other fathers find that this does not work, particularly if
the children are not encouraged to cooperate. If you find that
things you buy for your children regularly do not come back
with them and they are left short at your place, then you may
have to insist that most of their gear remains with you. But
be generous when you can. And *never* buy into petty games
such as: *'Your mother should have sent more clothes'* or *'You'd think
she could've put something decent on you!'* Don't put that kind of
pressure on the children. It's not their fault and, in any case,
such problems are easily overcome.

A second home for your children

Apart from activities and clothes, make sure that your place
feels like a family home to your children. Hang special photos
of them on the wall (showing times you have shared), and
photos of other family members and friends.

Take happy photographs and keep them in an album for
each child as well as in your own. They will love this later on.

Being part of their lives

Make contact with your children's teachers, coaches, doctor
and so on. Make sure they know who you are, understand the
family situation, and realise that you want to be involved in
your child's life. In between contact visits, don't underestimate
the worth of a congratulatory letter or card on success at
school or sport, or to wish them well in an exam.

Being part of your life

Encourage the children's relationships with their relatives and
friends, especially their grandparents. These people are impor-

tant to them. Try to build an extended family for your children based on your own home and community. Encourage them to get to know your neighbours and their children.

Distant children

Many fathers find themselves living a long way from their children. Distance creates problems for both fathers and children and makes it difficult to maintain steady relationships. It places many separated fathers in an insufferable position, especially if their children are at an age when they really need contact with Dad. Unfortunately custodial parents and the Family Court often fail to appreciate this.

> **After we separated my wife took the children and moved to another town. If it were not for my parents I would have no contact with my children. They drive me there to pick up the children for school holidays. With the child support that I pay I cannot afford to run a car or pay for travelling expenses. I write a letter every week to my children but I never get a reply. My daughter tells me that she writes to me. When I ring I get an answering machine and no one rings me back.**
>
> *Gerald*

If there is a distance problem between you and your children, don't despair. It is not ideal but it *can* work. Sort out the access arrangements that suit you, your ex-wife and the children and stick to them conscientiously. If you can afford to, take holidays close to the children and arrange (by consent or through the court) for extensive access over that period. Maintain the continuity of your relationship by weekly telephone calls (get a court order if you need it), by letters and cards. It will take effort. Be thoughtful and work hard at it.

> **Access has been difficult because my wife moved interstate. Eventually I moved to the same city but she then**

✔ Make your place a second home for your children.
✔ Sort out clothes, toys and games.

✔ Organise your time with them.
✔ Keep them in touch with family and friends.
✔ Don't forget letters, cards and phone calls.

moved to a country area three hours away. The good thing is that I still see the children regularly and my wife is reasonably cooperative. However, I feel that I do not see them enough.

Rob

Holidays

Do a bit of planning for the school holidays. Take as much time off work as you can manage so that you can be with them. Alternatively, arrange some childminding through an agency or a relative and tell your ex-wife about it. Longer periods of contact can be exhausting but are very valuable for deepening relationships. Make an effort and take it one day at a time. Find out if your children would like any particular outings or weekend excursions and plan these together.

You will find many ways to make contact with your children more pleasant and successful. The key is to *devote* yourself to it and to get organised. It will not happen by itself. It takes a lot of effort and time. But, with that effort and time, it *does* get easier.

QUESTIONS	POSITIVE THOUGHTS AND RESOLUTIONS
★	★
How am I managing my changed role?	This is the start of my new life as a real father.
★	★
What do I do when I feel lost and full of recriminations?	It's not always easy but I'll stick at it.
★	★
What have I done to show I'm unselfish with my time?	I'll get organised.
★	★
How can I make sure that I am a competent father?	I will be dedicated: contact times are sacred.
★	★
Can I find more ways to stay in touch?	I will work on my value as a person and as a parent.
★	★
What have I done to keep my children in touch with their friends, grandparents and extended family?	I will identify problems and deal with them.
	★
	I will develop a no-nonsense attitude.
	★
	I will work out a way to sidetrack negativity and develop a positive attitude to change.

As far as possible without surrender be on good terms with all persons.

Desiderata

7

Overcoming Problems in Child Contact

With shift work, contact with the kids became more difficult. My ex-wife simply refused to cooperate. She would change arrangements at the last moment. If I complained she would hang up the phone. She refused to share the travelling so I had to pick up and deliver the kids every time. This meant round trips of over five hundred kilometres each time I had the kids. The pain, anger and frustration were continually with me. When I used to drop the children off and go to leave, my daughter would cry. I can still hear her crying out, 'Daddy, Daddy', as I drove away. My son started biting his nails. My ex-wife would ring and accuse me of upsetting the children.

Alan

Nothing causes more problems for the separated father than access to his children, or contact as it is called these days.

As with many of the subjects in this book, it is difficult to lump all situations together, because there are as many patterns of contact as there are separated parents with children. Some of them are settled by agreement between the parties. Others, regrettably, have had to be hammered out by the Family Court.

Some men are fortunate enough to have few problems in contact with their children. They and their wives are reasonable people and their children are brought up in a cooperative atmosphere. Lucky people! They are the exceptions. Unfortunately, much of the research indicates that true cooperative parenting is rare in separated families, and there is a lot of anecdotal evidence to support that.

> **I'm lucky as I have a really good relationship with my first wife and with the children. But it didn't happen by chance: we had to work on it and there were difficult times.**
>
> *Mark*

Effects on fathers

Contact is rarely easy. This needs to be said right from the beginning. Sure, there are the good and rewarding times, when everyone is happy and things are going smoothly. But more often than not, no matter how careful you are to sort out and organise contact, something will go wrong. There are a lot of separated fathers out there who are finding it tough and who are feeling guilty that they are not really enjoying access to their children. *Don't worry, you are not alone!*

> **I find access tough. I pick them up at the end of a busy week at work. I have to shop and cook their dinner. Sometimes they're tired and don't want to come. Saturday is a constant round of activities and we never**

stop. On Sunday they miss their friends but don't want to do anything about it. In all of this I feel very much alone. By Sunday night we are all exhausted and I'm relieved to take them home. But it's worth it and I'll never stop.

Colin

One Australian study reported that contact problems caused separated fathers to be sad, restless and unable to sleep. Over 50 percent of fathers claimed that contact visits were always or sometimes emotionally demanding. Most complained that the visits were too short and a lot of fathers felt that they were losing influence over their children. About three-quarters resented the loss of day-to-day contact with the children and the fact that they could not always share holidays with them. Many were still feeling hurt about the separation and almost half were sometimes or often unsure of their role now that the marriage had ended. Over three-quarters of the fathers surveyed were worried about the effects of the separation on their children.[94]

The pain

Many fathers cannot accept the loss of daily contact with their children and become desperate if they are unable to have regular access. They can become demanding and extreme in their actions: running themselves ragged by waiting to pick up the children after school (a source of embarassment to the children if it is not by agreement); calling on them at home at inconvenient times (thus annoying them and their mother); always wanting to take them out. In the end everyone becomes fed up and the situation explodes.

Some fathers find contact visits emotionally draining and painful in that they remind them of what they are missing. Contact confronts them with feelings of loss and failure. Sometimes they counter this by dropping out and staying away from their children.[95] Many men find it difficult to cope with the limitations of fortnightly contact and little in between. It's hard for them to keep up with the needs and interests of the children. Their parenting becomes superficial.[96]

> **The best thing about contact is to see my son's love, trust and acceptance of me. The worst thing is sending him back after the access period is over.**
>
> *Wayne*

Some problems and solutions

*   *I have been the breadwinner, with little involvement with my children. Now I am with them for long periods of time and I don't know what to do.*

Relax and listen to them, talk to them. Learn to *be* with them. Play with them, but leave them alone at times. Talk to other men and get ideas. Link up with other families.

*   *One of the children does not wish to go with me this weekend. He wants to spend time with a new mate.*

Take his mate with you if you can. Otherwise, persuade him that the boy can wait for another day and that you have made plans. Enlist the help of your ex-wife if this is feasible. Remember, too, that children in *intact* families often get 'no' for an answer!

*   *My daughter (or her mother) tells me at the front door that she is ill and cannot come.*

If this seems genuine, wish her lots of love and good health and withdraw gracefully. Perhaps return with flowers. If it is not, then tell them firmly but calmly that you know it is nonsense and that you are not going to allow this to go on. Talk privately to your daughter and ask her what the problem is.

*   *I have children of different ages and each wants to do something different.*

Make suggestions, ask them to compromise and decide. If it remains a constant problem perhaps you will have to make arrangements for separate contact.

* *They hate my cooking.*

Such complaints can come from sullenness or from the mischief of your ex-wife. If the food is okay, eat it and suggest that they do the same and brush off the criticisms. If it leaves a lot to be desired, do a cooking course and practise. It won't take long to learn. Ask the children for a list of their favourite foods.

* *They are cold towards my new partner.*

This will take time. Be patient and introduce your partner to the children gradually. But don't take any nonsense and don't let them be rude to her.

ONE MAN'S STORY

I moved into a two-bedroom unit. The children had their own beds but my ex-wife said that the sleeping arrangements were 'inappropriate'. She stopped my contact and I did not see my children for three months. When I rang to speak to the children she would not allow it. I went to court. I could not afford a lawyer but I had joined DADS and they helped me with the documents. I got fortnightly access. Shortly after, she tried to change it again and I had to take her back to court. Since then it's been okay. But she sometimes cons the kids into doing something else on a contact weekend and they ring me and say they can't come. She makes no attempt to 'make up' the lost weekend, so I don't see the kids for a month. I'm at the stage where I just cop it and I'm grateful for what I get.

More serious problems

There are other problems that are complex and deeply rooted. These will need more careful attention and more radical surgery. For instance, one of your children announces that she hates you and will not see you any more. Another develops behavioural problems at school which are suspected to relate to your separation. Clearly, these situations call for sensitive handling, for careful communication between you and your ex-wife, and for counselling from a good therapist. The most important thing is to identify these problems and to do something about them. Most can be solved if there's a readiness to acknowledge the problem and to get help. However, if there's a lack of willingness on your ex-wife's part or yours, then the problem will remain or, at best, will be pasted over in some way.

It may be that some problems in your relationships with your children will never be solved. Perhaps you will just have to live with them and do your best. Identifying them, thinking about them and talking to a wise friend or counsellor will all help. But in the end you may just have to accept that there are some things that you cannot change. If that sounds excessively gloomy, remember that you are not the only one in this boat and that it happens in many families.

> **For the first few weeks, every time I picked them up the children would be upset. My daughter would sob and beg me to come home. My son would tell me that there was nothing wrong between my wife and me. They were obviously being schooled by their mother. All I could do was to talk to them and to console them.**
>
> *Martin*

It happens in all families

Remember too that there are plenty of problems for parents and children in so-called 'normal' homes. There's a tendency for separated parents (and others!) to imagine that they are the only ones that have problems with their children and that it's the separation that has caused these problems. This is not always the case: children will have problems quite independently of the marital situation of their parents. They may be caused or contributed to by the separation but they may not: they may simply be the growing-up problems that they would have encountered in any case.

You just have to do your best to cope with them as they arise.

Try to develop the art of active listening in order to promote effective communication and awareness. It's up to you to try to talk gently with the child, to listen to what he or she has to say, to attempt to identify the difficulty and to do something about it. Sometimes honest, caring communication is enough; often it's not, and some form of action is required. The services of a child counsellor may be needed.

Some men find it useful to keep a journal about their contact, identifying positive and negative behaviour. This acts as a record and assists in planning reactions. Writing things down can be effective as a *slow-down, step-back and examine-calmly technique*. It may also help to seek the insights of an independent person to review the patterns emerging in the journal.

Gentle but firm

In building a good relationship with your children, attitude is all-important. Be reasonable and loving, but be firm. You do not have to take nonsense from yourself or from anyone else; you should not take it from your children. Don't be angry – or if you are, control it – and don't lose your temper.

For instance, perhaps encouraged by your ex-wife, the children might complain that you are not paying enough child support. You know that it is not true. So, after listening patiently for the sixth time, you will have to say: *'Look, Jack, what you are saying is just nonsense! You know it's nonsense and so does Jill. You are old enough to know right from wrong. I suggest that you put that rubbish right out of your head, because that's what I am going to do.'*

Behind children's anger

Sometimes behind the *'nonsense'* lies something else. Be careful to listen for the real problem so that you can identify it and deal with it. Remind yourself that children suffer in the initial stages of separation and divorce. It hurts them. It is foolish to imagine that everything's okay and they'll get over it in an instant. They *will* get over it, but only in time and with careful nurturing. In the meantime they must be allowed to express their pain and anger, their tears and disappointment. You may even have to accept a temporary rejection by one of your children. If a child is determined or adamant – and particularly if your ex-wife is not cooperative – you can't force the child to see you. Stay in touch as best you can – letters, cards, telephone calls – and the situation may pass.

> **I was really close to my daughter. When I left she thought I had deserted her and the family. She said she hated me and for three years she would have nothing to do with me. She is now coming to terms with the situation and we are seeing one another again. It will take time.**
>
> *Scott*

Conflict

There is plenty of evidence that parental conflict causes both low self-esteem and behavioural problems in children. Persistent conflict, inside and outside of marriage, can seriously disadvantage children. Poverty and lack of emotional support are also significant factors.

One study found that conflict surrounding contact harms a child's wellbeing.[97] Children can take a certain amount of conflict providing that it does not interfere with their relationships with both parents (remember, too, that no family is completely free of conflict). However, this study showed that *continuing* conflict not only makes contact unpleasant but can hinder a child's development.

Other research indicates that a majority of separated fathers experience conflict with their ex-wives at access visits. A large majority regard their relationships with their ex-wives as poor, and say that their discussions about the children are stressful and hostile.

> **The best thing about access is getting to be with the children. The worst thing is coming into contact with my ex-wife and her hostility.**
>
> *Damian*

So the message is: cut out conflict and make contact with your children enjoyable. If your wife is the source of the conflict there may not be a lot you can do. Try talking to her or ask a good friend to talk to her. Suggest counselling. Further strategies are mentioned in Chapter 11.

But if *you* are the source of the problems then there is a lot you can do. Look honestly at yourself. Analyse the situation: what things are causing the problems? In your dealings with your ex-wife are your responses reasonable? In your dealings with your ex-wife, are you breaking the cardinal rule: never fight with your wife in front of the children? Are you grilling the children? Do you need help from a counsellor or trusted friend?

The beginning or end of contact periods is no time for serious discussion between you and your ex-wife. Don't let it happen. Insist that adult discussion or dispute take place on different occasions – occasions quite separate from access. Do your best to minimise stress at contact *changeover* time. Ideally your children should look forward to coming to you and later to going home to their mother.

Violence

No matter how you feel in conflicts with your ex-wife, remind yourself that any violence or tendency towards violence on your part is not acceptable.

Even if you feel provoked in the extreme, recognise that violent reactions will ruin your contact with your children. Frustration and anger can be hard to bear (particularly if you have had contact denied or hear lies your ex-wife has told

FOR REDUCING CONFLICT

- ✔ Develop a personal stress reduction technique to assist contact.
- ✔ Rehearse positive strategies in your mind.
- ✔ Eliminate or reduce contact between yourself and your ex-wife.
- ✔ Wait for the children at the front of the house without going in.
- ✔ Alternatively, organise a neutral pick-up/drop-off address.
- ✔ Refuse to discuss problems with your ex-wife in front of the children.
- ✔ If the situation deteriorates communicate with her through a mediator or a lawyer.
- ✔ Communicate through letters (using reasonable and non-inflammatory language).
- ✔ Watch for signs of 'changeover' stress in the children.
- ✔ Diffuse these by loving talk and encouragement. Be cheerful yourself and not mournful. Be positive.
- ✔ Show your children that you have enjoyed being with them.

about you). But convince yourself that you will have to learn to deal with these feelings without physical response.

> We lived together for about six years and had one child. I did not want to separate but she made it obvious to me that she wanted me out. She was abusive and intent on provoking me to violence. I saw the family doctor who sent me to counselling, and this helped me to see that the only real option was for me to leave.
>
> *Leo*

If you are inclined to violence – even if there has been only one incident involving your wife or child – don't hesitate for a moment! Talk to a counsellor about how to manage your anger and control your responses. *Get help and get it quickly before you lose your children, their respect, your own self-respect and all hope for a decent relationship with your children and your ex-wife.*

Besides individual counselling, programs specifically designed for the treatment of persons given to violence are available in the cities and in some country towns.[98]

Marital violence is a serious problem for many married and separated women and their children. There is no excuse for men hiding their heads in the sand and pretending it does not exist or is a minor problem. It must be recognised and dealt with. It is the product of disturbed minds and attitudes. It is also seriously criminal.

There are men who suffer violence at the hands of their wives and ex-wives. If this is happening to you, seek expert help immediately. It may be necessary for you to limit or stop all contact with her – particularly if it occurs in front of the children – until she modifies her behaviour.

> **When we turned to violence I knew the marriage was over. It doesn't matter who started it and it only happened a couple of times. It told me that it was too dangerous for us to live together. We could have hurt or killed one another. On the last occasion it happened in front of the children. They were terrified. I walked out of the house the next day.**
>
> *Don*

Things you can do

Let's have a look at some contact problems that you *can* do something about, precisely because they are within your control.

But first, remember that contact is not just for you. It is principally for the benefit of your children. Nor is it a fight with your ex-wife for the love and loyalty of the children. Don't compete with your wife for their love. If you are decent there will be plenty for both of you.

Dedication

Contact is something that you can't afford to be selfish about. You must be generous and dedicated. It's often hard work, particularly at the end of a busy week in your job; you may not feel like getting in the car and driving to pick up the children. You are exhausted, or unwell, or you have not had time to shop. You would much prefer a drink and an early night with your new partner. Perhaps at this stage you have not even introduced her to your children and so you might not see her at all while they are with you. You will miss your game of golf and a dinner party with friends.

Let's face it: contact sorts out the men from the boys! The selfish separated father will turn up when it suits him and sometimes not at all. He will not allow the children to interfere with his own life. The children will have to 'fit in' to his weekend rather than the other way round. He is unreliable, unpunctual and uncaring.

Punctuality

With contact visits, regularity and punctuality are vitally important. They tell the children you care, and underscore the fact that something good between father and child is continuing despite the separation. Structure and order are important to children, helping them maintain some sense of control in a situation they often feel is out of control. This in turn promotes emotional security. Be responsible and be faithful. The children will love you for it.

> **Through all our problems my son knew one thing: he could rely on me. I never let him down. I was always there for him.**

Franco

Not only pick them up on time but get the children home on time, too! Remember, young children get tired and on a Sunday night they will look forward to going home. This is normal. It is not a sign of their disapproval of you.

Dropping off

If you have a choice between picking up or dropping off your children, choose the drop-off every time! In this way you are in control and can ensure that weary children are home at the appropriate time rather than having to rely on the punctuality (or lack of it) of your ex-wife. **Some say that the ideal arrangement is for the wife to deliver the children to you, thus demonstrating her approval of their contact with their father, and for you to take the children home, indicating your acceptance of their place with their mother.**

Respect for your ex-wife

Avoid using contact to pull your ex-wife down in the children's estimation. If you meet criticism avoid the temptation to reciprocate. There's no need to make a point of disagreeing with her ideas. If a real dispute arises handle it in a cool and gentle way. Show the children that you have your own standards, but don't ram these down their throats. With discipline, be firm and reasonable.

Allowing time for change

Don't expect too much too soon from the children. Give them time to adjust: it's a big change in *their* lives, too. Be honest with them and try to explain what has happened. Allow them to express anger and hurt and to cry. They, too, must be allowed to deal with their loss and grief. However, it won't help them to keep raking over it. What's done is done. Try to inject some positive thoughts into your discussions about your new family situation.

Spoiling the children

Be sure not to overcompensate and spoil your children. Don't allow them to take charge and don't tolerate pouting, sulking nonsense. If met at the front door with *'I won't come if you don't take me to the movies'*, you might try: *'How about we talk about that when we get home'*. But if it comes to a stand-off, be prepared to reject all forms of emotional blackmail and walk away without the children if necessary.

Don't try to *buy* your children's affection. It doesn't work! By all means show them a generous spirit. Steer a middle course: be generous at Christmas, birthdays and special occasions. Remember the occasional special treat or outing. But don't get them into bad habits.

You do not have to spend loads of money on them or plan exciting expeditions and experiences for them every time they come. Do reasonable things, enjoyable things, and sometimes stay at home. You don't have to entertain them every moment they are with you. Be honest and unapologetic about what you can afford and what you can't.

Re-establishing contact

If you have not seen your children for some time, you should do your best to restore the link. Approach your ex-wife and if it has been your fault then admit this and tell her you want to try again. Be honest about it!

Start by taking the children to a familiar or favourite place, or on an outing with familiar people. Then take them home and help them settle in.

Young children

Young children can sometimes become upset during access. This is not unusual and gentle reassurance normally fixes it. Long, tearful telephone conversations with their mother are to be avoided. If, however, the problem becomes chronic, contact the mother and take the child to her. If possible, discuss the situation with her and decide on possible strategies. Perhaps shorter visits or taking along a familiar relative will solve the problem.

✔ Remember that the whole point of contact is to foster the development of a good relationship between yourself and your children. They have more right to that than you have. It's a fragile right: abuse it and you lose it.

✔ Contact is not designed solely for your benefit, much less for your consolation. It's principally for the good of your children. So have fun and give them your time generously and without resentment. It must be a positive thing. If no one is enjoying it, work out what's wrong and change it!

✔ Try to be a person who is good to be with, fun to be with – a helpful and positive person. When your children get to the mid-teens they will decide who they are going to spend time with. Once independence is declared, they will feel no obligation to relate to *any* parent, whether absent or present.

✔ Unless you make yourself a person worth knowing, your children will choose to survive without you!

✔ As with fathers in all families, you'll have some good times and some bad times. You'll get discouraged, but don't give up. It's hard work, tough and sometimes exhausting. But in the end it's worth it and, along the way, you'll be rewarded by enough positive

experiences to convince yourself of that.

✔ You can get better at it. There are no university degrees or college diplomas in parenting. But there is learning to be gained if you are open to it. There are books, tapes, courses and talks that can teach you a lot. You can learn from talking to fathers in a similar situation.

Don't be too stressed about children's upsets or outbursts. They are not signs of rejection and should be handled with love, tact and confidence.

Remember that children sometimes suffer stress while waiting to be picked up by their mother. Deal with this gently with a lot of caring talk and encouragement. You might also find an opportunity to speak to your ex-wife about ways of avoiding the strain.

On the other hand, a young child who has been emotionally close to you will sometimes show signs of distress when she or he has to return home. Don't be foolish and crow triumphantly about this! It is not uncommon and it doesn't last for long. Rather, talk sensibly and sensitively to your child: *'Look, I know that you get upset when you have to go home. I do, too. We'll miss one another, but it's not long before you can come again, and we'll have a beaut time. Now, we must both be brave about this.'*

Older children

Encourage older children to bring their friends to stay or for special outings. Don't become unnecessarily upset if they or their mother tell you that they can't come one weekend. It's not necessarily a sign of rejection or your wife's fault: it's probably simply because they are growing up and they have other things to do.

Children of different ages

Contact can be difficult if the children are of markedly different ages. You have to adjust and compromise. There are some things that children of all ages can do together. You can also organise separate activities. Ask for suggestions and cooperation and listen to what they say. Sometimes you can organise a babysitter or playmate for one and spend time with the other.

> **Kids are different. My son likes to get up early and do things with me. My daughter likes to sleep in. I think you have to find out what they like and what they're good at. We stick to the simple things: cricket, Monopoly, wrestling, and the old-fashioned things like walks in the park, fishing and playing cards.**
>
> *Ron*

There may be situations where a separate contact visit for each child is necessary.

Meeting refusal

What do you do when you get a telephone call or you turn up at the door and your child refuses point blank to go with you? Firstly, don't panic! The situation often passes. Perhaps the child was bored on the last occasion and wants to do something else with a friend. Perhaps you have arranged something that she does not want to do. Perhaps she has had a tough week at school or an emotional upset and wants some time to herself. She might be ill or overtired.

On such occasions, resist the temptation to make a scene. The sensible thing to do is simply to say: *'Okay. I hope you'll feel better tomorrow. Is there anything you need? Give me a ring during the week. I love you a lot.'* And then turn around and walk away. Don't hassle the child.

If you can speak to the child's mother about the problem then do so. Only as a last resort should you threaten legal action, and certainly not in front of your child. Of course, if it happens too often then you have to do something about it.

Difficulties with long visits

Longer contact visits can present problems for a father. One is lack of confidence and fear as to how you'll cope, particularly if the children are very young. Such problems can be worsened by an oversensitive mother who may become concerned about such things as your living conditions, hygiene or food. Both you and the mother should develop an easygoing attitude to such fears. But be reasonable: if it's early days and there have been a few problems, understand her fears and gently allay them.

> **My ex-wife didn't want to have anything to do with me. But when I moved into the unit and our daughter started coming over for weekends, my ex-wife started to make noises about unsuitable accommodation. I set up my daughter's bedroom really nicely and she was tickled pink with it. The next time my wife dropped her off I invited her to have a look at it. She didn't want to get out of the car but her curiosity got the better of her. She had a quick look, said 'Not bad!', and left in a hurry. I've had a few complaints since, but they have been trivial and haven't worried me.**
>
> *Andy*

Special days

It's upsetting when a parent wants to monopolise the children at Christmas and birthdays. Be reasonable in working out with

THE BIG PICTURE

Don't tax yourself with unnecessary fears and worries such as: *How are the children feeling? Are they enjoying being with me? Will they come again?* You can only do your best and the rest is up to them. It's not a one-way street, and sometimes you have to remind yourself *and them* of this.

Many separated fathers fear losing their children's love. This insecurity is easily picked up by the children and is an obstacle to an easy and comfortable relationship. It smacks of dependency and indicates that the *father* needs to develop as an independent person.

Many problems are overcome with genuine love and common sense. Remember, words are not enough: hugs and kisses are important and so is lots of unselfish caring. Some fathers find it hard to express affection in tangible ways. Learn to be free and relaxed and natural in showing your children that you really love them.

your ex-wife the children's movements on these occasions. It can be a tough time for you if you cannot see your children on such occasions or if your contact is limited and strained. It's understandable that you will be sad and depressed. However, try not to get too stressed if you are without your children during these times. Tell yourself that there's more to life than the festive season.

If you are childless and at a loose end on Christmas Day, don't waste time feeling sorry for yourself: organise a lunch with relatives or friends or with other men in the same situation as yourself, or do some voluntary work helping other people less fortunate than you. Then, when the children *do* come, have your Christmas dinner – or birthday party or whatever. Children can get a kick out of having two birthdays or two Christmas dinners.

> **She would never let the children come on Christmas Day. The best I ever did was to have them on Boxing Day. I suppose it was to punish me for 'leaving' her, something for which she was as responsible as I. It was tough at first but after a time I adjusted to it and just kept their presents for whenever they turned up. There was nothing to be gained by making a fuss of it.**
>
> *Greg*

Emotional baggage

Some fathers who have not accepted and adjusted to their separation can present a pathetic picture to their children. These men spend the time complaining about what's happened to them, how they've lost their homes, how much money it's all costing them, and what a terrible person their mother is. The children may be forced to have divided loyalties – or either despise or feel sorry for them. Be careful not to load your emotional baggage on to the children. They should not have to bear such burdens.

A US study found that many divorced men fell into *victim-like* thinking. These men were preoccupied with their own needs at the expense of their children's. They displayed a contemptuous attitude towards their ex-wives and encouraged their children to be disrespectful. They were irresponsible with access and child support. They created conflict.[99]

If you come anywhere near this description, do something about it quickly! You have a duty to provide your children with emotional security. You will fail in this responsibility if you yourself are not emotionally secure and tend to *lean* or depend too heavily on them.

Try not to *need* your children too much; it's not healthy for any parent or child. In the process of moving from *victim* to *survivor* it is vital for the separated man to accept personal responsibility for himself, for what is happening in his life and for his responses to it.

Keeping your balance

Resist the temptation to spy on your children's mother through them. Avoid asking too many questions. They and their mother have the right to privacy. Your intrusions here will be seen as signs of immaturity. Be emotionally strong. Don't worry about their mother's new boyfriend (if they're happy, good on them!). The children will always acknowledge you as their father, unless you muck it up and turn them off you!

Sometimes you can take things too seriously and read too much into what the children say (*'I don't like Mum's boyfriend; I want to live here'*). Often these are passing thoughts and are better ignored. Keep it all low key and in perspective – no big deal, life goes on. Maintain your sense of humour!

> **At the beginning she said I could have whatever contact I wanted, but over time she has changed her mind and become more protective. The best part is playing with the kids and the kisses and cuddles. The worst thing is when they talk about my wife's boyfriend.**
>
> *Martin*

✔ Don't involve children in decision making that should be reserved for you and their mother, such as where they will live or go to school.

✔ Support their mother when you can and don't criticise her in front of the children. It's healthier to be as positive about her as you can.

✔ Avoid loyalty conflicts – placing children in situations where they have to take sides, yours or their mother's; the children will see right through this and will hate it.

✔ Avoid sending messages on important matters through the children: communicate directly with your wife.

✔ Insist on reasonable standards of discipline, hygiene, cleanliness and consideration in your home. The report, *'Dad lets us do what we like'*, is not something to be proud of.

✔ If items of clothing tend to be forgotten or lost, make a list of the clothes that the children bring with them. And after longer periods of access make sure that you return them with their washing done! It's not difficult to organise and their mother will appreciate it.

QUESTIONS	POSITIVE THOUGHTS AND RESOLUTIONS
★	★
What are the most enjoyable things I can do with my children?	I will listen to my children.
★	★
What activities do I know will cater for their needs?	I will identify problems with contact visits.
★	★
How have I ensured that I'm not spoiling them?	I will find someone to talk to if I am having problems adjusting to my new situation.
★	
In what ways might I be placing emotional burdens on them?	★
★	I will be loving but firm with my children.
How have I made sure that there is no violence, tension or conflict in my relationship with their mother?	★
	I will try to avoid conflict with their mother.
★	★
What things show me that I am out of balance and that I need them more than they need me?	I know we will move through this stage.
	★
	I will make sure they have a good childhood.

Speak your truth quietly and clearly; and listen to others, even the dull and ignorant; they too have their story.

Desiderata

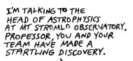

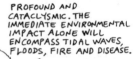

8

Your Relationship with your Ex-wife

Access has been a huge problem. I find it incredible that a government can implement a system to steal huge sums of money from the non-custodial parent but won't lift a finger to deal with the problems of access. I don't know how they can sleep. She obstructed access. I applied for legal aid but was knocked back. Four counselling sessions, four solicitors, four years and $15,000 later I have finally got basic contact orders in place. It was a fight the entire way.

Gavan

The other source of problems in your contact with your children – after yourself – is, of course, your ex-wife. Count yourself lucky if you are one of those who has the support of his ex-wife in making contact work well for all concerned. You are one of the blessed ones! No doubt your former wife is entitled to consider herself in that same category. All too often this is not the case.

Contact obstruction

In one study, 45 percent of fathers claimed that contact visits were opposed by their ex-wives and 49 percent reported frequent breakdown of contact arrangements. Some 60 percent complained of conflict with their ex-spouses on contact visits.[100] In American studies, between 20 and 40 percent of custodial mothers regularly interfered with access, and more than half admitted to it.[101] In another Australian survey, 80 percent of men described their ex-spouses as obstructive of access.[102]

Keeping an open mind

Let's assume that you have got your act into shape and are doing all you can to be a good father and a reasonable ex-husband. Problems can arise because of your ex-wife's attitudes.

Firstly, be careful not to blame her for every difficulty that appears. Some may not be her fault. Don't be alarmed, for instance, if on the odd occasion one or other of the children does not want to go with you for a contact visit. This does not always mean that your ex-wife is being difficult or that the child has a problem. It could be as simple as sickness or fatigue, a desire for solitude or even a better offer. Don't react foolishly. Take it in your stride. It may cause your ex-wife more inconvenience than it does you, especially if she has made plans. It happens in the best of families. Of course, if it occurs repeatedly then you will have to dig deeper and deal with it.

Being realistic

Don't blame your ex-wife for being *human*! She is prone to the same emotions that you are. She must be allowed to make mistakes too. You must remind yourself that being a single mother is not easy. She will have periods of intense loneliness and fatigue. She will feel vulnerable and exposed. She may have to deal with all the emotional difficulties of the children adjusting to the family break-up. Even if you are paying for her support and that of the children, she may perceive her future as extremely fragile. She may envy you your *freedom*!

Here you are, being jealous and resentful of her position – enjoying life with your children – and she sees *you* as the lucky one, the person with all the independence and time to do what he wants. Try to develop a respectful and sympathetic regard for her, appreciate what she is doing and assist her when you can and if she will allow it.

> **I see my daughter four times a week. She is still very young. My ex-wife and I have different parenting styles but we have sorted out most problems and it is working well. The Parenting After Separation course helped.**
>
> *Rick*

The uncooperative ex-wife

Regrettably there are some women who seem to derive pleasure from 'bugging' their ex-husbands. Firstly there are the 'little' problems. You turn up and the children are not ready, so you spend half an hour waiting outside in the car. She sends them in the clothes they stand up in and with nothing more. While they are with you, she telephones several times per day and unsettles them. She forgets to tell you about the birthday party they are expected to attend (with presents that you have to buy).

There are plenty of other irritants. They are the 'little' niggling and needling things that are infuriating and unnecessary. But you must learn to recognise them for what they are: they are 'little' when compared with really serious problems and are matters with which you can easily deal (and even learn to laugh about!). Talk to her about them, by all means, but if you don't get anywhere don't let them beat you. There are ways of coping and getting around things like this. You can always get clothes for the children. You can always make that party if you want to, and (who knows?) it may be an opportunity to share something with your children and meet their friends and their parents.

Perhaps your ex-wife refuses to cooperate in delivering or collecting the children. Well, if you cannot change the situation perhaps you'll have to do it all yourself. If your ex-wife is unresponsive to court orders or persuasion, and you want to see your children at regular times, you will just have to swallow your pride and cop it! (If this is not a valid claim for a Child Support deduction then nothing is!)

> **I am still involved in my daughter's life, but that is due entirely to my own efforts. My ex-wife does little to encourage it. But as time goes by I am confident that my daughter will respond to me off her own bat.**
>
> *Charles*

The big problems

The 'big' problems are the ones that really cause trouble. These are the problems that arise when your wife, in defiance of your agreement or Family Court orders, refuses you contact with one or all of your children, or allows only limited contact, or allows contact but makes it as difficult and unpleasant as she possibly can.

With serious problems like these you will, of course, talk to your ex-wife, or try to. There may be tense scenes and bitter telephone calls. Be prepared for the fact that your efforts may be futile and you will be forced to resort to a solicitor who may have to write threatening letters to your wife. Often these legal efforts will also be futile and you will be forced to resort to the Family Court, with or without the solicitor. And – worst of all – the processes of the Family Court, through hearings and counselling, may also be futile and you will be left with the problem, and with frustration and a great deal of financial and emotional expense.

That may sound negative, but it is a reality for many men. In many cases the above steps do work, and so I certainly do not want to discourage you from making the effort. Indeed, in most cases you will feel obliged, for your own and your children's sake, to exhaust every possible avenue to ensure that you have some contact with your children.

> I think that some people, especially those of low intelligence, are prone to emotions such as anger which can cloud their judgement and lead them to do strange and irrational things. If there's also low self-esteem – as in my ex-wife's case – then this combination leads to weird behaviour. They hit out at the person whom they see as being responsible for their low opinion of themselves. In my ex-wife's case she was really angry with her father, but she transferred that anger to me. She punished me through the children.
>
> *Harold*

The vicious cycle

The reality is that for many separated fathers the pattern is all too common: frustration, argument, solicitor, court, orders, frustration. And so the cycle goes on. You can get all the orders in the world from the Family Court and yet get little or no compliance from your ex-wife, and therefore little or no satisfactory contact with your children. The inability or unwillingness of the court to deal with this is a scandal.

As Bettina Arndt says:

'*The court's impotence in the face of the continuing defiance by women of access orders has a long history.*'[103]

ONE MAN'S STORY

Access worked for a while. Then her new boyfriend started to interfere and there were some nasty incidents. After they moved into their new house everything started to change. She became difficult with access; she refused to give me the phone number. She changed arrangements at will. Things became progressively worse. She stopped access for nine months so I took her to court. It took eight months and $15,000 to get a hearing and I got fortnightly access. But she continued to be difficult. She created scenes and she was abusive. The kids were constantly upset. After I started going with my fiancee, things got even worse. There were more nasty scenes. Then she notified the court that I had abused the children. DOCS investigated and found nothing amiss. A short time later she stopped access again. I was in court three or four times a month and my legal costs were in excess of $60,000.

In the end I simply gave up. The situation was so horrific for the children, myself, my partner and my parents, that I was unwilling to go on. It was an unwinnable situation. She has achieved what she set out to do: my children are no longer mine. I can now accept that situation but it's tough. Friends told me that I should go on fighting to see my kids. But they simply do not understand the stress and turmoil that is involved in the fight. You can't go on forever.

Very few people understand the pain suffered by a devoted father (not to mention the effect on the children) whose ex-wife uses the children as a weapon to 'punish' him for leaving home, or simply as an exercise of power. For him, access becomes a hopeless, impossible, frustrating mess.

To begin to understand, consider the following scenario:

Sometimes the children come, sometimes they don't. He's met at the door with excuses. He receives a telephone call asking him to have them on one of his 'off' weekends (after he's made other arrangements). He is informed by the children on another occasion that they can't come until he has paid for their music lessons.

*He goes back to court for more orders, hoping that contact with the legal process and some expression of displeasure from a judge might shame her into reasonableness (a formal rebuke and order for costs would be asking for too much!). Nothing of that nature occurs. She is charming with the counsellor, modest with the judge and perfectly agreeable to the orders. She leaves the court knowing that she has 'won again', because nothing changes and nothing happens to **make** her change.*

He remonstrates with her outside her home. A loud argument ensues with lots of shouting and insults. An overzealous neighbour notifies the police and she then obtains an Apprehended Violence Order preventing him from coming to the house.

After protracted and unexplained absences, in desperation he begins calling at their school at lunch time or after school just to say hello to his children. This lasts a week or two before the mother convinces the school authorities that this is harmful to the children and not within the court orders. On the next occasion a teacher or the children themselves tell him to stay away.

After months of all this, unless he is a fierce warrior or a peculiar individual, he retires, hurt and beaten. He is drained, financially and emotionally. He has no more stamina for the fight. He closes up like a sea anemone.

*She basks in her victory (or does she, I wonder?) and then slips easily into the role of the **victim** ('I have to do it all on my own, you know; he has lost interest in the children'). And the little contact that father and children have supports her public stance.*

This is the vicious cycle.

The separated father is thus portrayed to the world – and to his children – as a 'bad man'.

He sinks into the role of the vanquished, at once grateful and resentful for the small amount of access he is allowed. The children are initially confused but, like all children, they are resilient and learn to cope with and accept the new regime and his status as a remote father.

The truth is that he is effectively sidelined, or separated from his children. Who knows how much damage this causes both father and children?

> **Contact with the children has been very difficult. My ex-wife punishes me through the children. Initially she would refuse access. Then we went to court and the solicitors worked out a plan. I only see them one week-end every month. I do all the travelling: two hours each way. She refuses to cooperate. She blackens me in the eyes of the kids. My four-year-old son screams when he has to go home.**
>
> *Gus*

The power of the custodial parent

Under the present system, once a custodial parent captures the hearts and minds of the children and uses them against the other parent, there is little that the absent parent can do. When this realisation hits them, many separated fathers simply give up and all contact with the children is lost. Others cling to whatever they are allowed, but it is not a healthy and true relationship any more.

Whatever the dynamics in the marriage were, the custodial parent is now in the seat of power. In this scenario many a wife plays the *victim* role for years, using access to punish the husband for his 'betrayal' of them and the family, and bringing up their children with *that* idea of their father. If young enough at separation, the children will very likely accept this caricature of their father into their adult years and sometimes forever. This is pure indoctrination and in reality a form of child abuse.

A common occurrence

If this happens to you, the first thing is to assure yourself that it is a common problem: you are not the only one! It has happened and is happening to separated fathers all over the country. Lawyers have told me that the most commonly recurring cases in the Family Court are about denial of contact.

The sad fact is that for many fathers contact becomes so limited and unpleasant that they simply cannot tolerate seeing their children in those circumstances. So they stop trying and stay away. What a loss for them and for their children! Others struggle on in difficult circumstances trying to maintain whatever contact they can with their children.

> I have no relationship at all with my ex-wife and children. The marriage was hopeless and I moved out. She then poisoned the children's minds and made any kind of relationship quite impossible. My daughter was eighteen and my son fourteen. I decided to 'let them go' and work on myself. In the circumstances I think it was the only reasonable thing to do. I got the chance of a job in the city so I came here to make a fresh start. I think it's worked for me. I'm hoping that the children will eventually come looking for me and we can start again.
>
> *Costa*

Sorting it out in your mind

The next thing is to sort out in your own mind just what is happening and why. Identifying the problem contributes to peace of mind and acceptance. You immediately say: *'Well, that's easy. The problem here is my ex-wife. I'm doing all I can, paying the maintenance, making sure they are living comfortably, and trying to establish a relationship with my children, and she is doing her best to muck it up!'*

But you must go deeper and try to understand just why she *is* doing that.

Shortly before he became President of the new South Africa, Nelson Mandela said: *'We must develop absolute patience and the ability to understand the fears of others.'*

You must try to understand what's going on in your ex-

✔ Work it out in your mind: what is the problem?
✔ Try to understand what's behind it.
✔ Try to negotiate a solution.

✔ Don't fight or be abusive.
✔ You can control how you feel about it.
✔ Positive thoughts lead to healthy actions.

wife's mind. It's a common syndrome. Even if she is the one who initiated the separation, she may still harbour a lot of resentment.

ONE MAN'S STORY

Colin's ex-wife felt betrayed by his departure from the marriage and she reacted bitterly to it. In her own eyes (and, she imagined, in the eyes of others around her) she felt diminished as a woman – particularly as he had replaced her with another – and diminished as a wife and mother. She felt a failure and she believed that people would look on her as such. She had been a full-time mother and wife and she thought that part of her reason for living had been taken away from her. Her place in society, her identity, the way she defined herself, were all under threat. She felt rejected. She felt financially insecure. She was angry, depressed and vengeful. She wished to punish him for what he had done to her. Because Colin was no longer in the house, the only weapon she had that would really hurt him was their children.

ANOTHER MAN'S STORY
Derek's wife asked him to leave and he did. She said she had lost all love and respect for him and despised him. She said she wanted nothing more to do with him and did not want him to have any further contact with the children. She had fallen in love with another man whom she thought was a much better person and father than Derek was and she believed the children would be better off without him. She convinced herself that what she was about to do was for the good of the children. She was impervious to argument.

On the other hand, some women are not consciously trying to hurt their ex-husbands. Instead, they harbour a perception that if the ex-husband has a close relationship with the children he will hurt them as he has hurt her. And dealing with a hurt child becomes the responsibility of the custodial parent. She thinks that she can avoid this problem by limiting contact.

Other women, of course, have had bad experiences with their husbands. Drugs, drink, violence and abuse may have caused or contributed to the separation. No reasonable person would blame such a woman for limiting contact between the father and her children. It becomes a matter of protection.

The father removed

It must be acknowledged that many separated women want to restart their lives without any reminders of their former marriage. They discourage or deny contact between father and children. They leave town. They seek a new husband. They engineer in the children what is called 'parental alienation syndrome'.[104] In other words they seek to cut the father out of the children's lives and out of theirs.

Worst of all was the first Christmas after the separation. On the last one we were a family and had fun opening

presents under the Christmas tree. This time there were no children. Despite the support of family and friends I felt empty and lonely. Although the Family Court orders provided for a shared Christmas my ex-wife refused to allow the children to come. I did not see them until New Year's Eve. She has kept this up over the years despite more court orders. Not once have they been with me for Christmas or birthdays and not once – until they got into their teens and started to do things for themselves – did they give me a Christmas or birthday gift, or even send me a card. Her malice knew no bounds. She allowed me just enough contact to preserve the myth of fatherhood and justify child support but not enough to permit me to feel involved in the lives of the children. I became a pale uncle.

Clive

Each of you who is saddled with a particularly trying situation has his story. What you must do is work it out coolly in your mind. Rationalise it and know the problem that you face. Whether you can do anything about it is another question. But you *can* do something about yourself and how you let the situation affect you.

You are not responsible for what has happened but *you are responsible for how you react to it and how you handle it.*

Reactions of the children

The next thing to do is to think about the effect of your ex-wife's attitudes and actions on the children. When a wife is either denying access or making it difficult and unpleasant, the children are deeply hurt and troubled. They see and know what is going on. Consciously and unconsciously they react to it. They are already upset over the separation. They now are confronted with the spectacle of their mother not simply punishing their father by refusing access but also, through her obvious attitude and criticism, creating seriously negative images of him in their minds.

Whereas before they have had reasonably warm and loving feelings towards him, they are now confused. If she calls on them to take her side in the dispute and in her feelings towards their father, they will be more confused. Their loyalties have not been tested in this way before and the experience will cause them emotional stress and possible psychological harm.

This experience sets up a harmful *dissonance* in the mind of children. They love their father; they love their mother. But they see that there is no love between father and mother. What *should* happen is that they are assisted (by counselling and by a patient mother or father) to accept the reality that their parents do not like one another but that *they* can go on loving each of them in their own way. What *often* happens is that the children resolve the dilemma by falling in with their mother's line and forming an artificial hatred for their father. Others, caught in a no-win situation beyond their control, feel penalised and powerless. Not being able to cope, they withdraw from both parents and at times become depressed, sullen, antisocial and cynical of committed relationships.

This is a very serious matter. It is an assault on the innocence and love of children. It involves a loss of innocence. The children's trust in the reasonableness of their parent's relationship, their security in their own relationships with each parent, and their right not to have their loyalties tested, are all betrayed. They have been conditioned to identify their father as a loving and caring figure. But now their mother is telling them that he is a bad man who does not care for them at all. The resulting dichotomy is seriously harmful to their development and to their personalities.

Denial of contact is child abuse

When a mother unnecessarily denies her child contact with the father and puts the child through emotional turmoil this is a form of child abuse and should be recognised as such.

It abuses the children as persons in that it injures their minds and harms their peaceful development. It also abuses their right to love both parents without interference from anyone. The time has come for society *and the court* to recognise that the unreasonable refusal or misuse of child access by a custodial parent is child abuse.

Let's call it what it really is. And let's call recalcitrant custodial parents what they really are: *child abusers*! Perhaps attaching the correct title to this syndrome will cause the people with power and influence to sit up and take notice and, hopefully, to do something about it. Emotional abuse is now recognised as the most prevalent and most destructive form of child abuse.[105]

The results of emotional abuse

Studies in the United States have demonstrated the suffering and the intense longing experienced by children for their absent parents.[106] Uncomplicated child access has been shown to ease this distress.

Among separated families, the classic dysfunctional model is the distant, uninvolved, unsupportive and non-custodial father, and the chronically embittered and vengeful custodial mother. Children from such families display low self-esteem, depression, sullenness, aggression, poor school performance and antisocial activity.

A custodial parent's abuse of the children through refusal to allow proper contact should be seen as a powerful ground for a change of residence for those children.

The abusive father

The difficult father can be a child abuser, too. I am not talking about sexual and physical abuse. Those more obvious forms of violence need special treatment and cannot be accommodated here. They have been given plenty of exposure in popular and scientific literature. Special programs are available for both victims and abusers.

I am referring here to the father who himself makes contact a constant trial for his ex-wife and children. He makes everything difficult. He causes scenes when he picks up or delivers the children. He insults his ex-wife. He fights with the children. He is never punctual. Sometimes he simply fails to turn up at all. He makes abusive phone calls. He respects no one's privacy. He pumps the children for information on his ex-wife. He complains to them about how unfairly she is treating him. He involves them in legal proceedings. He involves them in disputes about money. He demands their loyalty. In short, he is mean and miserable.

When this behaviour gets to the point where it makes the children unhappy, depressed and disturbed, then it should be called child abuse. *The father is then an abuser.*

Be particularly careful that you do not let this happen to you. If you are a supersensitive and aggressive person, a situation like this can creep up on you. It may be a reaction to difficulties in contact which you feel are beyond your control. It could be that your ex-wife is deliberately engineering a scenario to make access as onerous as possible.

Stephanie Dowrick says:

'That is partly an issue of control. When the woman acts in a way which disrupts the man's certainties – about how things should be; about who is in charge – he frequently acts with rage to protect himself against unwanted feelings of fear and vulnerability. His outbursts of rage may be far more energetic than his expressions of love have ever been.'[107]

Fighting

Calm yourself, think about it and get help. You could easily lose the respect and love of your children if you react too savagely to these problems. Many men are *'fighters'*. I don't mean that in a physical sense. But such a man is aggressive and overreactive in his attitudes. When confronted with obstacles his natural tendency is to come out fighting! When told the children are too ill to see him he accuses his ex-wife of lying. When the children want to spend time with their friends he accuses them of lack of love for him.

If this is you, then stop yourself before you harm yourself and your children. You must stop 'fighting'. You must stop fighting against what has happened to you: your separation and divorce and all that that entails. This fight will only create a tension in you that will sour your life and your relationships, particularly with your children. A good honest relationship with a therapist or wise friend will allow you to express and release negative emotions of anger and depression, and to search for positive reactions and strategies.

The actions of the recalcitrant mother are sometimes caused or contributed to by a stupid and aggressive ex-husband. He can easily fuel the fire! The non-custodial father needs to look critically at himself and to take responsibility for his actions before he blames his ex-wife.

QUESTIONS	POSITIVE THOUGHTS AND RESOLUTIONS
★	★
What are the causes of my contact problems?	I will do my best to make contact work.
★	★
How am I separating the small problems from the big?	I will cope with difficulties.
★	★
What do I do to stay in control of my reactions?	I will not blame her for everything.
★	★
What steps do I take to stop myself being abusive or a fighter?	I will understand her fears.
★	★
How will I know when I need help and someone to talk to?	I will reason with her.
	★
	I will talk to someone about how I feel.
	★
	I will support moves to identify abuse of contact as child abuse.

. . . many persons strive for high ideals; and everywhere life is full of heroism.

Desiderata

9

Repartnering

As for repartnering, I used to feel I needed a relationship with a woman, as if I were incomplete without it. Now, after time and therapy, I have grown into independence. This has been the greatest gift of all. I really feel independent. I have a girlfriend but we do not live together. It's a really healthy relationship.

Dirk

Why are most men in such a hurry to remarry after divorce? Are we such insecure creatures that we need a woman to make us feel complete? Surely we don't kid ourselves that women need *us*! Does it have something to do with the way we are brought up? Shall we again blame our mothers? Are we, deep down, just lonely and misunderstood little boys? As Shakespeare said, in *Hamlet*: '. . . *they say an old man is twice a child*'. Are we so inept that we need someone to look after us? Or is it a *macho*/power complex that drives us to have someone to dominate and control?

Some experts identify an emphasis on strength and independence as central to male identity. This starts very early with young boys learning that they must be **strong** and not **weak**. They feel pressured to achieve emotional independence from their mothers before they are ready for it. This leads to many young men feeling inadequate and turning to a woman to provide their emotional **prop**.

At separation, men usually lack the emotionally supportive network necessary to help them deal with their loss. They are vulnerable and are prone to seek a woman who can fill this gap.

The drive to repartner

Whatever the reason, the fact is that no less than 23 percent of men remarry within twelve months of their divorce. And that does not account for the hundreds of others who enter de facto relationships.

The Australian Institute of Family Studies looked at remarriage in the early 1980s.[108] It found that 39 percent of men and 25 percent of women remarried within two years of separation. After six to eight years of separation, 70 percent of men had remarried compared with 52 percent of women. However, almost 80 percent of remarried men and women said that they had lived together before remarriage.

If you lump together both marriage and de facto living,

within three years of separation more than 50 percent of men and 30 percent of women have repartnered.

Not content with that, about half the separated men and women take on partners who have emotional and financial responsibilities for the children of their first marriage. And within three years of the new relationship, about 20 percent of men have new children to support.

> **Repartnering brought new problems. She wanted a child and I didn't. In reality she was living with a person still saddled with the problems of his first marriage. I was a mess. It has not been good.**
>
> *Brendan*

Too quick?

Now, I know we should not make rules or generalise about such things, but it seems that too many men repartner too quickly. Of course, some have already fallen in love with another woman before their divorce or separation. They will scream at me: *'What do you expect me to do? Fall out of love?'*

No, not at all. But even in such cases, a breathing space would be good for all parties concerned. A man really needs it. He has so much to do, mainly about himself! It could be that he's plainly pathetic and needs to learn to boil water and to look after himself: if he's no good for himself he'll be no good for anyone else. But quite apart from the extreme cases, every separated man needs time to sort himself out. He will have to reorientate his life, and very likely will need counselling for his hurt, guilt and sadness. He will also need to make new friends. Above all he needs the space and time to learn to live as an independent person.

> **Inevitably baggage gets carried over into new relationships. The important thing is to be aware of it.**
>
> *Tom*

So, even if you are enjoying a good and positive relationship and thinking of making it permanent, there's a lot to be said for living separately for a considerable period of time.

A gradual introduction

Before you even get to the stage of living together, it is wise to introduce your children to the idea of your new partner in a gradual fashion. Remember, you are not the only one with feelings. Many men are insensitive in this area and expect the whole world to rejoice and to accept immediately their new woman. It can come as a shock to them when they find that their parents are suspicious, their friends are doubting and their children hate her. Keep a level head and don't despair, but give everyone, especially the children, time to get used to the idea.

With the best will in the world, children may be upset at the prospect of any woman other than their mother in their father's life, let alone in his bed. At worst they will see it as a betrayal of them and their mother; at best they will regard it as highly undesirable, a nuisance and a threat to the stability of their lives. *Remember – children love stability*. If the present order in their lives is suiting them, they will hate to have it changed. Your new partner will be identified as a threat to that order. If they were upset at your leaving home, they will be also upset at your repartnering.

Without trying too hard, and by letting the children know that your new friendship is not going to spoil their special relationship with you, you will find that in time your children will accept your partner. If you and she are sensible and patient they might even come to like her! Let them see that your newfound happiness and security mean that you have more time and affection for them.

The concept of another woman in bed with their father is one which they might take some time to accept. For some children this can be a shock and it is a good idea to avoid that situation until the children see that she has a place in the household and in your life.

Introduce them to your partner's children if she has any, and try to organise some joint activities. Tell them you and your partner are thinking of living together well before you actually take the step. And if you are fortunate enough to have an amicable relationship with your ex-wife, introduce her to your partner.

> **Repartnering brings problems. I was concerned at how wary my children were of my new wife. The attitude of my first wife did not help. However, in time it sorted itself out.**
>
> *Ron*

> **I have repartnered but it has not been easy. It has been a growing experience, difficult but joyful. My new partner has a good relationship with my children. The really surprising and disappointing thing is the change that my new relationship produced in my ex-wife. Hitherto we had an excellent relationship and communication. As soon as my partner moved in with me that all changed and has practically disappeared. I found this devastating. It has led me to conclude that we should not underestimate the revenge motive in ex-partners, even in situations that appeared cooperative.**
>
> *Peter*

Obviously remarriage can also rock your ex-wife. She may see it as the ultimate act of rejection. It may make her jealous and angry and cause her to say and do foolish things. Mind you, *her* repartnering can have the same effect on you!

> **My first wife caused so much trouble and disruption that my second wife could not handle the stress it caused us both. She left me. I was devastated. I maintain that my first wife destroyed our relationship. Had**

my partner and I been strong enough to stand up to her and tell her to back off, we would have survived.

Clive

After you separate, your new friends, both male and female, should be introduced to your children in a normal and natural way. If you are dating a woman, it is only fair that she should have the opportunity of getting to know your children and vice versa. Have her to your home during contact times for a drink or meal, perhaps with several of your friends. This will show the children that you are a normal social being and are enjoying the company of others.

They will soon wake up to the fact that a certain female

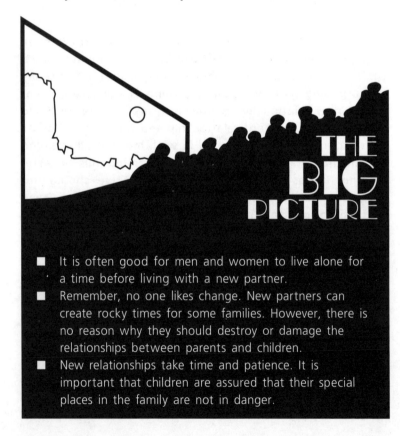

THE BIG PICTURE

- It is often good for men and women to live alone for a time before living with a new partner.
- Remember, no one likes change. New partners can create rocky times for some families. However, there is no reason why they should destroy or damage the relationships between parents and children.
- New relationships take time and patience. It is important that children are assured that their special places in the family are not in danger.

is special to you. Don't let this become a *big thing* for them or for you. Answer their questions honestly but leave them in no doubt that it is a completely normal and ordinary part of life. Reserve plenty of time for interacting with them alone. But do things together, too. Invite your friend to accompany you and the children to a movie or a picnic or restaurant, for example.

> **What made it easy was that my new partner at no time tried to be a substitute mother. She was just a friend. We were open and honest with the children. We reassured them that they had one mother and one father and that they both cared for them. We did nothing to undermine their mother or her relationship with the children.**
>
> *Phil*

Resentment

The appearance in your life of 'the other woman' marks a turning point for you, your ex-wife and your children. Almost inevitably your former wife will feel resentful and jealous (particularly if you have initiated the separation). It is the easiest thing in the world for her to give way to the temptation to demonstrate her disapproval through the children.

In these times keep talking to them, answering their questions patiently, and listening to them sympathetically. Don't lose your temper or become impatient. At the same time, however, be firm and confident. Correct any mistaken impressions that they have. If you handle the matter reasonably they, as everyone, will get used to the changes in time. Assure them that, although some changes will have to be made, their lives will not be greatly disturbed and, above all, that they will always remain special to you.

> **All my girlfriend was doing was being friendly. She would read the kids stories and help get them to bed. They were happy and of course told their mother.**

> Apparently she exploded. Next time the kids came they told me that they were not allowed to have anything to do with her. We felt we had to go along with this as the kids were young and would suffer if we made a fuss. My friend – now my wife – has always reckoned that this was wrong and we should have pressed on normally. I don't know. I thought it was best at the time.
>
> *Nick*

Interference

So what you get is the mother not *physically* interfering with contact but teaching the children to be cold, and sometimes rude, to your new partner. In other words, she is giving them *physical* permission to see you and your partner but not *emotional* permission to enjoy the visits. It's a brutal game. It is harmful to the children as it places on them burdens that they should not have to bear. It fosters a dilemma and encourages duplicity. No one has the right to play with the emotions of children in such a serious and damaging way.

On top of all that, it is also deeply hurtful for your partner. You must show her care and understanding through these difficult times. Be sensitive to her feelings. Don't shut her out. Involve her, but don't drag her into your family difficulties. Above all, don't allow any of the children to be rude and cold to her, not even for the sake of peace.

> I have repartnered. It has not been easy, especially for her as she has had to go through the legal nonsense and the associated trauma with me, plus the ongoing problems with my ex-wife.
>
> *David*

Talk to your children

'Look, I know what is going on and I know what's behind it. It's not fair to me or to Helen. It's rude and dumb. You

- ✔ Don't expect too much too soon.
- ✔ Stay cool and avoid overreaction.
- ✔ Remember your children's feelings.

- ✔ Remember your partner's feelings.
- ✔ Being too threatened or sensitive will impress no one.
- ✔ Do your best and ask others to do the same.

know that she is a good person. Now I am not asking you to love her or even to like her. But I do ask you to treat her decently, to speak to her nicely and not to rush out of the room when she comes in. I will not have you being rude to her.'

Show them in no uncertain terms that you consider what their mother is doing to be wrong and that you will not tolerate it. It is unfair to your partner and an affront to common decency if you give way and put up with this situation just for the sake of humouring your children and their mother.

Speak or write to your ex-wife and point out the harm that she is doing. Go to counselling and try to get her there, too. This should be no-nonsense, directive counselling. She should be told that her actions, words and attitude amount to manipulation and abuse and that she should cease immediately. Perhaps a good *talking-to* from a grandparent or friend would help.

ONE MAN'S STORY

A friend of mine had repartnered. The first wife was really playing up and making things difficult for him and the kids. It was the 'other woman' syndrome. She sent him solicitor's letters complaining about the way he and his wife were treating the kids. She did her best to muck up access. She infected the kids with weird and spiteful ideas of him and his new partner.

After six months of this the new partner had had enough. So she got on the phone to the ex-wife and told her so in no uncertain terms. She told her there was no cause for all the vitriol. She did not intend to interfere with her role as the mother of the children. All she wanted to do was to live peaceably with her husband. 'I'm not going to hurt the children, nor am I trying to supplant you in their eyes. I only want to be friendly. So lay off! We are simply not going to tolerate this nonsense any more.' And it worked. The ex-wife started to behave herself and things were pretty peaceful from then on. I think that's the way to handle the situation.

Your ex-wife's new partner

Ex-wives' new partners can cause problems too. You can strike the type who wants to take over the family (including your children) – the *managerial* type. Then there is the reasonably decent bloke who has been filled with crazy ideas about you by your ex-wife. He starts to interfere.

> **Another problem was the new husband. For whatever reason he took a protective and interfering position. I could deal easily with my ex-wife when he was not there, but if he was around, things were tense. I think some new husbands really want to muscle in and make up for lost time. They want to take over the family, and can become a real nuisance in relations between you and your ex. They need to be told to butt out!**
>
> *Gerry*

Gerry's advice is sound. The new man needs to be told to mind his own business. However, how best to do this is tricky. Talking to your ex-wife out of his presence might be useful. Otherwise a joint mediation session may be called for.

Your children's feelings

Be aware of and alert to what your children are saying. Be careful not to put them down or discount them by presuming that all their ideas come from their mother. Teenage children react poorly to being treated as if they are just repeating what they have been told and therefore are not capable of having feelings or ideas of their own.

Children can be hostile to their father's new situation independently of their mother's attitude and even contrary to it. They may feel sorry for their mother and reject the '*new woman*'. They may see this as a way of getting Mum and Dad back together again. They may be insecure in their relations with her and her children.

Reassure your ex-wife of her undiminished role in your children's lives. Assure her that your new partner can never be a mother to them, and that she is not trying to be.

What your new partner can do

You may need to contain your new partner's enthusiasm for your children, particularly if she has none of her own and is trying too hard to create a good impression. She will have to learn effective ways to relate to your children and to be sensitive in matters such as discipline. She should be careful not to undermine the children's mother in any way. Particularly in the early days the relationship between your partner and your children needs to be carefully handled. Don't force her on to them. Allow the relationship to grow slowly and naturally. Encourage her not to be a mother but to be a friend.

Assure your children that your love for them is unchanged.

If problems remain, keep on doing your best. With time and effort, most children come to separate fact from fiction.

The threatened father

The separated father can fall into the same trap if he is on his own and he hears that his ex-wife has formed another relationship or, worse still, remarried! He may feel *he* is the lost and rejected one. He becomes jealous and hurt and may act in an infantile way. The children will see this and will not like it.

If this has happened to you and you feel like that, it is important that you arrest such irrational and stupid feelings before they get the better of you and make you appear like a real fool. You must remind yourself that endings and beginnings are part of life and they can be productive of real growth. Ending one relationship and starting another can be good for people. Let go of anger and suspicion. If he is a decent person, don't resent your ex-wife's new partner or his relationship with your children. Allow yourself to like him – and to like your ex-wife, too! It won't hurt you and it will show your children that you are a mature adult.

> *When his ex-wife repartners, the separated father may fear that the new man will undermine his position with his children. If he reacts irrationally and childishly and with resentment, the children will pick this up very quickly.*

So when your children say: 'John's a great guy, he took us all to the movies', be cool and don't worry about it. Don't be threatened. It's not a competition between you and the new man for the affections of your children. Look on it positively: instead of just two, your children are going to have *four* significant persons in their lives – their mother and her new partner and you and yours if you have one. All of these people have something to offer your children in terms of experience, life skills and, hopefully, affection. It can be a rich life.

QUESTIONS	POSITIVE THOUGHTS AND RESOLUTIONS
★	
In what ways might my new relationship be moving too quickly?	★ I will be single again and enjoy it.
★ How do I go about introducing my new friend in a gradual way?	★ I will enjoy a variety of relationships.
★ How can I ensure that I am sensitive to my children's feelings?	★ I'm not going to rush anything.
★ What should I do if I feel threatened by my ex-wife's new man?	★ I will reassure the children of my love for them.
★ What are the advantages for me in living alone for a while?	★ I will not tolerate nonsense. ★ I will be cool and patient.

Nurture strength of spirit to shield you in sudden misfortune.
Desiderata

The three ages

10

Stepfamilies

Repartnering has not been easy. We both carried baggage from our first marriages. I was emotionally unstable for some years. She didn't understand or like the easy relationship I had with my first wife.

Arthur

One of the problems most commonly reported by men who have repartnered is that of the jealous second wife. This arises when a man's new partner is resentful of his obligations to his first wife and children. She wants him all to herself. She resents and is jealous of the time, money and emotional energy he expends on his first family.

If they have their own child or children, this resentment and jealousy usually increases in intensity. It can become a niggling and destructive force which causes heartache and bitterness for the adults and children. It can poison relationships.

There is no easy cure for a jealous wife. Counselling can help, of course, but you yourself have to do a lot of the work.

You need to be aware that your new partner may feel extremely insecure about your affections, the ex-wife becoming almost like 'the other woman' in her eyes. This could become a problem if your ex-wife and you regularly communicate. Reassure your partner. Restate your commitment to her and your new family. Be supportive.

ONE MAN'S STORY

My new partner was jealous of my easy relationship with my children and also with my ex-wife. She resented the time and money I spent on them. She felt that a lot of this could have been spent on her. My ex-wife used to ring me a lot about legal problems and my partner saw this to mean that she was still in love with me. I thought I was only being decent. She imagined my children did not like her. This was not the case at all. She was simply trying too hard and expecting too much. She suffers from low self-esteem. We have talked about these problems and things have improved somewhat. We've learnt to cope. It's really her problem.

Taking a stand

However, if the situation gets out of hand and her attitude is totally unreasonable, you will be well advised to take a stand.

You will have to make it clear to your new partner that you are not going to allow this conflict to continue. It has to be settled and laid to rest, otherwise your life together will be intolerable.

You must first clarify your position in your own mind and then put it squarely to her. You might say something such as: *'I love you and our children and my main job is to share this family life with you. And you know that I do that now as well as anyone. But look, I have two other children who happen to live with their mother. I've got to love and care for them, too, and that means spending money and time on them. You've got to understand that.'*

Convince her to join you in some counselling, argue and discuss your differences. Try to sort them out. *Do* something! Don't let it just fester away, hoping that things will improve with the passage of time.

Of course, it could be that she has reason on her side. It could be that you *are* spending too much time, money and energy on your absent children and not enough on the child or children that you have had with your second wife. Or perhaps your ex-wife is involving you too much in their affairs, or is too dependent on you.

It sometimes happens that a father shows an obvious preference for the children of his first marriage over those from his new union. Sometimes, however, he might neglect the children of his first marriage to the advantage of those of his present relationship.

These and other problems have to be explored and solutions found. It is extremely valuable to have a wise counsellor to help you do this.

One very practical solution is to engage a mediator and to agree to be bound by the plan that he or she proposes.

In an extreme situation it may even come to a 'last stand' scenario. That is, you may be forced to let your new wife know that you are unwilling to continue in the relationship if you and she are not able to arrive at a workable agreement on these matters.

Preparation

Of course, prevention is always better than cure. If you are considering repartnering you should talk seriously to your prospective partner about your feelings and obligations to your children. You must make it clear to her that she can never have you 'all to herself', that you (and she to some extent) will have to share involvement in the life of your first family. Tell her in no uncertain terms what it will mean in practice: time, money, phone calls, holidays and the like. If it appears to be a problem for her then you had better reassess your relationship.

Now, before you can talk about it in such a realistic way, it is absolutely essential that you have thought it all through very carefully. Many men are very good at kidding themselves that everything is going to be all right and that their new wives will be perfectly understanding. This tendency betrays a lack of thought, common sense and responsibility.

> **Right from the start I let my girlfriend know what she was in for. My situation was not simple. My ex-wife and daughter lived in another State. I travelled to see her once a month and occasionally she would fly over to me. I also travelled a lot in my job. I put a three-year plan to my new partner. She said she didn't think it would work but she'd give it a go. It was tough-going and for a while she left me. But I continued to talk to her and to explain how I felt about my daughter. She softened and so did I. I became more caring towards her. We are together now and doing well.**
>
> *Mal*

Melded families

Whenever it happens, whether sooner or later, remarriage or repartnering often brings with it an amalgamation of families. When children are concerned, no matter whose they are and where they live, there will *always* be problems. This needs to

✔Warn your new partner about your existing responsibilities.
✔Fulfil your obligations but do not neglect your new family.

✔If there are problems, talk them through.
✔Seek counselling or mediation.
✔Take a stand.

be stated and accepted right from the start: the melding of two families into one will always bring problems for all concerned.

There are difficulties that arise within the melded family itself – between children and parent, between children and step-parent – and these tensions will inevitably impact on the adults and their relationship. There will also be problems between a parent and absent children. There is evidence that separated men who live with new partners are among those who have the most contact problems with their children. So many men report that access had been relatively peaceful until the 'other woman' appeared on the scene.

The problems in a stepfamily situation can be handled successfully and the experience can be an enriching one. But the man who looks at it through rose-coloured glasses and thinks that everything will be perfect is in for a rude shock, and perhaps a series of them!

There may be cases where a partner's children are open to the idea of a new relationship for their mother. The more common experience, however, is that they simply don't want you there. They form a barrier around them and their mother. You are the intruder. You tend to retreat, wounded and hurt, and dreadfully disappointed at how things are turning out.

It took me a long time to break through the resistance of my new wife's children. It wasn't that they positively disliked me. It was rather that they feared that I would distract their mother from them and interfere with the routine of their lives. They gradually came to realise that these things would not happen. It involved a lot of effort, trial and error and sensitivity on my part, and being willing to shut up and take the back seat on occasions. But it's worked: we now are good friends.

Darryl

Stepfamilies – the golden rules

Such families can be made to work and most difficulties can be overcome. However, you need to be aware of and convinced of the essential rules. Here they are . . .

1. Accept wholeheartedly that a stepfamily is different. It's different from what you have had before and it's different from the so-called 'normal' family. Don't try to ape the 'happy normal family'. You now have persons living together who never meant to live together. Their lives are upset. They are sometimes angry. It's all very strange. Don't kid yourself or others that everything's wonderful!

2. Accept that stepfamily life is going to be tough-going for a while. You have to get used to each other. Everyone has to change a little. Ask one another for some give-and-take. On the other hand it can be a lot better than what any of you had before.

3. Don't try too hard. Simply try to be a special friend. Don't try to be a 'father' or even a stepfather to your partner's children, and don't call them 'stepchildren' (except in rare cases where that is what everyone wants). Don't insist that they call you 'Dad'. They won't want to. Let them use your first name.

4. Don't expect them to love you, or even to like you. Conversely, don't expect yourself to love or like them. These are things that must grow naturally if at all. Respect one another, yes, but remember that respect has to be earned.

5. Don't imagine that your difficulties are unique. Plenty of stepfamilies and plenty of 'normal' families have all the same problems. Not all biological parents get on well with their offspring. Remember it's hard for the children, too. They did not choose to live with you. Attend a 'parent effectiveness' course.

6. Don't compare yourselves unfavourably to the 'perfect' happy family next door which seems to be totally without problems. Don't regard yourselves as a second-class family and don't let others treat you like one. Try to improve your own self-image and that of the whole family by acting and speaking confidently and with no apologies to anyone. Remind yourself that there are many different kinds of families.

7. Talk through the problems and try to resolve them. Air your difficulties with your partner and, at times, with her children. Don't let them fester away. Perhaps a *family plan* should be agreed on, written down and signed by adults and children. This could be in the form of a contract with everyone contributing agreed clauses. Listen to the children and try to understand the feelings behind their words. Tough talking and tough decisions are sometimes called for. A family meeting could be the way, or isolating a child for a talk. One can envisage possible exchanges:

> 'Tell me straight what it is that's upsetting you.'
> 'I don't like you living here: it's my father's house.'
> *'I don't blame you, but be fair: your mother invited me to live here and she consulted you. And as soon as things are settled we'll buy our own place.'*

> 'I don't like you telling me what to do. You are not my father.'
> *'You're right, and I don't want to be. In future I won't tell you, I'll ask you. But when I do, I want you to remember that this is not a boarding house, it's our home, and you*

are old enough to do your bit to make it work for everybody.'

8. Don't retreat into passive indifference in order to preserve peace in the home. Nor should your partner allow this. You have the right to live comfortably, to be consulted and to make a positive contribution to the household.

9. Foster, don't impede, good relations between your partner and her children. Give them time to themselves and let them know that you will not interfere in their special relationship. Be sensitive to their family dynamics: one child (most likely the eldest) may have considered himself the head of the family and will feel threatened by you. Don't knock him off his perch. Allow him his place.

10. Never criticise their father, no matter how hopeless he is, even if they ask you for your opinion. Remember 'blood is thicker than water'! Encourage them to stay in touch with him.

11. Don't let them get away with playing one parent against the other.

12. Get all the grandparents on side. They can be great allies, and they have considerable influence on the children. Encourage the children's relationships with members of their extended family and with their friends.

13. The physical organisation of the home is important. Ideally, each child should have a room, but of course this is not always possible. It may not work to have older siblings, especially from different families, bunk in together for an extended period. However, all things are possible with effort and encouragement plus a respect for private space and possessions.

14. Both physical and temporal space are important. As for any couple, you and your new wife need to get away at times. Have an outing, see a show, spend a weekend away. Guard the privacy of your bedroom.

15. *'Love me, love my kids'* and *'It's either me or the kids'* are

unfair demands and should never be uttered by either partner. Such attitudes indicate that your relationship is unsound. Let your partner know that she counts in her own right, not just as a substitute mother for you and your children. If that's all you want, get a housekeeper!

16. **Don't expect your partner to love and 'mother' your children** unless she and the children all want this and their own mother does not object. But insist that they treat her decently.

17. **Friction with children is a major factor in the breakup of a relationship.** So if you value the relationship for its own sake (it'll die if you don't), you must nip these complications in the bud. There might conceivably arise the extreme situation which calls for 'the parting of the ways'. If there is a problem child who rejects all efforts at reason, refuses to behave decently, and is persistently defiant, rebellious and hostile, then serious steps must be taken. A change in custody, or at least a change of home, might provide the solution. Parents have the right to a reasonable life. They must also look after their own relationship.

18. **The decision to have your own baby is a very personal one** and should not be lightly undertaken. Don't do it to cement your relationship: it won't! And if you do, involve the whole family in the planning, birth and care. *'Two of mine, two of yours and two of ours'* is a nice thought. But nice thoughts can turn into expensive and trying situations. You must think and talk to your partner and seriously consider the question: Do we really want this?

19. **To discipline or not to discipline?** How far should you become involved in the disciplining of your partner's children? How much should you discipline your own children when they come on access visits? These are not always easy questions. Remember that the biological parent can check her children in ways which you can't. She can even scream and lose her temper and they will forgive her. But they won't afford you the same indulgence. Talk to your partner: there are lots of things that

she can solve with a minimum of fuss and some that only she should attend to. However, there is no need for you to take a back seat here: you are entitled to insist openly on basic standards of cleanliness, hygiene, punctuality, decency, consideration and respect. Be a minimalist – that is, don't be too fussy or rigid.

If your partner tends to overcompensate for her children's father by spoiling them, tax her about it. And if *you* try to make up for the times that you are not with your children by spoiling them during access visits, then check yourself and listen to your partner. If you communicate with her and with the children you will work out a parenting plan that will accommodate both families and will generally work for all. Treat *all* the children fairly, evenly, consistently. But respect each of them as an individual.

20. Be positive in your relationship with your partner's children. They are unique individuals whom you can get to know and understand, to like and even to love. They can add value to your life and you can to theirs. Take the trouble to find out about their world, their interests, their likes and dislikes. Be a friend rather than a parent to them. Don't be drawn into the role of the enforcer, no matter how much that suits your partner. Don't look on your relationship with them as competing with the relationship with your own children. On the contrary they can be complementary and mutually enriching.

Show interest in the doings not only of your own children but also in those of your partner's children. If you live with them in a family situation there will be plenty of opportunities to show them that you are genuinely interested in their welfare, that you can be relied on to help. You don't have to become a doormat, and they won't respect you if you do. But if you are honest, caring and tactful they will eventually come to respect you and, who knows, even to like you!

QUESTIONS	POSITIVE THOUGHTS AND RESOLUTIONS
★	
In what ways have I realised that my melded family is different?	★
	I will prepare for repartnering.
★	★
What am I doing that could be seen as trying too hard, expecting too much?	I will balance the new and the old.
	★
	I will be fair.
★	★
How am I viewed by my stepchildren?	I will talk to my partner.
★	★
How well are we communicating and listening to one another?	I will not try too hard.
	★
	I will accept that life is different.
★	
What can I do to show them I care?	

Go placidly amid the noise and haste, and remember what peace there may be in silence.

Desiderata

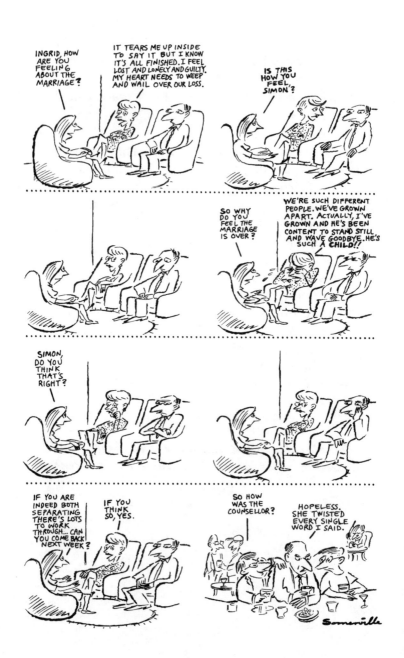

11

Solving Disputes

Some lawyers are good, some are bad, but I have a poor opinion of the system as a whole. My ex-wife always got legal aid and I got an ordinary lawyer until I ran out of money. How fair is that? Then I appeared for myself and didn't do too badly. The judges were pretty good to me, but it was an ordeal and all rather unbalanced. In the end I wondered if it really mattered what anyone said: the result seemed predictable.

Adrian

What do you do when you have problems with contact (or, indeed with any family law issue)? Firstly, go through the process of identifying the problems and, if you can, the reasons behind them. Give the issues some thought.

Then, try to talk to one another about the problems. It's really sad to see that the first thing most couples do in times of trouble is to **reach for the lawyers**! In most cases this is not necessary. A lot of things can be sorted out with reason and common sense, by yourselves or with a counsellor or mediator.

> **We had to do something. When my wife and I separated my son (eight) came with me and my daughter (six) stayed with her. It wasn't working out. On the advice of someone from DADS I went to the local Community Justice Centre and made an appointment. My wife agreed to come. We had some mediation and sorted out a parenting agreement. They typed it up for us. Then we took this to the nearest Local Court and the magistrate approved and stamped it. There were no lawyers and it didn't cost us a cent.**
>
> *Dean*

Some advice

★ At this stage, try to *stay away from lawyers and the court*. Ask your ex-wife – plead with her if necessary – to go to counselling or mediation with you. Suggest that she choose the venue. With the help of a counsellor or mediator devise a *parenting plan* (see heading below) that establishes a pattern for contact with your children.

★ *Keep a diary.* Make notes on contact, child support and anything else that might be useful for the future. Note incidents, dates and conversations. This is for your own protection and for use in counselling

or mediation sessions, and also in court if it comes
to that.

★ *Talk and/or write to your wife.* Even if you are able
to communicate in person with her, it sometimes
helps to put things down on paper. You are able to
crystallise your thoughts and to express them without interference from your emotions. But remember
that *the written word remains forever* and can
always be used against you. What you write can turn
up later in court in the form of an affidavit. So be
gentle and reasonable in your choice of words. Don't
be offensive; that will only deepen hurt and prolong
bitterness. Tell her how important it is for the children that they have a good relationship with each
parent. The children will not thank her for what she
is doing when they grow older.

★ *If these steps fail,* then usually there is only one
thing left to do: to approach a solicitor or barrister
and, possibly, the Family Court. But, before you do,
contact one of the *men's support agencies* listed at
the back of the book. This can save time, trouble and
money.

Counselling

Traditionally men have been slow to use counsellors or therapists
but it seems that this is changing. Good counsellors can produce
good results. Suggestions on where to find them can be obtained
from contacts with other men and from men's groups.

If you happen to end up in court, before you get too far
you will be required to attend counselling. This is generally in
the form of *conciliation* rather than therapeutic counselling.
You may not feel comfortable with this process but you should
not hesitate to go.

> I consider that the counselling I got was a major con-
> tributor to my survival. The counsellor was able to put
> things into perspective and this helped heaps in my
> wife and me coming to terms with the situation.

> *Len*

The counsellors of the Family Court are often criticised,
mostly by men. Sometimes the complaints are justified: like
anyone else, counsellors are human and can make mistakes.

> From the outset each of the court counsellors was a
> woman. In my very first session I was immediately
> asked: 'Did you physically abuse your wife?'! There had
> never been any suggestion of abuse. I felt an anti-male
> bias right through. I got the impression they considered
> men unable to manage, care for and love their children.
> Women were seen to have these qualities as a matter
> of course.

> *Louis*

Often the criticism is unwarranted. It comes from fathers
who are hurt and are experiencing strong emotions. Many are
sometimes unable to make rational judgements about the
difficulties that they and their wives are experiencing. They
resent being told certain things about themselves and their
behaviour. They are annoyed that the counsellors do not agree
with their points of view.

But instances of counsellors being too sympathetic with the
wife's point of view, or at least perceived to be, can happen when
the woman is further 'down the track' in managing her situation
(especially when she has initiated the separation), and the man
is still reeling from the shock and floundering with his emotions.
Joint counselling in such cases is a waste of time and can be
counterproductive. The husband needs individual counselling,
perhaps from a counsellor different from his wife's. A good
counsellor will recognise this and point him in the right direction.

Counselling in relationships is usually a waste of time. Personal counselling is fine. I have had over a year of individual counselling in personal development and it has been useful. I am also in a men's group which meets monthly. We share experiences and emotions with total honesty. This has been very valuable.

Patrick

When you go to joint counselling, be reasonable. Don't expect too much from your counsellor: he or she is not a miracle-worker and can only work with the information that you and your wife present. Be open to advice and be open to criticism. But if you feel the counsellor has it wrong, don't just sit there and say nothing, and then go outside and tell everyone that the counsellor was biased in your wife's favour. *Tell him or her what you feel!* Discuss the situation in depth. Argue with them if you will. But don't just retreat into hurt silence. It takes a bit of work, and you have to do your bit! If, in the end, you are convinced that the counsellor is unreasonable or unwise then say so and ask for another counsellor.

I went to counselling and found it worthwhile. The counsellor – a woman – and I were on the same wavelength. She recommended some useful books. I think men have to learn to be honest with a counsellor, to say what they believe.

Len

Courses

The Family Court Counselling Service runs special 'Fathering After Separation' programs for men. There are other organisations and individuals who conduct similar courses.[109] Check the list at the end of the book.

Mediation

There is yet another step that you can take which may produce a solution and avoid a nasty fight in court. Mediation is a means of settling disputes. A mediator is a person (not a judge) who will sit down with you and your wife and listen to what you have to say. In a non-adversarial and non-confrontationist manner, he or she will ask questions, make comments, suggest alternatives – all with a view to assisting the two of you to come to a workable solution to your problems. If you come to an agreement you can ask the court to ratify it. You may not need a lawyer at all.

Mediation is less costly than hiring lawyers and going to court. Mediation is now established in Australian legal systems, and is proving a successful means of solving disputes. It is provided for in the Family Law Act, and several registries of the court provide mediation. There are also private agencies that offer mediation services.[110] All you have to do is to go to the front desk of your nearest Family Court Registry and ask for some literature on the subject. If you have a solicitor, he or she should know all about it.

Early studies of the results of mediation in the Family Court are encouraging: the success rate is high. It's not surprising that when two people agree to something there is a better chance that they will stick to it than if it is forced on them by the court.

In at least three American States couples in dispute are obliged to use a mediator before resorting to litigation. In Australia the Family Law Act encourages people to settle their disputes by mediation and counselling rather than in court.

Parenting plan

One of the best ways for parents to look after the interests of their children is to work out a *parenting plan* which covers all aspects of their children's lives and their relationships with them. This merits consideration whether or not your contact with your children is proceeding smoothly.

A parenting plan is a written agreement between you and your ex-wife which contains a pattern for your contact with your children. It might contain broad principles setting out your mutual concern for the welfare of the children. It will list the logistics of your contact with them, the frequency, times, holidays, special arrangements and the like. It could contain as much detail as you agree on. It could also include a provision for the referral of disputes to a nominated umpire and an agreement to accept his or her decision.[111]

Talk to your counsellor, mediator or lawyer about such a plan. It may make things much easier you, your wife and your children.

Lawyers – choosing and using them

Lawyers are not all bad. Most separating couples need advice on the Family Law Act and on their duties and responsibilities. And unfortunately some people *have* to go to court. Good lawyers will give good advice. Good lawyers will give good service in an area which is notoriously difficult.

Your choice of lawyer is crucial. As with all professions, standards vary. Don't go to just anyone: personal recommendation by someone with experience is best. Find a relative, friend or workmate who has had actual dealings with a good solicitor or barrister and who is happy with the service received. There is often someone in DADS, a separated men's association or a men's group who will be able to give you the name of a good lawyer. Some contacts are listed at the end of the book.

There are undoubtedly excellent lawyers who achieve good results for parents both within and without the Family Court. They are not all motivated by the '*don't get mad, get everything*' philosophy. But the legal system is adversarial and you can't blame a lawyer for doing his best for his client when he knows that the law is on his side.

If you become disillusioned with the performance of your lawyer, don't hesitate to find another. You will be expected to settle your account with the first before the papers are released to your new solicitor. But be reasonable about this: don't expect him or her to satisfy all your demands or to agree with everything that you say and do. Your lawyer is only human and cannot be expected to achieve the impossible. And a good solicitor or barrister will not agree with you if you are wrong.

Take advice

Also, be open to advice. Be aware that you, like other newly separated men (particularly in the early stages of their separation), can be self-righteous, opinionated and pigheaded. Even if you are not the root cause of your problems, you might require some good advice. You might not like it but it may be sorely needed.

The cost of legal representation and court proceedings is a serious problem. The limitations of legal aid are extreme and a separated man with any kind of wage or salary will never qualify. You should talk to your lawyer about the possible range of costs that will be involved in pursuing your application both inside and outside the court. Ask him or her to set out in writing how much you will be charged and for what services. There are plenty of lawyers around these days who charge legal aid rates or close to them.

A solicitor's letter

What does not cost a lot of money is to ask a solicitor to write a courteous but firm letter to your wife. The letter will outline your complaints and direct her attention to current court orders. It will indicate your willingness to take court proceedings if those orders are not complied with. *But if you are not so willing, don't do it!* If you merely threaten and then don't follow through you have lost your bargaining power.

> I knew I couldn't get all I wanted from the court, but I was determined to fight on. I reckoned I owed it to the

kids and myself. My ex-wife would only agree to fortnightly access and I wanted more. It was a dreadful
time. In the end the court gave me three weekends each
month, so I don't think I did too badly. My solicitor was
really good but it cost me a small fortune.

Tony

ONE MOTHER'S STORY
We tried everything to settle our dispute about
where the children would live. We went to
counselling, we attended many mediation sessions,
both in the court and at a private agency. We had our
lawyers file applications in the Family Court. In the end
common sense and reality prevailed and we were able to
come to an agreement without the intervention of the court.
It took a lot of effort, concentration and heartache. It also
took a lot of time – about eighteen months – but I feel that
the time was important. It was a process of slow and painful
education. We all grew up a lot and got used to our new
lives.

The Family Court

The last port of call under the present regime is the court
hearing. This can be a traumatic and sometimes destructive
experience, not to be lightly entered into. However, there are
times and situations when such proceedings are necessary, for
your own benefit and for the good of your children.

You will do well not to expect the world from your solicitor
or barrister, nor from the judge and the result that he hands
down. You will have to accept the decision, at least until
circumstances change and you feel in a position to have the
court review the orders.

What is most likely to impress the judge is a reasonable
approach and a caring attitude, both from you and your legal
representative. Displays of temper and petulance from either
of you won't do you any good at all. If your advocate is being

unnecessarily rude and aggressive, tell him so and ask him to stop. If you feel he is incompetent, sack him and ask for an adjournment so that you might find another lawyer. But, in all things, be reasonable and be seen to be so.

Self-representation

It is possible for you to act for yourself, but it is not easy. It takes a bit of intelligence, a lot of courage, and the ability to express yourself in a reasonable way both on paper and in the courtroom. Although judicial officers are generally sympathetic, it is impossible to avoid the impression that they would prefer you to be legally represented.

The other big problem is that representing yourself places you in direct contact with your wife or her lawyer. Normally it will be the latter because, if she is not working, she will qualify for legal aid. You will, therefore, be carrying the burden of negotiation yourself and, if that fails, the job of contesting the matter in court, with all its intensity, emotion and frustration. This process is extremely stressful. Cross-examining your wife is unpleasant and is not calculated to produce better relations.

More and more men are now representing themselves in court proceedings, either through lack of money or because they see the futility in throwing away $20,000 or so for a fairly predictable result. If you decide to go down that road then help is available. Handbooks[112] and the occasional course will not make you a lawyer but they will certainly take a lot of the mystery out of the process. Again, contact with a men's support group will put you in touch with others who have done it.

In family law proceedings, sworn affidavits have to be filed before the hearing. A good compromise is to hire a lawyer to help you draft your affidavits and then conduct the case yourself.

Futility of continued efforts

Is there anything further that you can do? Under the present regime, no. You can keep going back to court if you will, but that is expensive and mostly futile. Generally speaking, the Family Court is unable or unwilling to do very much by way of enforcement of orders.

> Frankly, the Family Court system stinks. From my point of view it is biased towards the woman. I felt caught up in the system, in a no-win situation. Once the lawyers or police were involved, any attempt at resolution of our differences went out the door. I felt that I was no longer dealing with my wife but with the whole system.
>
> *Tom*

The options

What can a separated father do if he suffers constant frustration over contact with his children?

There seem to be three options at present:

★ **he fights all the way with solicitors, barristers, conferences and hearings in court**
★ **he stops trying, goes away and lets go of his children**
★ **he takes a middle course, pressing for counselling, mediation and perhaps one court hearing but no more**

The third option may be a reasonable way to go for the frustrated father, if only for his own sake. Because even if it doesn't work he will learn from the experience and will be able to reassure himself (and the children at a later time) that he did his best to stay in touch with them.

In the end, what often happens is that you are left to accept the situation as it is. You have to learn to muddle through, to do the best you can in the circumstances, and not to expect too much. This amounts to a *'letting go'* of your children, a recognition that your relationships with them will change, even perhaps become tenuous. While this is a depressing thought and hard to accept, it may well be the reality. It should not be, but it is. You can do no better than your best,

ON SELF-REPRESENTATION

✔ Talk to someone who's done it.

✔ Get help with your affidavits.

✔ Prepare your case.

✔ Visit the court and watch other cases.

✔ Rehearse your submissions with a friend.

✔ Take all your documents to court.

✔ Call the judge 'Your Honour' and the magistrate 'Your Worship'.

✔ Briefly outline what the application is about.

✔ Produce only evidence that is relevant to the case.

✔ Learn the difference between asking a question and making a statement.

✔ Don't make statements in court: you make submissions to the judge on interim applications and at the end of the case.

✔ Keep your cool. Don't lose your temper. Be polite.

and to show your children – to the extent that you are allowed – that you love and care for them.

The *'don't give a damn'* attitude

Sometimes putting on the *'I don't care'* or *'I couldn't give a damn'* attitude can work. The husband withdraws. He stops going to court, stops telephoning and pleading, stops chasing his children. He simply tells his wife and children that he is not prepared to be mucked around any more: *'It's not good for you*

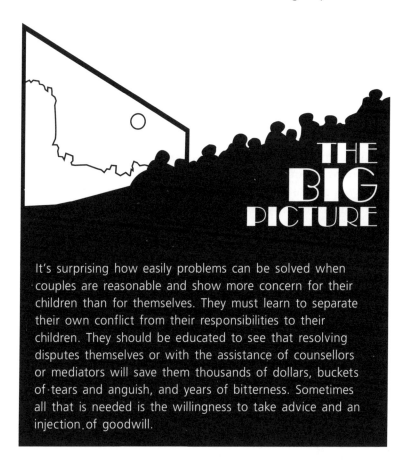

THE BIG PICTURE

It's surprising how easily problems can be solved when couples are reasonable and show more concern for their children than for themselves. They must learn to separate their own conflict from their responsibilities to their children. They should be educated to see that resolving disputes themselves or with the assistance of counsellors or mediators will save them thousands of dollars, buckets of·tears and anguish, and years of bitterness. Sometimes all that is needed is the willingness to take advice and an injection.of goodwill.

or your mother or me to keep having these troubles. I really love you and I want to see you. If you want to come, please ring me and I'll pick you up. But if you don't want to or are not allowed, I can't force you and I'm not going to try any more. I'm going to get on with my life.'

Some fathers have found that letting their ex-wives know they cannot upset them any more has resulted in better conduct.

On letting go

Most separated fathers have to 'let go' of their children to some extent. This is difficult and painful. Some may have to let go completely and accept that they have been blotted out of their children's lives. This can be agonising and remain a source of lasting sadness.

But a word of encouragement here: *don't give up too soon!* The early stages of your separation and divorce are very difficult and painful. The initial period of your access to your children will be the same. It takes a lot of sorting out, a lot of trial and error, tears and heartache. Ordinarily it will not be easy for you, your children or your ex-wife.

If you can get through this early stage with wit and wisdom (and a bit of luck!) you will find that *it does get easier!*

Stop paying?

If you are denied contact with your children it is tempting to use the only weapon that you have left: child support. When all else fails, you may feel like saying to your ex-wife: *'You won't let me have a decent relationship with my children, so I will not support them!'* After all, you reason, the children are not going to starve to death and it just might work.

However, if you think it through you will probably come to the view that it's not such a great idea after all. One reason is a practical one: you won't get away with it. Either the Family Court or the Child Support Agency will get on to you and force you to pay. It is one area where those institutions get serious about enforcement of orders.

Moreover, it will only give your ex-wife and children a 'stick' to hit you over the head with: *'He never really cared about us!'*

The other reason is more positive and meaningful. It is important for you as a father to be able to say to yourself and to your children that you are and will always be a decent father, who loves and cares for your children, who supports them as much as you are able, and who will maintain as close a relationship with them as is in your power.

Doing your best

You will demonstrate that care and love in a practical way by generously paying for their upkeep despite the difficulties you have with contact and even in cases where it is denied. You will then be in a position to assure them, some years down the track when they are old enough to make their own decisions and start questioning your role, that you did love them and that *you always did your best*.

This is asking a lot. It is far from easy to shell out money for children whom you rarely see. But be aware that children *need money*. Children who grow up in poverty are seriously disadvantaged and poverty is sometimes a result of divorce. It is not the children's fault that you and your wife separated.

Take the long view. If you are a decent person and a good and caring father, eventually your children are going to come to recognise that – no matter what rubbish their mother is feeding them. Children are very adept in sorting out fact from fiction and right from wrong. Hang on to that thought and hope for better times.

Keep on trying. Stay in contact. Stick at it.

> **It was a fight all the way. Initially she tried to cut me out of the children's lives. We spent a lot of time and money in court. I got all the orders in the world but she didn't care a fig for them and gave me limited access. However, I kept my cool, paid the maintenance and used every opportunity I found to show the kids I cared. I think they knew this and they must have put pressure on her because over the years things got better.**
>
> *Ben*

QUESTIONS	POSITIVE THOUGHTS AND RESOLUTIONS
★	
If there are problems, what are the best options for dealing with with them?	★ I will opt for a parenting plan.
★ How can I best communicate with my ex-wife?	★ I will press for counselling. ★ I will be open to advice.
★ What can I do to avoid going to court?	★ I will avoid court if I can. ★ I will try mediation.
★ Who can I talk to in order to get help?	★ I will always pay for the support of my children.
★ What must I do to show that I am really doing my best for my children?	★ I will continue to love my children and to be there for them.

But do not distress yourself with imaginings.
Many fears are born of fatigue and loneliness.
Desiderata

12

The Court –
A Failure for Families

I had reasonable access for a couple of years and things were not too bad. Then for some reason she stopped it and reported that I was abusing the children. She applied in the Family Court for access to be stopped and it was. Police and DOCS investigated and concluded that there was no basis for the allegations. The police believed that they were fabrications. It took eighteen months to get a hearing in the Family Court. At the hearing the judge refused to admit evidence of the police investigation. The hearing lasted four days but we had to wait over eight months before the judge handed down his judgment. It was in my favour and I now have contact with my children. But I had not seen them for two years. Aged five and eight, this was devastating. The whole process, from the time access was refused to the time it was restored, cost me two years of my children's lives, $40,000 in legal fees, and sent me bankrupt. There's got to be a better way.

Vince

The *Family Law Reform Act 1995* reformed the law and procedure relating to divorce.

Some of its aims were:

★ to eliminate the high costs, delays and indignities involved in the old fault-based divorce law
★ to simplify, and remove undue formality from, court proceedings
★ to introduce counselling
★ to provide for the effective enforcement of custody and access orders

In some areas the Act has been successful. Indeed, in abolishing the old grounds for divorce and replacing them with the single ground of irretrievable breakdown, the Act, in one stroke, rid us of the concept of fault and did away with the nonsense that entailed. For this, and for the emphasis on conciliation, we should be forever grateful.

Failed system

It must be said, however, that – despite the efforts of judges, registrars, counsellors and lawyers – the Family Law Act and the Family Court have in many ways failed to live up to their promise. The system is not achieving all of its aims. For many separated mothers and fathers it simply does not work.

Court proceedings are costly to the extent that protracted litigation is really available only to the wealthy and those in receipt of legal aid. Contact orders are not being enforced. The trappings of formality have reappeared with the reintroduction of wigs and gowns for judges and barristers, and with more solemnity than Lionel Murphy and the early judges ever envisaged.[113]

I didn't like the system at all. I was intimidated by the lawyers, documents, court and judge. I was not in control of any of it. I felt very vulnerable in the whole

process. So I was determined to settle it rather than press on to a hearing. I settled for less than my due.

John

The deficiencies in the family law system are widely recognised.[114] In 1992 the federal government set up a committee to examine the working of the Family Law Act. The committee presented a report to the government and changes to the law were drafted.[115] Some recommendations have appeared as amendments in the *Family Law Reform Act 1995*.[116] The law is fine in theory but flawed in practice.

The Family Law Act looks good on paper. It says all the right things. I just don't understand why the court does not interpret it the way it is written. I think the court system stinks. It sets people against one another. It produces anger and resentment.

Owen

The areas that cause the most problems for separated men (and often for women too) are the court's handling of contact problems, enforcement of orders, relocation of the custodial parent, the cost and adversarial nature of court proceedings, false allegations of violence and abuse, child support and property division.

These matters are discussed here and in the next couple of chapters.

Parental responsibility

The *Family Law Reform Act 1995* came into force in June 1996. It has introduced important changes to the Family Law Act and more amendments are to follow. Separated men will hope that the government has the courage to carry through with the process of reform.

The accent in the Family Law Reform Act is on *'parental responsibilities for children'*. *'Custody'* and *'access'* have been eliminated and replaced by *'residence'* and *'contact'* orders. These and other *'specific issues orders'* are called *'parenting orders'*, and there is provision for *'parenting plans'* to be presented to and approved by the court.

A prime object of the legislation is to encourage couples to use counselling, mediation or arbitration to decide issues and to settle disputes. Indeed the court must order the parties to attend counselling if that is considered to be in their best interests.

The best interests of the children

The law sets out the *'best interests'* of the child as its primary consideration. Whereas the Family Law Act has always insisted on the **welfare** of the child as its primary concern, the Family Law Reform Act expands this to a requirement that the court consider the **care, welfare and development** of the child.

Section 60B is worth quoting in full:

(1) The object of this Part is to ensure that children receive adequate and proper parenting to help them achieve their full potential, and to ensure that parents fulfil their duties, and meet their responsibilities, concerning the care, welfare and development of their children.

(2) The principles underlying this object are that:

(a) children have the right to know and be cared for by both their parents, regardless of whether their parents are married, separated, have never married or have never lived together; and

(b) children have a right of contact, on a regular basis with both their parents and with other people significant to their care, welfare and development; and

(c) parents share duties and responsibilities concerning the care, welfare and development of their children; and

(d) parents should agree about the future parenting of their children.

Sole custody

Contrary to the American practice of making orders that actively promote access to children, here in Australia for many years the practice of the court was to make orders for settled sole custody with access for, but no interference from, the absent parent. Access was seen almost as an optional extra! This has led to an 'overpowerment' of the custodial parent, often to the exclusion of the non-custodial parent from the children's lives. In plain language it means that the court has allowed custodial mothers the power to do what they want. The result of this has been that most divorced men in Australia *'end up virtually estranged from their children – sometimes by choice but very often because of deliberate obstruction [by] custodial mothers'.*[117]

Both parents

It is of some comfort to separated fathers to see that the Family Law Reform Act has finally dealt with this malaise. The new Act enshrines both the right of children *'to know and be cared for by both their parents'* and the duties and responsibilities of both parents *'concerning the care, welfare and development of their children . . .'*[118]

In other words there is a presumption of *joint parenting*. What separated men, women and children now need are clear signs that the Family Court is taking this seriously.

The 'friendly parent'

Separated fathers will also be heartened to read, in the new Act, provisions which insist that when it comes to making orders for the *'care, welfare and development of their children'* the court must take into account the behaviour and attitude of each parent to the children and to their parental responsibilities.[119]

This comes close to the situation in some American jurisdictions which provide that in custody orders the court will consider, among other factors, which parent is more likely to promote access, that is, who is the *friendly parent*. Many commentators are now suggesting that, given the evidence that contact with both parents is more important to children than where they live, the child's principal residence ought to be with that parent who is most likely to foster and maintain relationships with the other parent and the child's wider community, namely grandparents, relatives, friends, school and activities.[120]

I believe that in custody and contact disputes the court should give great weight to the 'friendly parent' concept. This will mean that in cases where one parent demonstrates an inability or unwillingness to allow the children to maintain relationships with both parents and where the other parent is reasonable, there is a good case for making the latter the custodial parent.

Enforcement of orders

By far the most galling problem for separated fathers is the court's inability or unwillingness to enforce its orders, in particular contact orders. It is not difficult to get orders from the court, but their enforcement is another question altogether.[121]

> She moved to Queensland and refused me contact with my daughter. When I took it to court she failed to answer the summons. I obtained a warrant and travelled to Queensland with federal police. We seized my daughter and brought her back to Sydney. She then travelled to Sydney and appeared in court. She applied for custody and I agreed. Contact orders were made. She never complied with them. I had no contact for twelve months so I went back to court. The case was moved to a Queensland court but she still failed to appear. She told me: 'Take me to court if you like. What are they going to do to me? They won't put me in gaol!'
>
> *Jason*

In the Family Law Act there are extensive provisions for the enforcement of court orders, stretching from bonds and fines to imprisonment. The Family Law Reform Act has added a whole range of injunctions which can be used against offenders. The new Act provides that if a person interferes with a residence, contact or other order of the court, then that person has to justify what he or she has done.[122] It also provides that where a person has interfered with an order the court can take any action that it considers appropriate.

But there is an immense gap between theory and practice. In practice, the custodial parent can get away with just about anything! Under the present system, in protracted access disputes the caring father will always lose. He soon learns that there is no redress or cure from the court. So he goes away and distances himself from the family. She wins. All a difficult mother has to do in the current climate is to keep up the disruption until her husband retires from the fight, and the court will neither chastise nor correct her.

> I think the family law system is rotten. It is biased against the man and towards the woman. It is hamstrung by the blinkered views and expectations of the parties which are fed by adversarial lawyers. The court has traditional/stereotypical views on family roles and these largely dictate the determinations and orders of the court.
>
> *Damian*

Everyone – the Joint Select Committee, the court, the Australian Law Reform Commission, professionals and litigants – agree that the Family Court is *'underutilising'* its powers to enforce access orders.[123] The greatest number of complaints about the court arise from its failure to enforce its orders.[124]

Where's there's a will there's a way

It's all very well to have enforcement laws on paper; what is required is the will to make them work.

For most separated fathers the principal source of frustration with the Family Court is its prevailing philosophy. It appears to be: *We can't change your ex-wife's attitudes or behaviour when she herself is unwilling to do so; we can't enforce court orders if she is defiant, and we really can't smooth out access for you. We are not in a position to supervise your relationships with your ex-wife and children. We don't want to upset the children. Therefore, we can only encourage you to do the best that you can with the situation.*

This is not good enough. What is needed in the Family Court is a new spirit and a determination to promote cooperative parenting in the terms of the new Act.

The judge could see what was going on. In fact at one stage he asked her if she was using the children to punish me. She admitted she was! But at no stage did he chastise her for that. All he did was to make more orders for her to flaunt.

Dennis

Courage in the court

The court needs to be willing to act with firmness and with a certain measure of flexibility. I do not mean that the court should be whimsical and act precipitously without a proper hearing and consideration of all the evidence. But if there is evidence that some arrangement is not working, or that the previous orders are ineffective, then the court should not be slow to act.

The Family Court is rightly concerned with the welfare of the children. However, in many cases it seems that the court is overburdened with considerations of the *immediate* welfare of the children in contrast to their *long-term* benefit. For instance, the children may be upset in the short term by a change in custody and access, but it may be to their everlasting good. The court should avoid taking the easy way out of such dilemmas. Too often, I suspect, the court identifies 'the best interests of the children' with the avenue that causes them least immediate disruption.[125]

The problems for **children** in the current family law system are widely acknowledged. *'However, the focus of the court remains on the parental contest and it would be fair to say that the processes of family law litigation do not always serve the needs or interests of children or allow their effective participation.'*[126]

It's time for the judges of the court to be courageous and firm. If one parent persists in mucking up access then something should be done about it, and if that involves a transfer of custody to a father or the imposition of a fine on a mother, then so be it! Similarly, if a father, through violence, abuse and drink, has rendered contact thoroughly unpleasant, then let the court deny him access until he learns to behave himself.

Quick to stop; slow to enforce

The complaint of fathers is that the court is quick to stop contact but slow to enforce it. The Family Court never hesitates to stop and punish men who are abusive, who breach court orders or fail to pay child support. *'But when it comes to taking sanctions against custodial parents who deny access to their children, judges have traditionally gone to water.'*[127]

I firmly believe that fines and orders for costs would be effective in reducing non-compliance with court orders. Imprisonment is not a reasonable option except in the most extraordinary circumstances. Perhaps community service on access days would be a useful penalty for a recalcitrant custodial parent.

> In the two years after our separation I spent $60,000 in legal fees for court cases directly attributable to my ex-wife's obstruction of contact with our children, and on her baseless allegations of harassment. In not one of these cases were her actions justified and yet I was never successful in applications for costs. Eventually I ended up appearing for myself.
>
> *Daniel*

Judges have been reluctant to impose financial penalties on a wife on the ground that she can't afford it or *it will take food out of the children's mouths* or it will merely involve a shift in maintenance payments. This idea needs to be discarded. It does not apply to parking and traffic fines. Why should it in the family law arena? There is nothing like the sting of a moderate fine to remind defaulting parties of their responsibilities! They can always pay by instalments.

Further non-compliance with orders or refusal to pay a fine or costs could be dealt with by community service orders or even the extreme measure of a suspension or reduction of maintenance payments.

The ultimate sanction is, of course, the removal of the children from the care of a consistently recalcitrant parent. If the court is serious about the ultimate good of the children it must grasp this nettle. The court must let defaulting parties know that it means business. The word will soon get around.

It is unfair that the innocent parent has to go back to court and pay legal costs in order to enforce orders that the court has already made. The court itself should accept that burden. Attached to each Family Court there should be lawyers – in-house or from Legal Aid or private practitioners on a duty roster – who will press the enforcement of orders on behalf of an aggrieved parent. Costs should be paid by the guilty parent.

Moving away

The traditional unwillingness of the Family Court to interfere with the right of the custodial parent to live wherever he or she likes has been disturbing. This right has often meant taking the children to live interstate or a long distance away from the non-custodial parent.

This rigid view has undergone some modification in later cases.[128] However, the court has continued to place the interests of the mother ahead of those of the children. Judges continue to observe that if the mother is not allowed to live where she wishes she will be unhappy and if she is unhappy the children will be unhappy. Imagine the reaction this gets from a father contemplating the prospect of his children's living a thousand kilometres away!

The court's attitude on this matter has not been soundly based and has been more concerned with avoiding immediate problems than with solving them. It also conflicts with the principle that the children's, not the parents', welfare is paramount.[129] Several cases speak of the court's unwillingness to interfere with the freedom of movement of the custodial parent unless it is proved that the move will adversely affect the welfare of the children. What this fails to acknowledge is that a breakdown of healthy **regular** access **does** affect the welfare, happiness and development of the children. The Family Court has not accepted this.

Black and white

The *Family Law Reform Act 1995* offered hope of a real change in the attitude of the court to this problem. For the first time we have written, in black and white, recognition of '*the child's right to maintain personal relations and direct contact with both parents on a regular basis.*'[130] In fact, the practical difficulties and expenses involved are matters that the court must take into account in making orders that are in '*the best interests of the child*'. Surely these new provisions would force the court to take a stricter view of a shift in residence that would substantially limit regular contact between child and parent.

Unfortunately, the desired change did not come.

There was both good and bad news for separated fathers in the Queensland relocation case.[131] The good part is that the court recognised what the Family Law Act says about children's need for regular contact with both parents. The bad part is that it does not accept that **regular** needs to be **frequent**.

The good part is that the court held that the decision to relocate must be in the best interests of the children. The bad part is that it continues to equate the best interests of the children with those of the mother.

Separated fathers should not be too disappointed at the result of this case, as there is much of positive value in the judgment. It was also a case that had its own special features. There is every reason to hope that in future the court is going to subject applications by custodial parents to relocate to a more rigorous scrutiny.

The really worrying feature of this case was that the court justified its decision as being in the best interests of the children concerned. The result – allowing the mother and children to move a thousand kilometres away from their father, relatives, friends and school – was presented by some commentators as a victory for the children's interests. It was no such thing. It was a loss for the children because these relationships will be diminished. It was a victory for the mother because she will be free to pursue a new life with her new partner. The case continues the court's preference for adult relationships over those of children.

Three problems

The Queensland case reveals at least three problems in the court's attitude to relocation issues. One, it is not difficult for a custodial mother to persuade the court that the children's welfare is so inextricably linked with her own happiness that if the latter is denied then the '*quality of her motherhood*' will be diminished and this will harm the children ('*what's good for the mother is good for the kids!*'). Two, the court is still imbued with a preference for adult satisfaction over and above that of children ('*children can cope, adults can't!*'). Three, children's relationships with an absent parent can be sustained by contact which is *regular* but not necessarily *frequent* (half the school holidays are good enough!).

Arguments may rage about the first two, but the last concept is absurd. It's only lawyers and judges who could come up with a concept as nonsensical as that!

It is difficult to see any indication that judges really appreciate the intensity of the love between father and child and their mutual grief at being separated for long periods of time. Rather they view the unimpeded peace of mind of the mother as intrinsically linked to the welfare of the children, and the children's relationship with their father as secondary to that.

Or is it because there is a belief in the Family Court and among family law professionals that, at a pinch, children with a good mother can really do without their father, or, at best, regard him comfortably as a figure in the background? I suspect this belief is alive and well. It flies in the face of the more reasoned and researched view that a father is a figure of critical importance in the development of his children.[132]

> My ex-wife decided out of the blue that she and the children would like to live in Queensland. There was no good reason for this. I fought the move in the Family Court. She told the judge that her parents were intending to move to the same place. There was no evidence of this and it turned out to be nonsense, but the judge accepted it. He allowed her to go and gave me access during school holidays. No one had asked the kids about their feelings. They went and within two months were back in town and have been here ever since. Apparently the kids jacked up and wanted to come back.
>
> *Harry*

Separated fathers look forward to further development in the court's attitude to this problem. If a custodial mother wishes to change her residence in a way that will prevent regular (*frequent*) access between child and father, the onus should be on her to prove that such a change is unavoidable and will not be detrimental to the child's welfare. Secondly, the right of a father and child to regular contact ought to be given the same status as the right of a custodial mother to live where she desires, and should be put ahead of the needs of her new relationship. Sometimes the best solution will be for the relocating mother to let the children live with their father.

Regular contact

The difficulties in the enforcement of contact orders should be seen in the context of the need of the children to maintain close and regular contact with the absent parent.

Let's face it: maintaining a good relationship with someone means that you see them often and regularly. The notion that an absent parent can have a meaningful relationship with children he sees only three or four times a year is nonsense. It doesn't matter how long these visits are, they are no substitute for weekly or even fortnightly contact.

> **I no longer feel involved in the life of my son. He lives in another State and I only see him for three weeks a year. I ring him once a week.**
>
> *Wayne*

Court costs and delay

A further area of concern for separated fathers is the cost and delay of family law proceedings in court. The ordinary person simply cannot afford it. Many men have exhausted their savings on fighting in court for orders which were theirs by right and ought never to have been opposed.

Then there is the delay factor. If a dispute cannot be settled or mediated, the matter has to go to a hearing before a judge. It may take a year or more before the court is in a position to hear the case. In the meantime the errant behaviour continues and this can work untold damage to the relationships involved.

> **My ex-wife wanted to stop my contact with my little boy. She tried all sorts of things but I wouldn't go away. Finally she accused me of sexually abusing my son and we ended up in court. After an interim hearing all contact was suspended. I could not even have supervised contact. I have not seen my son for nine months. So far it has cost me $5000.**
>
> *Dean*

The adversarial system

The adversarial system works well in the criminal law arena. But it should never have been applied to family law. We have gone down the wrong path. Unlike criminal law, in family matters after separation we are concerned with **truth**, the truth about the nature of future parenting that will best provide for the **care, welfare and development** of the children. This truth cannot be discovered through examination and cross-examination of witnesses by advocates pushing their own barrows and promoting the interests of their clients. It involves human and socio-economic issues. It can only be discovered by careful, calm and objective enquiry.

ONE MAN'S STORY
To win in the Family Court you've got to lie. Telling the truth won't get a man anywhere. My ex-wife and boyfriend gave evidence that they had a stable relationship and would continue to live near the children's schools. Eight months after the judgment they had broken up and she had moved three times. The judges are impressed by people who know how to perform and by experts. There's little common sense or wisdom in their judgments. They simply do not get at the truth. It's a secret court so people don't know what's going on. It's a scandal.

The adversarial nature of our court system makes the experience tense, unpleasant and emotionally draining. Even before the parties get to the terror of cross-examination, the allegations in the affidavits are enough to set them at one another's throats. After documents are exchanged and accusations levelled, any hope of future peace is destroyed forever.

Before that, the stage is set for confrontation when court documents – applications, summonses and affidavits – are served on an unsuspecting parent. The lawyers take over and often fuel disputes by encouraging their clients to insist on their 'rights'. And then there is the formal and alien atmosphere of the courtroom itself. How can such an environment provide an outcome which is in the best interests of children?

> In a forum that pays scant regard to laws of evidence, where an alienated person, full of resentment and hatred and motivated by fear, can accuse a former spouse of anything he or she and an advocate can think up, how can even the most objective judge arrive at a meaningful ruling? Surely any person with the most basic grasp of the issues can see that this is the worst possible time to enter a system which is adversarial.
>
> *Desmond*

A new forum

Increased emphasis on conciliation and greater access to counselling and mediation are only part of the cure. In its present form the court system either does not work or is superfluous. A more radical approach is called for.

I believe we should start with the recognition that the court is not an appropriate forum for the establishment of parenting patterns after separation. There is a good argument that this could best be done through another and separate mechanism.

The Family Commission

The suggestion that there be established a new body (let's call it the *Family Commission* for want of a better name), quite separate from the court, is not a new one but is a proposal worth considering.

This Family Commission would have *Family Centres* in accessible locations and they would be made up of mediators, arbitrators, counsellors and social workers. No representation would be permitted except in special circumstances. Separated men and women would approach the Commission in person,

ONE MOTHER'S SOLUTION

Where decisions are made about the future care of children, I don't think that one person should be responsible for the final decision. Rather a tribunal of, say, three people should review the case, with a majority decision, and there should be a right of appeal. This would remove much of the present arbitrariness of the Family Court and its conflict of interest between the rights of adults and the rights of the child. The tribunal should make use of expert opinion where required and this should include the children's rights to be heard and to have their opinions taken seriously.

explain their problems and be given appropriate assistance by a team of professionals. A case-worker would be assigned to each couple and be accessible in person or by telephone.

The Family Centre would have an outreach function. Social workers would visit homes and supervise parenting plans devised in the centre. Early intervention would be a priority. It would be compulsory for couples to take their problems to the commission, which would become the normal place for settling disputes and sorting out parenting plans.

Each centre would have a *Family Tribunal* to arbitrate disputes that were not settled through mediation and counselling. The Family Tribunal would be made up of mature and educated persons (not only lawyers and social workers), who would sit in twos or threes to hear cases. The proceedings would be by way of inquiry.

The Family Court of Australia would be strictly an arena of last resort or a court of appeal, besides attending to the legal technicalities of divorce and property orders.

In getting at the *truth* of matters in dispute, officers from the centre would interview parents and children in their homes, as well as neighbours, relatives and others who know the husband and wife. Surely this would be wiser than relying on the opinions of so-called experts who examine a child and each parent for an hour or two and then make recommendations about what should happen. The role of grandparents

THE BIG PICTURE

There is little more that can be done with the Family Court in its current form. It's difficult to see any prospect of real change in the court while the iniquitous section 121 of the Family Law Act remains in force. This not only prevents fair reporting but excludes the court from public scrutiny, always a valuable check on judicial wisdom.

Despite reforms, the system remains slow, expensive, adversarial and ineffective. The new Act offered hope for ordinary people with its insistence on disputes being settled and parenting plans worked out away from the courtroom. But nothing has changed very much for hundreds of fathers and mothers who are frustrated in their attempts to obtain just and lasting solutions to serious problems that occur after separation.

A radical change is called for. A new body is needed to encourage and assist couples to sort out healthy patterns of parenting after separation and divorce. Right from the beginning of separation, couples must be set on the right track. Only in that way will their children be spared the negative consequences of divorce.

ought to be recognised here. In most cases they are sensible people who could provide valuable information on the care of the children to a counsellor or tribunal.

The Family Commission – its administrators, counsellors, social workers, mediators and arbitrators – would be imbued with a defined philosophy. This would be to treat all persons with courtesy and care and to act always in the long-term interests of the children and their parents. A no-nonsense approach would be followed — insisting that orders and agreements be honoured and breaches not tolerated.

Pilot study

Perhaps a pilot study carried out to test the idea would throw light on whether or not such a scheme would work.[133]

The reply of Family Court supporters to these suggestions is that such radical changes are no longer necessary. They point to the emphasis on counselling and mediation in the *Family Law Reform Act 1995*, to the efforts of thoughtful lawyers and judges to have the parties settle matters without litigation, and to the statistic that 95 percent of cases are in fact settled without the necessity of a final judicial hearing.[134]

However, these are not valid arguments for the retention of the present system. Indeed, on the contrary, they point inexorably to the conclusion that in 95 percent of matters the court itself is superfluous.

We do not need an expensive court system, with large and luxurious courtrooms, bewigged judges and lawyers, and complex procedures to facilitate the process of mediation and conciliation between separating spouses. Indeed such an atmosphere is generally not conducive to mediation. An application in the Family Court is a challenge to the other party: *'This is what I want and I intend to approach a judge to get it!'* Despite the best efforts of many lawyers, it inevitably becomes a contest with one party wanting to win. It's hard to blame a lawyer for wanting to use the system to get what is best for a client. Indeed a lawyer has an obligation to push a client's case and this usually leads him or her to attack the other party's case. This emphasises confrontation and creates hostility. Unfortunately it's clear that some lawyers foster litigation rather than conciliation.

Things to do

If you feel that you have been unfairly treated and are unable to change the situation, what is important is that you get over your initial anger and bitterness as soon as possible.

There are some other things that you *can* do. You can contribute to changes in the law by writing to your federal member of parliament and by joining fathers' associations, family law reform bodies and lobby groups. You may benefit from joining a men's group which offers personal support and an environment in which you can speak freely. Getting away from a narrow concentration (perhaps fixation) on your own problems and widening your areas of interest could have a positive and healthy effect on you.

ANOTHER MAN'S STORY

All I wanted was reasonable contact with my children. All she wanted was to cut me out of their lives. The boys were seven and nine. The case went for nine days. Allegations flew backwards and forwards with little intervention from the judge. My barrister cross-examined her for three days. I was cross-examined for two days. There were two psychiatric reports, one favourable to her case and the other to mine. Two friends who had known both of us for years gave character evidence but they were not allowed to express opinions. At one stage I was cross-examined for hours on incidents that had occurred in the late eighties and early nineties. I wondered what all this had to do with two little boys seeing their dad once a fortnight. It was ridiculous.

QUESTIONS	POSITIVE THOUGHTS AND RESOLUTIONS
★	★
What things must I do to qualify as a *friendly parent*?	I'll stay away from lawyers and the court if I can.
★	★
What efforts have I made to keep regular contact with my children?	I'll remind everyone that the children have a right to see me.
★	★
What am I doing about reform of the family law system?	I will do my best to make contact work.
★	★
What am I doing to balance my own needs with my struggle to be a good father?	I'll stick to our parenting plan.
	★
	I will live close to my children.
	★
	I'll lobby for changes in the system.

Avoid loud and aggressive persons, they are vexatious to the spirit.

Desiderata

13

False Allegations and AVOs

I was arrested by police in my own home, in front of my children, and with neighbours looking on. I was taken to the local police station, interrogated for several hours and locked up overnight. The next morning I appeared before the magistrate. I had never been in court before. The magistrate refused bail and I was transported to gaol. It was a week before I got out. I had never been in trouble before, had been in the same job for over ten years, and was well known in my community. In the next twelve months I had to appear in court over twenty times. All the charges involved false accusations by my ex-wife and each and every one of them was eventually dismissed by the court. Financially and emotionally it broke me.

Gregory

Criminal lawyers talk about the police *trifecta*. They mean those charges which police often bring (sometimes without justification) against troublesome citizens: *offensive language, resist arrest*, and *assault police*.

Regrettably, we now have a parallel in family law: *denial of access, apprehended violence orders (AVOs)*, and *false sexual allegations (FSAs)*. For many separated men, they often follow one another as night follows day. Lawyers who practise daily in the Family Court report that they are common strategies in the armoury of custodial mothers who want to limit or terminate children's contact with their fathers.

> **One lawyer said that he was surprised that my ex-wife had not accused me of sexual abuse of the children. He suggested that it would help my application for custody if I accused her new husband of the same! I couldn't believe what I was hearing.**
>
> *Chris*

Domestic violence myths

We all know that there are violent men and that some men abuse their children. But they are in the minority. The great majority of men are not violent or abusive, yet they are being branded and made to suffer for the sins of the few.

Violence needs to be viewed in its proper context and divorced from myths and gender arguments. The exaggeration in domestic violence statistics by feminists who portray violence as an all-male problem and ignore other forms of violence does not advance protection in our communities.[135] The greatest incidence of violence is that committed by young men against other young men. The incidence of male-against-female and male-against-child violence is undeniably significant, but so is that of women against children. In some studies mothers have emerged as serious abusers of children.[136] There is also growing awareness of a level of violence inflicted by women against their male partners.[137] All violence in our society must be condemned. It is wrong to strike another person, whether man, woman or child.

AVOs and protection

There was a clear need for anti-violence legislation and general support for its introduction in Australian States and in New Zealand. It has made a valuable contribution to the protection of citizens, especially women and children. It is immensely sad to see AVOs being perverted into a means of driving wedges between fathers and their children.

You need to know about AVOs so that you can develop a reasonable attitude to them and so that you will handle yourself with common sense and firmness if you have to go to court.

Courts in all Australian States and Territories and in New Zealand have the power to issue apprehended violence orders. Breaches of these orders and actions like stalking and intimidation are now offences and are punishable by fines or imprisonment.[138]

A magistrate in a Local Court may make an order against a defendant if he or she is satisfied on the balance of probabilities that the complainant fears violence to herself, children or property, and has *reasonable grounds* for these fears. It does not have to be actual violence. Threats are enough.

Harassment or molestation, stalking or intimidation, are also grounds for the making of orders. These include conduct that causes a *reasonable apprehension* of injury to a person or property.

The complainant

A person may lodge and swear a complaint herself or a police officer may do it for her. Indeed, the police are obliged to make a complaint on behalf of a person who a police officer believes or suspects has been or will be a victim of domestic violence, stalking or child abuse. However, the officer is not obliged to if he knows the person herself will lodge the complaint or if he believes that there is good reason not to make the complaint. In the latter case he must record the reason in writing.

You would think that believing there is '*good reason not to make the complaint*' would encourage police officers to refuse to have anything to do with frivolous complaints. Unfortunately, these days this is not the case. The police have come under such pressure from members of the public, politicians, the media and their own superiors that they are afraid *not* to press a complaint.

You can hardly blame them. Most people have heard about cases where a complaint has not been taken seriously and there has been a violent tragedy. In these cases the first to be blamed are the police and the magistrate who granted bail to the perpetrator.

Discretion

Nevertheless, it is not good enough for police to be seen to be jumping to the tune of every complainant and leaving it to the court to sort out the mess. Police should be trained to use the discretion that the legislation gives them and refuse to have anything to do with patently stupid complaints. It does nothing for the image of the police for them to be seen supporting spurious complaints.

It is encouraging to hear that chamber magistrates will soon be given a discretion to issue or not to issue a summons or a warrant on receipt of a complaint. A magistrate properly armed with education, guidelines and common sense can provide a real service in keeping unworthy complaints away from busy court lists. The magistrate can divert potential litigants from court and send them to helping agencies such as counsellors.

Something has to be done to stop women dragging men to court over something as trivial as raised voices or

> dirty looks, let alone completely false allegations.
> Courts should refuse to accept nonsensical complaints
> and magistrates should order costs against the false
> accuser. My ex-wife had me in court ten times on spu-
> rious applications and I beat every one of them. I had
> to take time off work but I could not get an order for
> costs against her.
>
> *Bernie*

In court it ought not to be police prosecutors who press the complaint on behalf of the complainant. It is good to know that there are moves afoot to change this. Solicitors from the Office of the Director of Public Prosecutions or local 'duty solicitors' should do that job. Although this is now provided for in the law, more often than not the police take on a role of support for the complainant rather than their traditional role of impartial enforcers of the law and of peace and good order. This is undesirable and should be changed.

Legal representation by means of legal aid or duty solici-tors ought to be readily available – subject to means tests – to both complainant and defendant. At present this is not the case. Complainants have access to domestic violence liaison officers (police officers) and to Court Assistance schemes. Defendants, unless they can afford legal representation, receive no assistance whatsoever. Yet experience has shown that rep-resentation often results in speedier resolution of cases.[139]

Getting a summons

If your ex-wife has sworn a complaint and is seeking an AVO, you will be served with a *summons* to this effect, telling you when you have to appear in court. The mere service of a summons is a nasty experience for an innocent father who is having problems with child contact and who knows that his ex-wife is merely using the process to harass him and to limit that contact.

> The police came to the door and gave me the summons.
> When they told me what it was about and I read it I
> felt sick in the stomach. I knew nothing about the
> allegations and I had no warning. I felt absolutely
> powerless.
>
> *Arnold*

The first rule is: *Don't panic!* It's happening all over the country to hundreds of separated men. Talk to men who have had similar experiences and see how they handled the situation. Many men successfully appear for themselves. It may or may not be necessary for you to arrange for legal representation. Before you do, check with the court to see if a duty solicitor will advise you or appear for you.

At court: facing the magistrate

- As soon as you get to court go to the office and ask for leaflets entitled *Apprehended Violence Orders – Information for Defendants*. Spend some time reading them.
- It's unusual for an application to be heard on the first day. Normally it will be adjourned to another day for hearing. On the first day the case will be *mentioned*, and that will give you an opportunity to tell the magistrate briefly what it is all about.
- If family law proceedings are underway, don't forget to tell the magistrate about these.
- A rather nasty shock for men/defendants in AVO proceedings is that the magistrate will talk about *bail*. This is because AVO applications automatically bring bail law into play. Where a case is not resolved on the first day in court, the magistrate will adjourn it for further hearing and will consider the question of bail. He will tell you about this and you can address him on the bail conditions. This is annoying but is simply part of the procedure, so don't let it stick in your craw.
- Right from the beginning, *protest your innocence and tell*

the magistrate the real reason for the application. You may say something like:

'*Your worship, I oppose the making of any orders with regard to this complaint. The complaint is completely unjustified, the allegations are spurious, and the complainant is using these proceedings as a weapon to stop my contact with my children. This application is an abuse of process. I am confident that I will be able to illustrate that and I will be asking for costs against the complainant.*'

The magistrate will urge you to talk to your wife or her lawyer or the police if this has not already happened. You need to know the options that are available to you. Apart from giving in and agreeing to whatever orders your wife wants – which I am presuming to be unacceptable – there are three options.

1. Undertakings. You may seek to settle the matter by giving mutual undertakings: you promise to do or not to do certain things and your ex-wife does the same. Or, you give undertakings yourself without requiring her to do anything. Once the undertakings are agreed on, no AVO is made and the complaint and application are dismissed. This is the easiest and least painful solution to the problem. It is not always acceptable to the complainant as undertakings do not have the force of orders and cannot be enforced. However, she may be reassured with the possibility of bringing a fresh AVO before the court, and the magistrate may simply adjourn the present application for a period of time to see how the undertakings work out.

2. Consent orders. This means that, without admitting that you are at fault in any way, you agree to the order that she wants or to mutually acceptable orders. The magistrate will then make the orders and you can all go home. But be aware that if that happens *an AVO is in place and if you knowingly breach it you commit an offence which can bring you back to court.* Indeed, once an order is made, if a breach is suspected or alleged you can be summonsed or arrested with or without a warrant. You will be brought before the court, bail will be in question, and a hearing on the breach will take place.

There's a lot of pressure being put on men to avoid a hearing by agreeing to orders. Police and court staff are trying to cut down the workload by persuading men that this is the easiest and quickest way to get the case out of the way. Often men are intimidated into agreeing to orders which are completely unwarranted. Then they find the orders are used as weapons against them. It's not on! Don't settle. Fight. You can't do any worse!

Ron

The making of an AVO is a serious matter, and for that reason you ought not to agree to it lightly. It has the advantage of being quick and inexpensive. If it will not trouble or inconvenience you in any way, well and good. But be aware of the pitfalls.

3. Resistance. The third option is to fight. If you know that the allegations are spurious and that your ex-wife is simply using the system to gain some tactical advantage over you, and if you have the money, time and courage to do it, then go for it!

You may win in the end and have the complaint thrown out of court. But be warned: sometimes AVOs can be difficult to defend because the magistrate only has to be satisfied *on the balance of probabilities* that the complaint is reasonable. Many men have had the experience of having a completely false and unreasonable complaint upheld by a magistrate.

Her AVO complaint was a set-up. The magistrate said he believed my evidence and did not accept that I was a violent person or that I would use violence (as had been alleged by my wife). Nevertheless he said that she did in fact have such fears, so he was obliged to make an AVO against me! He was wrong. I think the process has become a revolving door, a standard tool for a woman to take the moral high-ground in any matrimonial dispute.

Blake

Interim orders

If the matter is adjourned to another day, don't be surprised if the magistrate makes *interim orders* in favour of your ex-wife. These are temporary orders that will remain in force until the case can be heard. The magistrate will note your objections and the fact that the allegations are contested. But in most cases the magistrate will take little persuasion to make such interim orders that he or she sees as a prudent measure after reading the complaint. The orders will often be just what the complainant has asked for.

In fact, if a person has been *charged* with a domestic violence or stalking offence, the court is *obliged* to make an interim AVO against that person unless it decides that such an order is not required.

It is extremely upsetting to have an order made against you in circumstances where you maintain that the complaint is completely without foundation. But again, rest assured that it is part of the process and try to realise that the magistrate, having no opportunity to hear evidence and to test the strength of the complaint, has little alternative but to provide the protection that is sought – just in case the complaint *is* valid. At that point the magistrate does not know what your wife is up to.

Serious stuff

What you *must* do if an order – be it interim or final – is made by the court is *to take it very seriously*. Because although the order itself does not mean that you have been convicted of a criminal offence – and therefore does not appear on your record – *a breach is a criminal offence and can be punished by a fine or imprisonment or both.*

Make sure you get a copy of the order and understand precisely what it means. If there is any doubt ask for clarification. Then you must obey it to the letter, no matter how much that hurts. If the court is satisfied beyond reasonable doubt that you have *knowingly* contravened an order, then it will convict you of an offence which *will* appear on your criminal record and which can be used against you in future procedings and in the Family Court.

No matter how insulting or silly it seems, always obey an order of the court.

Keep notes and have a witness

Protect yourself against allegations of breach of orders by keeping a diary of events and conversations. If you fear that a blow-up is likely when you go to pick up the children, take a witness with you, ideally one who is independent from the family. If there are complaints about your behaviour with the children during contact ask a family member or a friend to spend time with you when the children are there. It's a real hassle but may stand you in good stead when next you have to appear in court.

Support

While this is going on, keep talking to your lawyer if you have one, and especially to men from family law groups who can give you advice and settle you down. Faced with false allegations, and traumatised by court hearings that are weighted against him, it is easy for a man to go into *emotional overload*. It is vital that he look after himself – his physical and mental health, his management of anger and depression.

> **Network support is very important. I got help from other men who had been through the same experience and I went along to a Family Law Reform association. They were a big comfort. I saw that I wasn't on my own and how common this problem was. I got a lot of support and good advice.**
>
> *David*

tips

✔ Keep notes of all contact with your ex-wife and children.
✔ Talk to other men with experience of AVOs.
✔ Get some legal advice.

✔ Look after your mental and physical health.
✔ Strengthen your spirit through meditation and stress management.

Police powers

The police have wide powers in the area of domestic violence. They can arrest a person with or without a warrant if they believe that he has either inflicted violence or threatened it. They can remove him from his home in these circumstances, whether or not they place him under arrest. They can enter a home without a warrant on the invitation of one person or if they believe that an offence is about to be committed. They can search for weapons and remove any they find.

An interim AVO will suspend any permit or licence you may have to possess firearms. A final AVO will revoke it. Indeed, once a final AVO has been made you will not be allowed to hold a firearm licence for ten years. If possession of firearms is raised against you in court you will be well advised to offer to surrender them immediately to the police. Otherwise you may have the nasty experience of the police turning up on your doorstep and searching your home.

An AVO can prevent you from entering or going near the matrimonial home even if you still own it.

Appeal

If you lose and have an AVO made against you, you have a right of appeal to the District Court. Here the case will be reheard by a judge. Again, if you have the money, time and energy, this may be a good option, particularly if the AVO is going to be used against you in the Family Court. Get a good lawyer if you can, but most judges will give you a reasonable hearing if you decide to appear for yourself.

If you win in court, ask for a costs order against the complainant. Magistrates and judges have the power to award costs if the complaint is *vexatious* or *frivolous*, and they should not hesitate to do so in those cases where it is obvious that the AVO was sought merely for tactical or improper reasons. Unfortunately there is no provision for costs against police complainants. Even if you don't get costs, it is to be hoped that the threat of such an order plus the experience of being cross-examined will dissuade your ex-wife from causing trouble in future.

What about *cross-claims*? If you have a real and serious basis for a cross-application for an AVO against your wife, then you might consider pressing a complaint. Similarly, if you think that such an action will deter her from pressing on there might be an argument for it. However, I wouldn't jump too easily that way. It will complicate and lengthen the proceedings and could be seen merely as a tactical ploy. Take some advice.

False sexual allegations

One of the classic ploys used by hostile mothers to prevent contact is the accusation of sexual abuse of a child by the father.

> **You really start to doubt your own sanity. I knew I had done nothing wrong but it went on for so long – investigation by the department, contact with the police, appearances in the Family Court, interviews with**

> the psychologist – that I started to ask myself: 'Perhaps
> I did do these things!'
>
> *Derrick*

There are few experiences so devastating for a father than to be accused falsely of sexually abusing his child or children. Of course you won't hear about it from the children. You will be lucky to hear any details from anyone! One of the really frustrating features of such allegations is that no one wants to tell you anything. It hangs above you like a black cloud.

It often comes to you by way of refusal of access and veiled excuses from your ex-wife. In New South Wales, for instance, you might be told by a child protection worker that the agency has some concerns about the children. Your ex-wife refuses to elaborate. You telephone the agency and are told that they are not in a position to give you any information. Eventually an appointment is made and you get to see the officer in charge of the file relating to your children.

> I was ushered into a small room by a severe-looking
> man who told me that he was a 'child protection
> worker'. He then immediately told me that my two
> daughters had been sexually abused. 'You have had the
> opportunity to do it', he said, adding triumphantly, 'and
> you must have done it.' I was completely, totally over-
> whelmed. In the one moment I had learnt that my two
> innocent girls had been the victims of sexual assaults,
> and that this 'child protection worker' believed I had
> molested them.
>
> *Bernard*

What to do

If you are wrongly accused in this way, you need to take a strong but patient stand.

I suggest there are three things that you must do right from the beginning.

Firstly, state clearly to anyone who will listen – departmental officers, magistrate, judge, counsellor, relatives, friends – what this is all about and tell them in no uncertain terms: *'These accusations are totally false. They have been dreamt up by my ex-wife in order to keep me away from the children and to cut me out of their lives. The children have obviously been coached. I would never dream of doing anything like that to any child, let alone my own. I deny it absolutely.'*

Secondly, contact other men and men's groups who have been through the same experiences. As with AVOs, networking is tremendously important. It will provide you with contacts who can support and advise you in this dreadful time. It will be of some consolation for you to realise that you are one of many.

Going on the attack may be worth considering. Immediately stop all contact with your child or children. Get a good lawyer and instruct him or her to make an application for custody of the child (on the ground of mental abuse of the child) – or at least for supervised contact until the drama is over. It may be good tactics to turn the heat on your ex-wife by telling everyone about it – family and friends – and ridiculing the allegation.

Thirdly, get a good lawyer. This is one area where, at least in the initial stages, you need the advice and assistance of a competent and experienced solicitor or barrister. But don't just run off to the family solicitor or to the one in your neighbourhood. This is a special area and needs a special lawyer. Get recommendations from other men who have been through the mill in dealing with allegations like this. In one of the divorce or men's support groups you will find someone you can talk to and who will shepherd you through the processes ahead of you.

Dealings with the authorities

What you do next depends on how the powers-that-be decide to handle your case. If the police have been called in, then regrettably it becomes terribly simple. You will eventually be arrested (a terrible indignity for a law-abiding person and a process that ought not to be used when a summons would be more appropriate). Cooperate with the police but, apart from denying the allegations in the above terms, say nothing and do not take part in any interview until you have spoken to a good criminal lawyer. Insist on being provided with all statements containing the allegations against you.

If the allegations remain with the department, demand to know what it is that you are supposed to have done.

> **I returned to the DOCS officer the next day. I demanded to know exactly what I was alleged to have done. Unbelievably, he refused to tell me anything, saying: 'We are not required to provide any information to the alleged perpetrator.' In a day I had gone from being the children's father and guardian, the person they were closest to in the world, to 'the alleged perpetrator'.**
>
> *Marshall*

Seek information

Make sure you take and keep notes of all your dealings with police and departmental officers. If the latter refuse to tell you what the accusations are, go immediately to the head office of the department and make a complaint. If that does not succeed, complain to the relevant State government minister, either directly or through your local member of parliament. The latter can be a handy ally in matters such as this.

Use *Freedom of Information* laws to obtain copies of the department's files and their contents. This can give you vital information. It is important that you get all details of the complaints and allegations as quickly as possible in order to avoid subsequent amendment and fabrication.

> **The memos in the DOCS file indicated that the two investigating officers had developed a 'gut feeling' that there had been some abuse despite the denials of the**

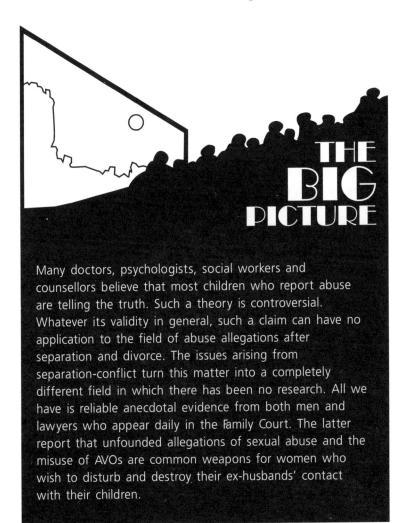

THE BIG PICTURE

Many doctors, psychologists, social workers and counsellors believe that most children who report abuse are telling the truth. Such a theory is controversial. Whatever its validity in general, such a claim can have no application to the field of abuse allegations after separation and divorce. The issues arising from separation-conflict turn this matter into a completely different field in which there has been no research. All we have is reliable anecdotal evidence from both men and lawyers who appear daily in the Family Court. The latter report that unfounded allegations of sexual abuse and the misuse of AVOs are common weapons for women who wish to disturb and destroy their ex-husbands' contact with their children.

children. Faced with the prospect of these denials continuing, one officer had made a note: 'If nothing else succeeds I'll say to the girls that someone has told us that your Daddy puts his finger in your vagina.'

George

Expert reports

State departments and the Family Court tend to call for medical and psychiatric reports all too soon in cases of alleged child abuse. Their excessive reliance on them is a matter of great concern. The reports will often conclude that the symptoms in the children are *'consistent'* with the alleged sexual abuse without canvassing other innocent explanations. If they are prepared by experts who believe that *children never lie*, or that *all men are violent*, then they call for careful handling.

> **The Family Court ordered a psychiatric report on the children. The psychiatrist who interviewed them wrote a report concluding that not only had I abused my daughters but my son too! There had never been any allegation of interference with him and he – like my daughters – protested that nothing of the sort had happened. The psychiatrist claimed that the children were lying 'to protect their father'.**
>
> *Jeremy*

Through your lawyer, and with the guidance of others who know, you will have to find a wise and intelligent psychiatrist and a paediatrician who will know how to debunk such claims. This will all cost money and time but is something that you cannot afford to ignore.

Counselling

At the same time, remember that you will benefit from some experienced professional counselling to help you manage this ordeal. It is an excruciating time in which your self-esteem and peace of mind will take a nose-dive. If you are in Family Court-directed counselling and strike the *'kids never lie'* philosophy, ask for another counsellor or find one independent of the court.

- ✔ Prepare for court: if appearing for yourself, read the 'Self-representation' section in Chapter 11.
- ✔ Prepare your cross-examination by writing out the questions you need to ask.
- ✔ Never agree to an order in advance of the hearing.
- ✔ Take court orders seriously.
- ✔ If you win, ask for costs.

The court

If proceedings have been commenced in a magistrate's court you should have them removed to the Family Court. With some exceptions, magistrates and their courts are not well equipped to deal with such matters. In cases where the department takes the matter to the Children's Court you should immediately file an application for *residence orders* or *contact orders* in the Family Court. This will give you some sense of control over what is going on and it may lead to the Children's Court proceedings being deferred or abandoned, thus saving time and money.

The Family Court has established procedures for dealing with abuse allegations. For the innocent father these are mostly tortuous, demeaning and slow. There's no point in expecting the court to conduct a speedy hearing, to pronounce you not guilty and to restore your contact with your children. That simply will not happen. Faced with competing claims from you and your ex-wife, the court has no idea of the truth of the matter and will do little to investigate it. It will be concerned with the *'best interests'* of the children and this may involve orders that will not suit you or your perception of right and wrong.

> The case took ages to come to court. There were many appearances and many adjournments and nothing much seemed to happen. My barrister told me that it would be a year before a final hearing. We asked for supervised access but that was refused even though DOCS had advised that there was no evidence to support the allegations. The psychologist's report noted what DOCS said but advised that it would not be 'prudent to re-establish contact at this point in time'. So I have not seen my son for five months.
>
> *Dave*

Supervised contact

You may be directed to counselling, when you consider it a complete waste of time. Show a positive spirit by cooperating. A separate legal representative may be ordered for the children. Indeed, if this is not done you should ask for it. Contact with your children may or may not be restored. If it is, it will always be in the form of *supervised* access. This is humiliating and stressful for you and your children, often it is quite unnecessary, and it can go on for too long. Nevertheless, it is better than no contact at all. At least your children can see that they still have a father.

Be careful to behave yourself impeccably during supervised access. Don't involve the children in the argument. Apart from giving them brief answers to any questions that they have, avoid talk of the drama and in no way criticise their mother. Don't school them on how to deal with the authorities or experts. After each session make notes on what has happened and what was said.

If the court or the children's separate representative calls for a psychiatrist's report, insist on being consulted on the choice of psychiatrist. Your lawyer and men's support group should know the good, the bad and the indifferent. Insist on being interviewed yourself and take advice on how to behave during the interview.

When to stop

The above is all very well and good, but the really big thing for separated fathers who have the misfortune to find themselves falsely accused of sexual interference is: *'How much should I do? How far should I go? I am suffering, the children are suffering, what hope is there?'*

The brute fact is that, under the present court system and its practice, when a woman is prepared to go to extraordinary lengths to capture the minds of her children and school them to press allegations against their father, there is little hope of a just outcome.

If she and the children persist in their allegations and there is material in the reports to support them, then you will *lose* – either completely, or partially through contact orders which are impossible and unpalatable. Remember, too, that family law proceedings are not about whether the allegations are true or false. The Family Court has decided that that is not the issue. It has decided that the issue for judgment is whether or not the children are exposed to *'unacceptable risk'*. In a real contest the court often takes the easy way out and opts for safety. You will end up the loser. As one judge said: *'Where there's smoke there's fire!'*

> The judge found that my ex-wife had lied and had planted the allegations in the minds of the children. He said that she had emotionally abused the children in this way. He also slammed the examining doctor for accepting that there had been abuse in the face of clear evidence to the contrary. But, unaccountably, he then proceeded to find that there was still an unacceptable risk to the children and ordered supervised contact! The only 'unacceptable risk' for them was from their

mother's actions in alienating them from their father. Why didn't the judge let me look after the children and order supervised contact for her!?

Malcolm

Winning the war

But even if you win the battle you may not win the *war!* By that I mean that if your ex-wife is determined to cut you out of the lives of the children, no matter how successful you are in court, she will win in the end. All she has to do is to pervert the hearts and minds of the children and to make their contact with you so stressful and such a test of loyalty that in the end *they* simply want the drama to end and will drop off. You can't blame them.

I had access to the children for two years before the trouble started. My ex-wife wouldn't talk to me about it but DOCS told me that she had made reports of sexual abuse of my son and daughter. Eventually the police charged me with these offences. In the meantime I went to the Family Court and got two hours' supervised contact once a fortnight. The charge involving my son was dropped by the prosecution before it got to court because of contradictory statements. The case concerning my daughter was heard in court and I was found not guilty. It was quite obvious that she had been 'brainwashed' by her mother. I had contact with the children restored but it didn't work. There was little contact and a lot of court! Counselling did not work. After a year I was told that the children did not want to see me any more. I decided to give up. It was a lost battle. There was too much trauma for me and the children.

Aiden

The only answer I can give is to suggest that you press on in court until you decide that it is futile and counterproductive

- ✔ State your denial right from the start.
- ✔ Contact other men.
- ✔ Get a good lawyer.
- ✔ Go on the attack.
- ✔ Demand information and statements.
- ✔ Consider counselling.

and heartbreaking. There comes a time when you realise that there is no hope for a good result, that you and the children are suffering too much. It is then time to *let go* and to get on with your life.

You can only hope that time will soften your suffering and perhaps bring awareness to your children.

ONE MAN'S STORY

I fought for custody of my children and lost. The judge made no finding in relation to the abuse allegations. I was given reasonable access but my ex-wife refused to comply with the orders. I tried contempt proceedings but she claimed that the children were now afraid of me and no longer wanted to see me. She left town. I decided enough was enough and I withdrew. I got on with life. The pain of losing my children gradually subsided. I kept faith with the idea that the perpetrators of this elaborate scam could never take away my love for my children nor their love for me. I was right. Some five years later my son contacted me from his foster family (his mother had kicked him out of her home). He was soon back with me. Two years later my two daughters also found their way back. After more than eight years of sad and unnecessary separation we're a family again.

QUESTIONS	POSITIVE THOUGHTS AND RESOLUTIONS
★	
What must I know about AVOs and false allegations?	★
	I will state clearly the real purpose of the allegations.
★	
What things should I do before going to court?	★
	I will seek out details of the allegations.
★	
Where should I go to get support from men and men's groups?	★
	I will be careful in dealing with my children and my ex-wife.
★	
What kind of diary should I keep of my contact with my children and ex-wife?	★
	I will obey all court orders.
★	
What benefits are there for me in therapeutic counselling at this time?	★
	I will do my best to maintain contact with my children.
	★
	I will look after my spiritual and physical health.

Keep interested in your own career, however humble; it is a real possession in the changing fortunes of time.

Desiderata

14

Child Support

I was enormously distressed over my treatment by the Child Support Agency. I could not understand how they could take so much of my earnings. There was no comeback: there was a 'like it or lump it' attitude among the staff. I know I was not always easy to deal with, but I was still in shock over the separation and I felt I had lost my children. To be hit with a demand for most of my salary really knocked me. I felt powerless and vulnerable and, above all, poor!

Maurice

For fathers with lots of money, child support is something that will not trouble them very much. But for those who are poor or of average means, it matters a great deal and can be a constant worry.

There was once a time when too many separated fathers got away with paying little or no maintenance. When a father defaulted or fell short, the community would step in and help in the form of social security payments. In those days even the Family Court considered that fair enough.

Well, of course, it wasn't, it isn't, and it is no more. Those days are gone. With the establishment of the Child Support Agency (CSA), together with a new philosophy in the court (that the obligation to pay maintenance lies with the parents and not with the community), it became easier for custodial parents to obtain and enforce payment, and more difficult for defaulting parents to avoid it.

In the past, two-thirds of non-custodial parents paid nothing. Now two-thirds pay up. This is a big improvement and it is to be hoped that the trend will continue. The CSA is a much needed vehicle for the collection of child support. But it needs adequate staff and resources, and it needs to be guided by fair principles.

Attitude

Separated fathers need to develop a positive attitude to the matter of child support. You and your wife brought the children into the world and it is up to you both to provide them with emotional, material and financial support. They have a myriad of needs: psychological, intellectual, artistic, physical – to name just a few. The satisfaction of these needs costs money. That's the brute fact. Whether it's schooling, clothing, holidays, sport or the bare necessities of housing, food and health, it's an expensive business. It's easy for separated fathers who do not have the daily care of the children to forget this and to delude themselves that it all costs less than it really does.

Don't kid yourself that your obligation ends if your ex-wife repartners and comes into a more affluent lifestyle. I can understand the envy of a separated father, struggling to support himself – and perhaps a new family – who is still asked to make substantial contributions in child support. He sees his children, ex-wife and new husband enjoying life in his former house, going on expensive holidays and generally enjoying a standard of living much higher than his.

But remember: they are still *your* children. They do not belong to her new man, no matter how it looks. They are still your responsibility and they will respect you for taking it seriously.

A generous spirit

And what about *generosity*? Surely there's a place for that here. It's too easy for separated men to become selfish, to think of themselves first, to imagine that they are being ripped off by their former spouses, and seriously to underestimate the amount of money it takes to keep two or three children in a reasonable degree of comfort. Think about the cost of goods and services; think about the demands of children spurred on by their peers and the advertising industry; think about the standard of living that you want your children to enjoy. Think about how deprived they will be without adequate support. Think about how much they were costing you before your separation.

And, while you're at it, think about how much you love them and how much you want to prove to them that you care. Talk to other sensible mothers and fathers about how much *they* spend on their children. Think about it – but then be reasonable and be generous.

Remember, too, that many studies point to poverty as a factor in behavioural problems in children. You will want to support your child both financially and emotionally.

Unfairness

However, it's easy to ask affluent fathers to be reasonable and generous; it's not so easy for a father on a modest or low salary, or a father with a new wife and family. It is obvious from the little research that has been done, and from the submissions to the Joint Select Committee, that many men have serious and justified complaints about the amounts of child support exacted from them by the court or the Child Support Agency. They see those amounts as unfairly high and they feel that their circumstances and the circumstances of their ex-wife and children have not been fairly assessed. They feel hard done by. They can't *all* be wrong!

> **I was paying $400 per week in child support. My ex-wife – at home with our three children – from child support, supporting parent's benefit, child allowances and rent assistance, was netting $600 per week (all after tax). No wonder she could afford to buy a home, service a mortgage and go on an overseas holiday. Meanwhile, I was left with $600 a month to live on and to provide a home for myself, my new partner and the children (who visited every second weekend). My partner ended up supporting me. A system that keeps the custodian comfortable and the provider poor is a flawed system!**
>
> *Bill*

In 1995–96 the Commonwealth Ombudsman received 2968 complaints about the CSA. Almost 80 percent of these were resolved in favour of the complainants. Only the Department of Social Security was the subject of more complaints.

Crippling burden

One study found that 27 percent of fathers claimed that the maintenance system was crippling them financially, forcing them to live with their parents or in shared accommodation, sometimes distant from their children.[140]

In another survey, many men felt that they could never re-establish themselves economically. Some chose to remain on the dole rather than see themselves as being 'ripped off' by maintenance and the tax system.[141]

> I was a teacher on $35,000 per annum. By the time I paid superannuation, Federation fees and medical benefits, the 27 percent of my gross salary that I had to pay had inflated to over 30 percent of my real, before-tax earnings. My ex-wife had moved interstate and I was flying my two boys home at my own expense. After daily living expenses I had nothing left. I rang the CSA and told someone that I could no longer manage the monthly payments. I was told: 'If you don't like it you can take it to court.' No one told me about the review process. I lost heart and gave up work for several months.
>
> *Frank*

The most recent assessment of the Child Support Scheme revealed that 16 percent of fathers were experiencing real hardship, especially those who had repartnered and had new families.[142] After talking to dozens of separated fathers I suspect the real figure to be closer to 25 percent.

On the other hand, there is also clear evidence that many women are dissatisfied with the performance of the CSA. It has been found to be slow or unsuccessful in pursuing recalcitrant fathers (the so-called *'deadbeat dads'*) for the payment of child support. Fathers must support their children, and defaulting fathers should be firmly pursued and quickly brought to account. A mother should not have to wait for months before this is done. It is obvious that the Agency needs more personnel and resources.

The real costs of children

This is a complex topic. There are so many imponderables. People have different ideas on living standards. The crucial question, of course, is: How much does it cost per week to support a child? *Not* how much do the parents *choose* to spend on it, but how much does it cost to keep the child in reasonable health and comfort. There are as many answers to this as there are parents, children and statisticians.

The CSA believes it has arrived at an appropriate formula and an adequate scale of payments for child support. The claim is made that this formula was *'based on research into how much it really costs to raise a child and was developed in consultation with community groups.'*[143]

Difficulties with the CSA system

The CSA system is unsound and unfair. There are at least three general difficulties with the current system.

1. The CSA scales are based on the proposition that ordinarily children should enjoy the same standard of living that they had before their parents separated; that the same amount of money should be spent on them.

Sometimes this can be achieved. But often it cannot. Often the ideal is not attainable and should not be striven for. After all, the very fact of separation is not ideal. By virtue of their separation, all parties will inevitably suffer a decline in their material standard of living.

2. How much it costs to raise a child is an extremely rubbery figure. Research is needed to establish the *real cost* of children, not simply what middle-class parents decide to spend on them.

The Australian Institute of Family Studies each year publishes estimates of the expenses involved in supporting children of different ages. These figures differ according to which approach to the data is used for the calculations.[144] However all figures refer to what those parents choose to spend on that child.

The 1993–94 Household Expenditure Survey revealed that the average weekly expenditure of a couple with two children was $973.[145]

> **The CSA is a good idea but the formula is wrong. My daughter is young and lives in another State. I have to travel there and rent accommodation if I want to see her. The CSA has refused to recognise all those costs. If I work overtime I'm expected to pay more. There's no way in the world that it costs $220 per week to keep a young child.**
>
> *Len*

Over-generous payments

What parents in intact families choose to spend on their children is of little relevance to the amount that separated parents are able to spend on theirs. My conversations with mothers and fathers from both intact and separated families indicate that some levels of the CSA scale are too high. Some mothers of intact families have been amazed to hear of the amount of money that the CSA exacts of separated fathers. Several have commented to me that they wish their own husbands were as generous!

As always, it's the poor and middle-income earners who are suffering, particularly those who are PAYE taxpayers. After paying child support, superannuation, medical benefits, transport and home costs, they are simply left with a pittance to live on.

> **I am a separated mother and my two children live with their father. I am on a secretary's wage and after a Child Support Agency assessment I have to pay over $450 per month to my ex-husband. He is in his own business and manages to understate his income. After that money is gone and after mortgage, rates, insurance and travelling expenses are taken care of, I have $68 per week to live on. It's pretty tough.**
>
> *Janet*

3. It is clear that the CSA scales are calculated according to a formula that fails to take into account the real needs of the individual who pays. Some fathers' groups argue that the

after-tax earnings of the separated husband should be the starting figure rather than his gross wage.

The problem I see with this approach is that, while wage and salary earners would be easily assessed, it is possible for those who are self-employed or in their own business to reduce, legally and illegally, their real after-tax incomes. The latter would end up paying less than employees on equivalent incomes.

Perhaps the better way to go would be to specify that certain expenditure – rent or mortgage, costs of earning a living, superannuation, medical insurance – be deducted from *gross* income before the application of the CSA formula.

Exempt income

Some particular problems with the system are as follows:

★ **It is not good enough that the exempt income of the non-custodial parent is based on the single rate pension whereas the custodial parent can earn more than average weekly earnings without affecting the maintenance.**

★ **If a custodial parent repartners, some allowance should be made for the resulting financial benefit, if any, in the calculation of child support. Similarly, financial benefits from a parent's business or employment that are not reflected in taxable income ought to be assessed and taken into account.**

★ **It is quite clear that the authorities have no idea of the ordinary costs of exercising access – transport, accommodation, holidays, excursions, food and clothing. These expenses are substantial and are a running sore for most separated men who have regular access to their children. Yet, unless they are exceptional, they are not taken into account by the CSA. This is unfair and needs to be addressed.**

> The children stayed with me for three weeks of the school holidays and we had a great time. It cost a lot of money. It came as a great shock to me to be told by my lawyer that not only could I not deduct these costs from my maintenance payments but I had to keep up the regular payments to my ex-wife at the same time! I couldn't believe it. She now owned the home and was working.
>
> *Dick*

Fathers with second families

The situation of a separated father who has repartnered and has more children is particularly precarious. The CSA allowance for new dependants is meagre and nowhere near as much as is exacted from him for the support of his first family.

> The greatest inequity of all in the child support legislation is that the non-custodial parent is unable to begin life again because there is not even enough money for basic living expenses, let alone trying to establish a new life and trying to get ahead. I am put in a terrifying situation where I am between a rock and a hard place. What am I supposed to do? How do I live with the fact that I do not have enough money to support my new family?
>
> *Ernest*

Staying at home

Another matter which needs to be addressed is the obligation of the *custodial* parent to contribute financially to the support of the children. The old idea of the mother as the caregiver and the father as the financier must go! *All aspects of parenting must be shared.*

This obligation is recognised in the Family Law Act and by the Child Support Act, but in reality it is only applied if the custodial parent – in most cases the mother – *chooses* to work.

The Family Law Reform Act provides:

(a) that children have their proper needs met from reasonable and adequate shares in the income, earning capacity, property and financial resources of both their parents; and

(b) that parents share equitably in the support of their children.

In these days when roughly 60 percent of all women with children (and over 70 percent of women with teenage children) are in full- or part-time work, it is unacceptable that a separated mother who can find work should be allowed to choose to stay at home except in special circumstances or through a joint decision with her ex-husband.[146] No longer should the Family Court or the CSA accept unchallenged the claim: *'I have to stay home to look after the children.'*

It is simply not fair that a man of ordinary means should bear the full financial burden of supporting his children when his wife is in a position to assist. Many men complain that the current attitude of the court and the CSA encourages women to stay at home no matter how old or young their children.

A change of attitude to this matter would solve a lot of problems, not least for women themselves. It should encourage custodial mothers to involve their ex-husbands more in family care and responsibility. Many men are just waiting for the opportunity. *There is abundant evidence that the most generous fathers – i.e. the best payers – are fathers who are involved in the lives of their children.*

There will obviously be cases where a woman cannot cope with young children and paid employment. Perhaps she has children with special needs, or is unskilled, or has been out of the workforce for years and lacks confidence, or simply can't get a job. The CSA or court counsellors should direct her to the appropriate agencies.

As the journalist Adele Horin puts it: *'Women need every help to maintain their links with the workforce for their own sakes, their children and the economy. And men need every encouragement to participate more fully in family life. Women **can** have it all, and so can men: the status and independence that come from work, and the pleasures of family life.'*[147]

Better work practices

To assist women to stay in the workforce, men will have to change their ways. They will have to be more involved in the parenting of their children. Efforts should be intensified to provide more and better childcare facilities, flexible working

THE BIG PICTURE

All decent men want to support their children both financially and emotionally. However, the payment levels currently imposed by the CSA are unfairly high and do not take real needs into account. Moreover, many women are not accepting their share of the burden of supporting their children. Recent changes to the child support scheme do not go far enough to correct the inequities of the system.

hours, job sharing, taxation rebates and the like. Managements will have to acknowledge the family obligations of both male and female workers.

A better way

The Child Support Agency ought to be the last port of call. It is only needed when children are not properly supported. Sensible parents, on separation, should sit down and talk about how they can realistically support their children to the best of their abilties. They know one another well enough to come to commonsense decisions and not to make impossible demands of one another. They know their incomes and expenses. They themselves, or with the help of a mediator, will be able to decide on a financial plan which will adequately support their children without impoverishing either parent. If their combined contributions are not sufficient, then the community must step in and augment the children's support by way of special social security payments.

Consideration should be given to replacing the current *review* system with a process that would see reviews conducted by sensible, mature and experienced members of the community (properly trained for this function) instead of by lawyers. Mediation along the lines of the Community Justice Centres could produce results that are realistic and acceptable to both parents.[148]

Payment of support

Let's look at some practical considerations that arise for separated fathers in their dealings with the CSA.

Of course, if you and your ex-wife can agree on a package without any intervention of the court or the CSA, then that makes it easy. If not, the CSA will do it for you, at least for couples separated after 1 October 1989. The Agency will apply a particular formula to your pre-tax earnings and issue an assessment to you and your ex-wife. You will then be expected to pay that amount on a weekly, fortnightly or monthly basis.

You may also come to a *private agreement* with your ex-wife and this can be submitted to the CSA. Bear in mind, however, that if your ex-wife is receiving any kind of social security benefit the CSA is required to assess your agreement and pass it on to the Department of Social Security for their approval.

You may pay directly to your ex-wife or to the CSA, which will send the money on to her. The CSA also has power to direct your employer to deduct the amounts from your paypacket. If you are recalcitrant the Agency has power to chase you and take you to court.

Review and appeal

If you are unhappy with the CSA assessment you may ask the Review Office to re-examine the figure. However, your complaints have to be based on solid financial considerations and not just on opinion. If you are still unhappy you can appeal to the Family Court. You will then need legal advice.

The CSA's number and address are listed in your telephone book and you can ring for information and assistance.

Coping with payments

What courses of action are available to men who are faced with crippling CSA payments?

Some simply put up with it, spend less and work harder.

> I knew I was being ripped off. She lied about her part-time cash employment. She and the kids were living comfortably and I had $60 a week to live on. I just couldn't be bothered doing anything about it. I lived simply and did more overtime.

Greg

✔ Try to come to an agreement with your ex-wife and avoid the CSA.
✔ Get expert advice and rearrange your finances.
✔ Talk to men who know the CSA system.
✔ Keep a diary, accounts and receipts.
✔ Ask for a review.
✔ Be courteous and reasonable with staff.
✔ Find a helpful officer and ask for an interview.

Remember the economy measures suggested in Chapter 2. Even if you are finding it tough there may be things you can do to control your income and expenditure. Perhaps you need financial counselling or a good accountant. Whether you are self-employed or on a salary you can often benefit from a talk with an expert tax accountant or lawyer.

You will find it useful to contact one of the support groups for separated men that are listed at the end of this book. Advice from men and women who have been through the system is invaluable.

Remember, separation and divorce can give you the time and opportunity to improve your earning power, either by extra work or study or by changing jobs altogether.

Be prepared

Satisfactory results can sometimes be gained through careful use of the *review* process in the CSA. This may lead to some of your expenses being taken into account and to a lowering of your payments. But you need to be well prepared. You have to be able to **prove** your expenses, so it is important to keep accounts and receipts, perhaps even a diary of financial expenditure. Keep in mind that the CSA will automatically increase your payments each year by the Consumer Price Index (CPI) inflation rate, whether you have had a pay increase or not. It is only by a review that you can counter this.

If you know that your ex-wife is not being honest about her own income, gather evidence to dispute it. A *Companies Office* search and a *Land Titles Office* search can sometimes tell you a lot about the financial position of a self-employed person. Sometimes some detective work is necessary. The CSA will not do this for you. It's up to you to assemble a good case, to prove your claims and, if you dispute them, to disprove hers.

> **I wasn't making ends meet. In desperation I cut out overnight access and made this part of my review case – that is, that I could not afford to have the kids overnight. You've got to think about your expenses and work through them. If you persevere and are lucky, you can succeed in a review.**
>
> *Andrew*

Find a person in your nearest CSA office who is helpful. Not all staff are competent and caring. Keep trying until you find somone who is. Write down his or her name and always ask for the same person, whether by phone or in person. Keep notes of your contact with the Agency. Generally it is better to deal with your contact in person rather than simply filling in forms or telephoning. Keep copies of all documents that you give to the CSA. Never use ordinary post: if sending documents use registered mail, facsimile or courier so that you have proof that the CSA has received the document.

Be reasonable

Be courteous and decent in your dealings with CSA staff. Don't argue. If you ring too often and too rudely you will quickly be identified as a *troublemaker*. You will often get the impression that they don't care about your expenses and needs and simply want to apply the formula. But remember that staff can only *administer* the system; they can't rewrite it for you! It's a waste of time and energy to get angry with someone on the other end of the telephone.

Certainly there are some who are incompetent and some who don't like or trust men. Use the *complaints* facility if you have to. But bear in mind that CSA officers are in a tough job. Government cutbacks in staffing levels and resources have resulted in huge workloads, poorly trained personnel and a high turnover of staff. Many parents complain that frequent changes in case-officers lead to lack of continuity and waste of time.

Self-employment

Self-employment is the easiest way of managing income. People in their own businesses have legitimate means of minimising their pre-tax income which are not available to the wage and salary earner. There are also opportunities these days for workers to be employed on a *contract* basis, providing it is done within the guidelines of the Tax Office. Talk to your boss about this. With the help of a good accountant you might be able to arrange your finances in a way that will allow you to live comfortably and still provide generously for your children.

If a contract situation is not open to you, you may be able to persuade your employer to put you on a package that allows you to take part of your salary in benefits such as increased superannuation, motor vehicle and other fringe benefits.[149]

Last, and definitely least, is the option of unemployment. Some fathers have been so impoverished by the level of child support exacted from them that they have chosen to leave work and go on the dole. While I appreciate that there may be financial and emotional pressures that drive a man to this extreme, I think that its disadvantages normally outweigh its advantages. It is a negative way of handling the problem and will do nothing for the man's financial and emotional security, not to mention his self-esteem. It could also impoverish his children.

> I decided that there was no other way out: the only way that I could cope with the property settlement, legal costs and child support and still survive was to resign my job. I got $30,000 superannuation payout and I was able to repay my parents the loan that had financed the custody case and living expenses. I gave my ex-wife some money for our daughter when I had it, but I could not have afforded the CSA rate. I stayed unemployed for a year and that gave me a breathing space, allowed me some time to sort myself out and to regather my strength. But I knew I could not stay out of work for long.
>
> *Joseph*

Property division

Closely related to child support is the issue of property settlement. Because she is living in the matrimonial home with the children, a custodial wife at settlement may receive 60–75 percent of the joint assets. This is because she has to accommodate the children, and also because normally she has less earning power than her husband. Yet in the child support payments that she continues to receive after settlement, there is still included a component that relates to accommodation expenses for the children. This is patently unfair. After settlement the property is hers for all purposes and forever. Any extra expense incurred because of the children's temporary occupation should come under the heading of maintenance or child support.

> I thought it was unfair that I only got 30 percent of the value of the house. By the time I left we had almost paid it off. I had to then borrow the money to buy

another home for myself and the children when they came on access weekends. After twelve years of marriage I had to start again. The children won't live at home forever, and after that she will have an asset worth half a million dollars.

Greg

The unequal distribution of property in favour of the custodial mother is based on biased and blinkered thinking in the Family Court. When a couple separates and the children reside principally with the mother, the concern of the family law system is to provide suitable accommodation for the mother and the children. The accommodation needs of the husband are not considered. Yet not only does he have to find a home for himself, he also has to provide accommodation for the children during contact periods, even if he has them only once a fortnight. In reality his accommodation needs are exactly the same as those of his ex-wife. If he has substandard premises his rights to contact can be imperilled. Quite apart from that, it is not fair and reasonable to expect a separated father and his children to put up with second-class conditions just because the children do not live with him permanently.

If there is a difference – because the children are spending more time with their mother than with their father – then that is not a *property* factor, it's a *maintenance* factor. How the husband pays it – through monthly maintenance or lump sum or surrendering part of his property entitlement – is his business. But it is an *accommodation* factor and should be notionally distinguished from the distribution of property.

Similarly, disparity of earning power is a *maintenance* factor and ought to have no bearing on property distribution unless husband and wife agree.

50/50 split

This is another area in which the Family Court has developed flawed principles. Matrimonial property (house, land, shares, family business) is a complex matter and you will need the assistance of a good lawyer to help you sort it out. The fundamental principle ought to be that, where there have been equal contributions, there will be an equal distribution of assets. But although there appears to be a move towards equal division, at present any property settlement or order will favour the custodial parent.

If you think about it, this is illogical and unfair. Whether she continues to live in the house or sells it and buys another, the custodial mother who ends up with most of the equity in the matrimonial home has been given a windfall that increases in value over the rest of her life, not just for the duration of the children's stay. That's the nub of the situation: this 'golden egg' that she receives at the expense of the husband is worth much more than the 'accommodation' factor by which it is presently justified.

The current practice of favouring the custodial mother in property settlement is the source of anger and hurt for most separated fathers. He sees it as the final seal on the loss of his home and family. Often he does not have the financial resources to buy another property. Why should one parent be impoverished in order to empower the other?

Property should not be considered in terms of the parents' needs and rights. The question to be asked is: **What are the accommodation needs of the children? What are the best arrangements for housing all parties so that the children can have substantial relationships with both their mother and their father?**

QUESTIONS	POSITIVE THOUGHTS AND RESOLUTIONS
★	★
What steps must I take to ensure that I am meeting my obligation to support my children?	They are still my children.
★	★
What can I do to avoid being *ripped-off*?	Bringing up children is not cheap.
★	★
Who do I contact to get financial and legal advice?	I will be generous and not mean.
★	★
What can I do to rearrange my finances?	I will get legal and financial advice.
★	★
What decisions must I make to reorder my priorities and lifestyle?	I will talk to men with experience.
	★
	The system should be changed.

Exercise caution in your business affairs: for the world is full of trickery.

Desiderata

15

Looking after Yourself

I know I'm a better person. Two years of Biddulph, Bly, Moore, Gilette, *Men's News*, men's groups and gatherings – how could I not have changed!? I got 'Father of the Week' at daycare. I was really stoked by that. It's all been such a wild trip. It was not my ex's fault. It was all about me, really. I had to find out who I was and who I wanted to be.

Ted

There *is* a life after divorce. I don't expect you to believe that or to be enthusiastic about it if you are in the early stages of separation. You can do all the right things, but there are some things that only time can fix. However, doing 'the right things' will positively assist your rehabilitation, while *not* doing them will retard it. In other words, life won't be easy for a while but you can make it easier or more difficult for yourself – it's up to you.

No one can tell us how to live our lives. Most of us are pretty stubborn when it comes to taking advice. This is a great shame as there is a lot of help out there which can make life easier for separated men.

The tracks of people's lives are different, but the *principles* on which the broad framework for reasonable living rests are the same.

I'm not talking about religions, philosophies or theologies. If you derive meaning, strength or wisdom from any of those, then good luck to you. But what I want to discuss here are human values, human activities, and how you feel about yourself and others. Of course, these might be critically affected by philosophical or religious beliefs. But they don't start there: they start right *inside you*.

It's not the only way to do it but one way of looking closely at yourself and your world – your very existence – is to divide it into *home*, *work* and *leisure*. In that world there's just you and *others*. in talking about the reorganisation of your life after separation, let's concentrate first on *you*.

You

Take time occasionally to sit down quietly and have a good think about yourself. Not many people do this. We tend to blunder through life, allowing things to happen rather than making thoughtful decisions; meeting the demands of the situations we find ourselves in rather than taking a long-term view. We rarely stop to think, to consider if there's a better thing to do or a better way to do it. We don't pause to reflect and ask ourselves: is this right for me or for those around me? How many people have *ever* asked themselves: What kind of a person am I? Am I content? Am I useful? Am I living a reasonable life? Am I happy with my home, my job?

I suspect we do not do this because we are not in the habit of **reflection**. We have not been brought up that way, nor have we been educated that way.

Once or twice a year, and certainly in times of crisis, we should do some reflecting. Sit down, or go for a walk if you will. Do anything you like, provided you are on your own and in a position to think in an undisturbed and undistracted way.

> **I always do my best thinking when I'm walking along a beach. There's something powerful in the movement of the ocean and something comforting too. I feel really rooted to the universe. The immensity of it all seems to get me out of myself and away from my problems. I see them in perspective.**
>
> *Brian*

As a separated man you will often have problems that tend to overwhelm you: relations with your ex-wife and children, court hearings, child support, how you are going to manage. But I want you to make a big effort to push those to one side for a while and try to concentrate completely on YOU, and you alone.

Talk to yourself:

'*I want to be a **whole** person, not just part of a person. I want to be useful to myself, to my family and to others. If I'm not content with myself this will affect my relationships and my work. If I'm no good to myself, I'll be no good to anyone else. I really want to get myself together.*'

Think about your *health* – your physical wellbeing, your mental wellbeing, and your emotional wellbeing.

Physical health

In the trauma of separation and divorce, your physical health usually suffers. Make no mistake about it, you can easily get run-down, and unless you do something about it you will stay down for a long time. Two things normally happen.

Firstly, the sudden change in your lifestyle (change of home, role, relationships) from that in which you have been settled for so many years, plus the grief, sadness and emotional turmoil that accompany separation, all have a draglike effect on your mind and body. It's something akin to physical shock. You have no energy or enthusiasm, you get headaches, you feel ill, you can't sleep, you lose your appetite, you get a hollow feeling in your stomach or a tight feeling in your chest. There may be other symptoms.

Secondly, you tend to forget about regular sleep, exercise and good food. You either neglect these essentials or you just can't be bothered. Or, like a lot of men, you are used to being looked after and you lack the confidence or the will to look after yourself.

In this condition it is very easy to sink into a second-rate existence of lethargy and depression, and to seek relief in alcohol or pills. Of course, there's no magic cure, but there are steps you can take which will not only alleviate the symptoms but will allow time – the only complete cure – to heal your spirit.

It would be a good idea to have a medical checkup from a good doctor. Be careful of alcohol and pills. The latter should be used only as a last resort when, with the advice of a doctor, you feel you are not in control. Get yourself into a fairly regular routine of healthy food, adequate sleep or rest, recreation and work. Be careful not to lose yourself in a mad frenzy of activity, in drinking sessions with sympathisers, in confessional dinners with relatives.

Get some physical exercise. I don't just mean golf or tennis once a week; I mean regular exercise, three or four times per week. It doesn't matter whether it's running, swimming, aero-

ONE MAN'S STORY
I don't know that I'm a better person. But I have moved on and I'm improving all the time. I have learnt about loss and grief and come through them. It's like coming through a dark night into a new day. I went through the drink and drugs stage. I now have a sense of purpose and less fear. Some people call it arrogance, others a well-placed confidence in my own accountabilities. I can make things happen for me. I feel empowered. I look back with some regrets, but overall the picture is positive. My attitude to money and possessions has changed: I see their value in terms of their utility. I generally try to make myself useful and of service to people. We have to learn to be centred and to know when we're off centre.

bics or walking (one of the best and cheapest) – do *something*! It helps the body and mind and it will help you to sleep.

If you have difficulty sleeping, don't torture yourself about it. Read a good book or listen to music or watch a bit of TV. Get a book or a tape on relaxation. There are good 'sleep-better' programs available. Take a few classes in yoga or relaxation techniques. They *do* work, and can give you a feeling of wellbeing and control that you've never had before.

In short, *look after yourself!*

Mental health

Much of the above applies here, too, particularly the bit about relaxation. Remember, stress is a killer! It causes illness and reduces our capacity to make good decisions. It affects our judgement. *'Wars start in the minds of men'*, as someone once wrote.

> I think physical exercise is very important. It seems to get the system moving and to prevent depression. Walking in sunlight cheered me. I also found yoga a big help. It helped me to cope with stress and even to move

around fairly peacefully. I slept better too and I felt healthier.

Duncan

There are courses on stress management, assertiveness and the like, and plenty of books on the subject. I have included some of the latter in the *Book List* at the end of the book.

Reading

Speaking of books, reading is a habit that can bring enormous peace and satisfaction. If you are already a reader, then you are a step ahead in the mental health stakes. If not, I suggest that your separation will give you the opportunity to develop this precious practice. Find a good bookshop and an intelligent bookseller, or a helpful librarian, who will guide your reading in the areas that you find interesting. It will do marvels for your mental health.

After my separation I was depressed and for some time found it difficult to concentrate. I could not read a book or newspaper. By chance one day I picked up an art book containing prints of paintings by a famous artist. I found that it gave me pleasure and peace simply to look at the pictures. I developed a love of art. Soon I was reading again.

Oliver

Expanding your horizons

There is something to be gained in giving some time to reading a daily newspaper. It's not just a question of staying abreast of current affairs: there is that to it, of course, and the information you gain will help you be a good conversationalist, and that's important. But there's more to it than that.

An intelligent reading of a daily newspaper gets you out

of yourself. It immerses you in the lives of others, in the life of your community, your country, the world. It stretches your mind, your interest, your understanding and, hopefully, your compassion. It's a mental thing and it adds a third dimension to your life.

It's easy and human to become selfish and narrow. We naturally tend to concentrate our mental energies on ourselves and on the people and things in our immediate vicinity. But if we go no further we may become insular. We allow ourselves to be limited by our home, children and job.

Writing

In difficult times some people find writing very therapeutic. Keeping a diary, writing poetry, short stories or a play, can all be cathartic and soothing.

> **I still feel the pain at times. I keep a diary, I write letters to myself. If I feel sad, I write about it. It helps. Initially I gained a lot of weight, I was depressed and did not sleep well. Now I'm doing better.**
>
> *Andrew*

It's possible to waste time watching television! Used intelligently, it can be refreshing and enlightening. But too often it is just an excuse for doing nothing.

Don't neglect your cultural life: music, films, theatre, art, are all important for a healthy mind. But watch the expense!

If you have a hobby or play a particular sport, keep it up. You may have to make adjustments, or choose another venue, but if you enjoy it don't let it go.

Keep some time for yourself. The busiest and most generous of men needs to make sure that he occasionally does something quite selfish and self-indulgent. He ought to watch his favourite show, go to a movie, eat at a restaurant, read a good book, or do something that he really enjoys. There are times when we all need to reward or spoil ourselves.

Emotional health

This is the tough one! How do you control and strengthen your emotions? There's no simple answer to this question. However, if you've attended to your physical and mental health as suggested above, then you've given yourself a good start. After that, it's a matter of choosing the strategies that will assist you to avoid becoming caught in *self-preoccupation*, a state which will prevent you from moving on in your journey. Talking to yourself, meditation, communication with friends and counsellors, are some of the tools that many men have found useful.

The benefits of being alone

Many men find safety in investing the emotional or soft side of their nature in their wives and families. When they lose their partners and children, they often lose the only people they have allowed to respond to their emotional needs. To compensate they tend to rush into new relationships. But without a period *alone* there is the real danger that they will take their emotional *'baggage'* from the first relationship into the second.

For some men solitude is frightening because they equate it with loneliness. It need not be like that at all. It is a wonderful opportunity to develop the 'inner' man, to foster your intellectual and cultural life, the *thinking/feeling* part of you.

When you become separated you have been given the chance to develop *'the capacity to be comfortably alone'*.[150]

This *period alone* gives a man – perhaps for the first time – the opportunity to develop responsibility for his life, for his past and present. It gives him the time to come to a point of positive self-esteem which forms the best basis for his parenting and for his relationships.

> **My time on my own gave me the chance to mature and to grow in confidence. When my first marriage ended I wondered if there was something wrong with me. Was**

there some flaw in my character which led to problems in relationships with women? By the time I met my second wife I was past that stage and, although a bit wary, I was confident that I would approach this relationship with more wisdom and common sense.

Wayne

Gaining control

'Getting your life into shape', 'sorting yourself out', 'becoming a real person', 'taking control of your life', 'getting on with your life', 'making it', all express the thing I'm talking about, and there are many other expressions. It's a condition not easy to define, and it can mean different things to different people. But, however you define it, the *feeling* is much the same for those who experience it. It is *'a comfortable sense of being at home in your own life.'*[151]

It's a feeling of being in control of your life; that is, that you are making things happen and managing to cope with the rest. Life is not perfect and you have your share of problems and heartaches. But you are on top of them and they don't tear you apart any more. You have accepted your situation and are starting to enjoy it. You are making it *work* for you.

When my ex-wife and children moved away I saw that as an end to a period in my life. It had not been a good period. My life as a man and a father was a mess. The separation challenged me to do something about that. I had not been facing my problems and now I had the opportunity to have a good look at myself. I went to my doctor and had some therapy. It's worked out over time. I have grown up and learnt to like and respect myself.

Tim

Self-reliance

Confidence in yourself is to do with being *centred*, focused, feeling that you are OK. It's being able to rely on the solid core inside you. The experience of separation has forced you to rely on yourself rather than on someone else. Perhaps you have made contact with your *self* for the first time, and you are stronger because you have survived and grown.

I have heard it said that you can never live successfully with anyone else until you have learnt to live with yourself. It's not that other people are unimportant. Indeed, relationships with others are enriching and necessary for the spirit. At times we need others. But it is only in solitude that you are able to dig deep enough to find out about yourself.

Becoming a real person is something each of us should have achieved much earlier in life. But few of us do. Perhaps that's because of our dependency on others. Perhaps it's because of immaturity or lack of opportunity. Separation gives us another shot at it. It's a chance worth taking!

> I think I'm a much better person. I am much stronger. I feel like I am now starting to 'grow up'. I feel now that I can say with certainty that I'm part of the human race because I've experienced grief, stress, pressure, tension, fear. It's made me look at life differently.
>
> *Arnold*

Suffering

It is the natural and logical process of life for a person to come to the realisation of his *aloneness or separateness or abandonment* – that is, the realisation that essentially we are on our own. This state of awareness is customarily reached through suffering. Indeed several weeks of pain can teach us more about ourselves than years of painless living. It does not happen to everyone. Some remain dependent and incomplete creatures all their lives. It takes suffering and struggle and

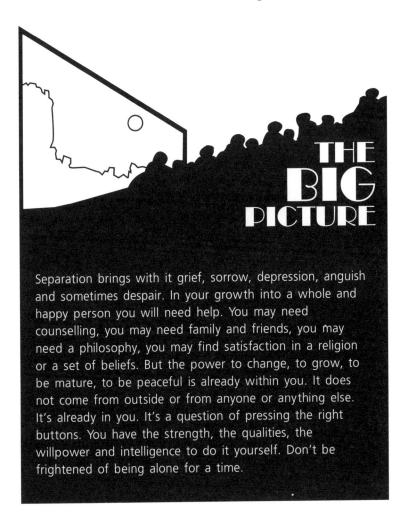

THE BIG PICTURE

Separation brings with it grief, sorrow, depression, anguish and sometimes despair. In your growth into a whole and happy person you will need help. You may need counselling, you may need family and friends, you may need a philosophy, you may find satisfaction in a religion or a set of beliefs. But the power to change, to grow, to be mature, to be peaceful is already within you. It does not come from outside or from anyone or anything else. It's already in you. It's a question of pressing the right buttons. You have the strength, the qualities, the willpower and intelligence to do it yourself. Don't be frightened of being alone for a time.

courage to face up to and to accept our aloneness. Some have the opportunity thrust upon them through the death of parents or spouses, or through desertion. Others come to it through a realisation that they are different and separate from their parents, spouses, friends and children.

Being alone will allow you to grow as a man. You will feel yourself healing, becoming more contented and peaceful as the months go by, becoming a stronger and more confident person.

Professional help

If you find yourself seriously depressed or stuck in sadness, don't hesitate to get help. We all need professional assistance at some stage of our lives, and we should not be ashamed to admit it. Seek out a good psychiatrist, psychologist or counsellor. Someone might be able to recommend one. Telephone your local community health centre; there may be a free counselling service in your area.

Some evening colleges and adult education institutions run courses for people coping with separation and divorce. Also available are programs in self-development.[152]

> I had personal counselling. It steadied me and I grew as a person. It took a bit of organising and cost money. But it was worth it.
>
> *Ted*

Men's groups

You might consider joining a men's group. Many men who have made giant steps in personal development have told me that they owe most of it to their involvement in a men's group. These groups provide mutual support, information and encouragement for their members besides being extremely therapeutic. I have listed some at the end of the book.

> I was more than lonely: I thought I was dead! I tried booze and pot until I realised that was hopeless. Mates got sick of my tripe so I got used to living alone. I basically lived in a cave for six months. Then I started going to a men's group. It has been my lifeline. I've been in it for two years now and I love those guys. I also had a great boss who really looked after me. Once I started to get my act together I noticed that support was there when I needed it. I now realise that loneliness was very

important to my journey. Bly calls it *Katabasis,* or the descent. The trick is not to get stuck in it.

Steve

A first step

In breaking a cycle of depression that can come to any of us, particularly after separation, a useful strategem is to decide to *do something*. It does not matter much what this is so long as it is a new activity and is reasonably pleasant. It might be a new hobby or a course of study. It might be some voluntary work. You might decide to paint your apartment or go to a gym. Whatever it is could serve to kickstart your recovery, to get you *out* of yourself, to be a foundation on which you can build.

I suddenly found that I had all this free time and I felt miserably unhappy. Out of the blue I decided to learn Spanish. Don't know why. I started to enjoy going to evening class and I met some nice people. Then I was introduced to bushwalking and a whole new world opened up for me. Relations with the ex-wife and kids are pretty hopeless, but I don't feel hopeless any more.

Peter

Others

Shift your scrutiny now to *others*. It is useful to examine your relationships with your children, your ex-wife, any significant people with whom you associate. Ask yourself how you can improve these relationships and identify the problems. Next, turn to the three components of your life: *home, work, leisure.*

Home

Examine your life at home and your attitude to it. Have I succeeded in turning my new abode into a real home? And into

✔ Do some thinking or meditating.
✔ Live in the present.
✔ Focus on what is possible even if it is not all you want.
✔ Set yourself reasonable goals.

✔ Accept your limitations and vulnerability.
✔ Recognition of your loss and grief is a step towards emotional strength.

a *second home* for my children? If not, what can I do about it? Am I treating it like a true home, am I happy to go home each evening, or do I treat it like a boarding house, spending as little time as possible in it? Do I still look on the matrimonial home as my only true home? Perhaps I should move towards a property settlement with my ex-wife so that I will have the funds to buy a place of my own. Or perhaps I simply need to spend some time finding a better place to rent or share.

Work

Am I happy with my job? If not, perhaps now is the time to look around for another position, or to commence a course which will make me more qualified or qualified in a different field. If I'm happy at work, how am I performing? Are there things that I can do better? Am I allowing my personal problems to affect the way I work?

Leisure

Time is precious! One of the real gifts that comes with separation for the non-custodial parent is the gift of spare time, especially over the non-access weekend. Like anyone else, you need your relaxation, your pleasures, your outings, your sporting and leisure activities. But don't waste that time! It can allow you to study, develop a skill, get a part-time job, start a hobby, or develop a particular interest. This could be the beginning of a whole new life.

Resolutions

Now that you have examined so many parts of your life, make a few resolutions. Then go away and put them into practice. And don't forget to do some more thinking in future. It may help you with the reasonable management of your life in this time of stress and pain. Make your life a thoughtful one. Life should be a gentle mix of making things happen and allowing things to happen, a combination of action and acceptance. Most people sit back and let things happen and then do nothing or take some action that is either too late or unwise. With thought and self-examination the happenings in our lives can be better managed.

> I feel that a lot of my life has been wasted through depression. Eventually I struck a wonderful doctor – a GP – who was willing to listen to me and talk to me and who referred me to a good psychiatrist. I was on medication and in therapy for several years. One day I made up my mind that I could do without my medication and therapy and I haven't gone back to it. I still talk to my GP, who is marvellous. I think I'm a better person, stronger, changed. After all I've been through I feel 'bulletproof'. My advice to men: get a good GP!
>
> *Brian*

QUESTIONS	POSITIVE THOUGHTS AND RESOLUTIONS
★	★
When can I give myself an opportunity to reflect on my new life?	I will stop and think.
★	★
What new activities can I develop to give me pleasure?	I will enjoy my home.
	★
	I will examine my life.
★	★
What am I doing to care for my physical, mental and emotional health?	I will keep healthy and fit.
	★
★	I will get some counselling.
What would it take to join a men's group?	★
★	I will make the most of my time.
How do I use my free time?	
★	
How can I enrich my work and home life?	

Enjoy your achievements as well as your plans.
Desiderata

16

Success as a Separated Father

At first I saw no future. I had a feeling of helplessness. But in time I learnt to step back and look at myself. I came to see that my separation from my family was just one aspect of my life. There were others: myself, my work, my relatives and friends. I was lucky in that I had fantastic support from my boss and workmates. I learned to focus on myself, to see that I was worthy and important. I decided that I was not going to let this beat me, that I would move on with my life and enjoy it. I can now help others who are going through the same problems.

Hans

The problems you have had with the family law system may not be overcome in your lifetime as a father. These problems may not allow you to be the father you want to be. The only way, then, to manage your fatherhood is for *you* to change! And you *can*!

There is a good argument that reasonable success in the business of being a separated father depends on the following.

Three basic attitudes:

★ *A good self-image* – or being reasonably confident and content with yourself.

★ *No bulldust* – this means you don't take nonsense from yourself or anyone else (at least not for too long). It means being totally honest with yourself and with others and demanding the same from them.

★ *A positive spirit* – a conviction that life is too good to miss. In other words, time is too precious to waste on depression, anger, hostility, pettiness, meanness and, in particular, negative thinking. As Auntie Mame said: *'Life's a banquet and some poor sons of bitches are starving to death!'*

Self-image

Each of us has, rightly or wrongly, a certain picture of ourselves. If asked, we can describe ourselves as a certain type of person: quiet or noisy, confident or shy, sensitive or tough, intelligent or dumb, ambitious or otherwise. But if pressed, rather than describing ourselves in terms of our inner personal characteristics, we will define ourselves as *others* define us: a divorced man, say, with two children who lives at Hometown and works in an office. If further pressed, we will then go on to talk about what we do at home and what we do at work.

This is fair enough as far as it goes. But it does not go far enough and there comes a time when every man (and woman too) should sit down and say: *'Hang on! What kind of person am I, really? How do I feel about myself? What qualities do I have?*

Am I a good person? Am I useful to myself and to others? Is my life of any value? Do I count? Are my actions good, bad or indifferent? Are my thoughts positive or negative? Am I content with myself and my life?'

Look at yourself

As we've seen, separation and divorce are excellent opportunities for a man to take stock of himself, to have a good look at himself and his life. Generally speaking, this will mean that he has to accept himself and develop the attitudes we discussed in Chapter 3. Until he does, he will feel unsettled, unhappy and directionless. The things around him have changed dramatically, and so he has to change too.

Loss of wife, children and home does not leave a man in a neutral position. He either grows or declines emotionally from the changes forced on him.

> **The worst thing was my realisation that the children and I did not have a lot in common any more, that I was not there for their growth and had little influence on them. The best thing has been my personal development. I am living my life my way. I see things differently, particularly about bringing up children.**
>
> *Greg*

In this process of redefining you must start with *yourself*, separated from others. This will mean *letting go of*, or mentally detaching yourself from, the people who matter to you – your ex-wife, your partner, your children, your parents, relatives and friends. You think about yourself not in terms of your position in a family or place or job, but in terms of how you feel about yourself, who you are, what you are about.

Now, the point of this is not to encourage you to detach yourself **emotionally** from your children and the others or to push them out of your life. Not at all! It is simply a mental process to help you to see yourself in a new light and to see your relationships with them in a new way, too.

Independence

'Letting go' does not mean giving up loving your children or not fostering your relationships with them (though in some extreme cases it may involve the latter). It does not mean that you are henceforth going to think and act selfishly without any thought for anyone else. But it does mean that you can see yourself independently of them. It does mean that you recognise that you have a life of your own, separate and not dependent on them, just as they have their own lives, separate and independent of you. You do not need to be defined only in relation to them. You are your own person.

> **The worst thing about it was guilt at not being there for the kids when I thought they needed me. I was paranoid about her influence on them. The best thing was getting out of a really bad marriage where we were staying together for the sake of the kids. I was able to start a new life.**
>
> *Barry*

Changing functions

Having put yourself on the right track in terms of your attitude to yourself, you are then in the right frame of mind to work on redefining your relationships with others and your attitudes to them. For the separated father there will be changes, whether you like them or not. So why not like them or, if you can't, at least accept them? Your new attitude to yourself will help you to do this.

It is particularly important – for them and for you – that you do this with your relationships with your **children**. Too many fathers refuse to accept the changes that separation and divorce bring. They imagine that they can still be exactly the same father that they were while living with their children. It's just not physically or psychologically possible! You can be as loving, caring and attentive as you will, but you'll be different. If you don't accept that, you've got a long way to go.

I know it's hard, but you *do* have to 'let go' – to a certain degree – of your children, if they are not living with you. You have to let go of the notion that you are the major decision-maker and influence in their lives. You have to let go of the idea that you will always be there for them and they for you. You have to let go of the feeling that they alone give meaning and purpose to your life.

> **There is a life for you beyond and apart from your children.**
> *'Your children are not your children. They are the sons and daughters of Life's longing for itself . . . you may strive to be like them, but seek not to make them like you.'*

These are the words of a wise man, Kahlil Gibran, in his book *The Prophet*.

Armed with your new self-awareness, you will not stop being a loving, caring father to your children. But you will be a *different* one and you will accept the differences. More than that: you will refuse to see your changed circumstances as a tragedy or a failure, but rather as an opportunity to forge new and interesting relationships with your children. Your separation can give you the opportunity to do more with yourself and with your children than you ever imagined.

No bulldust

It's easy to theorise, I know, and difficult to do, but we really must make a big effort to cut the nonsense out of our lives. There's a bit of it in all of us. We put up with it from ourselves and from others. It deserves a bit of thought. If we get serious and honest, most of it can be stopped. To stop deluding ourselves is a good starting point.

ONE MAN'S STORY
It couldn't have been much tougher. She took my infant daughter and went to live in another State without leaving a contact address. It took time and money to find her and then she made contact difficult. We went to court several times – in another State – and it cost me a lot of money. I had trouble with incompetent lawyers and I ended up running the case myself. In the end I got the contact orders I wanted. I have managed to stay in touch with my daughter and I now have a great relationship with her. It's been all my own work, with no encouragement from my ex-partner or from the Family Court. I was determined that I would not leave my daughter without a father. Because of my efforts I have been 100 percent successful and I feel good about that. It's been a huge achievement and working at it I have grown as a person.

> **The separation gave me the chance to have a good look at myself. I was angry about the separation and felt a failure. But my confidence grew as I worked on myself. I spoke to a counsellor and a psychologist. I did some reading and thinking. I now feel pretty good about myself and I think I can help other men who go through the same experience.**
>
> *Paul*

Delusion

What I mean is this: self-delusion is simply lack of honesty. It's amazing how we can kid ourselves! We can kid ourselves that we are good workers, when in reality we often only do enough to get by. We can kid ourselves that we are good neighbours, but we rarely show any concern for the people next door. We can kid ourselves that our separation was all our wife's doing and that we were blameless. But if we look at ourselves honestly we could find lots of areas in which we did not measure up. We say we love and care for our children, but often we put more energy into what's best for *us* rather than what's best for them.

Selfishness, self-centredness, self-righteousness, self-preoccupation are all facets of the same curse: the arrogance of a man who is taking rubbish from himself and spreading it around him.

So, next time you hear yourself telling your ex-wife that she and the children are always asking for money and that you are giving them more than enough, stop and think and ask yourself: *'Is this really true or is it just bulldust?'* If it's the latter, then correct your attitude and talk to your wife about it. Next time you find yourself telling your children that there's no way you can take them to a concert on Saturday night because it does not fit in with your arrangements and their mother should have consulted you first, stop and think. If you are honest and generous and flexible, you will **know** that you can manage it if you really want to. It's just rubbish to say that you can't!

By the same token, however, you are not obliged to take bulldust from anyone else. If your ex-wife *is* really bugging the life out of you for money and attention that is simply not merited, then tell her that you are not going to put up with it, that you refuse to discuss it further. If one of your children attempts to play on your guilt to make outrageous demands on your time and your money, do not hesitate to let him or her know that you do not intend to be 'conned'.

Nonsense

Separated men sometimes have to put up with a lot of emotional blackmail. There are so many instances: little children are sent to the door when he calls to pick them up, all dressed and ready to go. *'Mummy says we can't go with you until you pay the $50 you owe her!'* There's only one response to this: *'Tell Mummy I'm sorry but I can't take you to-day. I love you both very much.'* And then get in your car and drive away. Don't give in! If you do, there will surely be more similar occasions. Don't worry, the children will survive. And so will you!

If you are doing the fair thing, there's just no need in the world for you to take this kind of rubbish from anyone. Everyone has the right to a bulldust-free life! After all the discussion, listening, communication, talking, counselling and agonising, there comes a time when you have to say: *'Enough! I want a simple, peaceful life!'*

A friend said to me: 'As long as you let her see that she is getting up your nose, she'll continue to muck you around! Chill out and relax a bit!' So I did. I decided to look after me as well as the kids. I let them and their mother know that I would do my best but I would no longer react to any nonsense. It seemed to work. I felt more at peace.

Bruce

A positive spirit

Such a spirit is hard to come by in the early days of your separation but, further down the track, it is absolutely essential. It is possible for a separated man to drown in a sea of negativity. If you refuse to accept the separation and fail to come to terms with your new lifestyle, it is easy to become bitter and hardened.

Meanwhile, life will pass you by, and so will lots of nice people, people who would happily associate with you if you were good company. Nice experiences pass you by too, because you become too negative to encourage them. Like a distracted fieldsman, you drop the ball when it comes your way. If this goes on too long, you may become beyond redemption.

Redemption is only possible for those who are willing to learn. It is eminently possible for those who are willing to change. It is a sure thing for those who have a positive spirit.

A positive spirit is a state of mind in which you refuse to let adversity beat you but turn it to your advantage. You refuse to be passive and let things happen but rather set out to *make* them happen. You refuse to feel sorry for yourself, knowing that there are millions worse off than you. You focus on what is possible rather than on what is missing. You refuse to blame others for your problems and you accept control of your own life. You take *responsibility* for your decisions and actions.

> The hardest part was turning into a single dad, missing the boys, having to set up a flat, arranging access, etc. One weekend I took the boys away for a break. A mate and his kids came too. We were buying provisions in a shop and the woman behind the counter said: 'Giving the wife a break like good boys are you?' I said: 'Actually I've been giving her a break for two years now!' You've got to laugh at times.
>
> *Mark*

This positive spirit gives you the energy to change what you can and to accept what you can't. It maintains your sense of humour and your sense of reality. It prevents you from committing the unforgivable sin: taking yourself too seriously.

It also gives you the energy to go on living your life and even to improve it, notwithstanding the difficulties that come your way. You learn to suck a lot more sap out of life, to appreciate true values and true friends, to be aware that there is a wider world outside yourself and your family.

Success

The separated father will be sad at times, and perhaps the sadness of separation and loss of daily contact with your children will never quite leave you. Even after you achieve a good level of contentment you will have your bad days. Some incident will give you a 'flashback' and the blues. But despite that, you will learn to be happy with yourself and your life. You will remain committed to the changed but special relationship that you have fostered with your children. Good things will come to you because – by your positive spirit – you have gone out to meet them or encouraged them to come your way.

Similarly, good people will be attracted to you. You will be peaceful.

You will even get to the point of saying to yourself:
'I've made it! It's been tough at times and I've had some dreadful moments. But it's all been for the best and I'm glad it turned out this way! Life is better for me, my ex-wife and my children. I've grown and I feel I've made something of myself.'

This can be you! It's not easy for a while; at the start it's painfully difficult. But it **does** get easier in time. If you give yourself the chance of another life, if you open your mind to the possibility of a better life, and if you make a real effort, that life can be yours. Develop your self-reliance, cut out the bulldust, act with a positive spirit – and success will come.

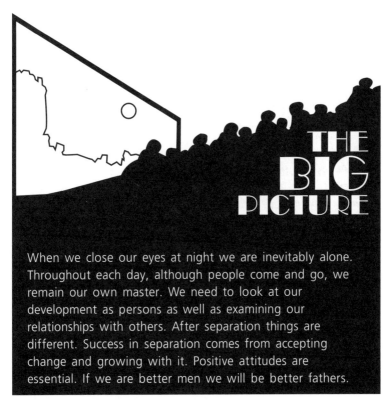

THE BIG PICTURE

When we close our eyes at night we are inevitably alone. Throughout each day, although people come and go, we remain our own master. We need to look at our development as persons as well as examining our relationships with others. After separation things are different. Success in separation comes from accepting change and growing with it. Positive attitudes are essential. If we are better men we will be better fathers.

QUESTIONS	POSITIVE THOUGHTS AND RESOLUTIONS
★	★
How can I show that I value myself as an independent person?	I will develop a healthy self-image.
★	★
What steps can I take to develop a positive spirit?	I won't take bulldust from anyone.
★	★
How do I deal with negativity, dishonesty and nonsense?	I will cultivate a positive spirit.
★	★
How can I accept and make changes in my life?	*I will learn to laugh again.*
★	
What must I do to succeed as a separated father?	

Therefore be at peace with God, whatever you conceive him to be; and whatever your labours and aspirations, in the noisy confusion of life keep peace with your soul.

Desiderata

Notes

1 K. Funder 'Motherhood, fatherhood', *Family Matters*, no. 30, pp. 34–37

2 Figures taken by the Australian Bureau of Statistics in 1992 showed that there were 268 000 men living apart from their children, but this did not include children over 15 years of age. On those figures I would estimate that in 1992 about 300 000 fathers were not living with their children. No comparable statistics appeared in the 1997 ABS survey. However, working on the number of children living apart from their natural parent, I would estimate that in 1997/98 the number of fathers living apart from their children (17 and under) has risen to more than 400 000.

3 Australian Bureau of Statistics *Family Characteristics*, Canberra, April 1997

4 New Zealand Government Statistics, 1998

5 *Sydney Morning Herald*, 15 April 1998, p. 15

6 C.H. Cantor and P. J. Slater 'Marital breakdown, parenthood, and suicide', *Journal of Family Studies*, vol. 1, no. 2, 1995, pp. 91–102

7 Peter Jordan *The Effects of Marital Separation on Men – 'Men Hurt'*, Research Report No. 6, Family Court of Australia, Sydney, 1985

8 Peter Jordan *The Effects of Marital Separation on Men – 10 Years On*, Research Report no. 14, Family Court of Australia, Melbourne, 1996

9 E.M. Hetherington, M. Cox, and R. Cox 'The aftermath of divorce', in Stevens, H. and Matthews, M. (eds), *Mother/Child/Father/Child Relationships*, National Association for the Education of Young Children, 1978

10 Don Edgar *Men, Mateship, Marriage*, HarperCollins, Sydney 1997, p. 306

11 The new word for custody is *residence*. But as the latter does not necessarily imply care and control, I continue to make use of the old term. The new word for access is *contact*, but I use both terms simply for variation of expression.

12 Steve Biddulph on fatherhood in *The Australian Magazine*, 2–3 August, 1997

13 Janne Gibson *Non-custodial Fathers and Access Patterns*, Research Report No. 10, Family Court of Australia, 1992

14 Peter Jordan *The Effects of Marital Separation on Men – 'Men Hurt'*

15 Peter Jordan *The Effects of Marital Separation on Men – 10 Years On*

16 ibid

17 Janne Gibson *Non-custodial Fathers and Access Patterns*

18 A. McMurray and A.M. Blackmore 'Influences on parent–child relationships in non-custodial fathers', *Australian Journal of Marriage and the Family*, vol. 14, no. 3, 1993

19 A. McMurray and A.M. Blackmore 'Influences on parent–child relationships in non-custodial fathers

20 'Holmes–Rahe Survey of Recent Life Experiences', *Journal of Psychosomatic Research*, vol. 11, 1967

21 For free services look in your telephone directory under *Community Health Centres*. Other professional counsellors are listed under *Counselling*.

22 Y. Walczak and S. Burns *Divorce: The Child's Point of View*, Harper & Row, 1984

23 J. Wallerstein and J. Kelly *Surviving the Break-up: How Children and Parents Cope with Divorce*, Basic Books, New York, 1980

24 J. Wallerstein and J. Kelly *Surviving the Break-up: How Children and Parents Cope with Divorce*

25 Constance Ahrons *The Good Divorce*, Bloomsbury, 1993

26 A. Ellis and R.A. Harper *A Guide to a Successful Marriage*, Wilshire Book Co, California, 1986

27 J. Pryor and F. Seymour 'Making decisions about children after parental separation', *Child and Family Law Quarterly*, vol. 8, no. 3, 1996, p. 242

28 Hamish Keith with Dinah Bradley *Becoming Single: How to Survive When a Relationship Ends*, Simon & Schuster, Australia, 1991

29 Barry Maley *Marriage, Divorce and Family Justice*, The Centre for Independent Studies, Sydney, 1992

30 Australian Institute of Family Studies *Parents and Children After Marriage Breakdown*, survey, Melbourne, 1987

31 Stephanie Dowrick *Intimacy and Solitude*, Mandarin, Melbourne 1993

32 J. Pryor and F. Seymour 'Making decisions about children after parental separation' *Child and Family Law Quarterly*, vol. 8, no. 3, 1996, pp. 229–42

33 Maggie Gallagher *The Abolition of Marriage*, Regnery Publishing, Washington DC, 1996

34 Barry Maley *Wedlock and Wellbeing*, The Centre for Independent Studies, Sydney, 1992

35 Barbara Whitehead 'Dan Quayle was right', *Atlantic Monthly*, April 1993

36 Bettina Arndt 'Last word on divorce and kids', *Sydney Morning Herald* and Melbourne *Age*, 8 November 1997

37 Constance Ahrons *The Good Divorce*
    Richard Glover 'Divorced from the facts', *Sydney Morning Herald*, 17 May 1993

38 Bryan Rodgers 'Social and psychological wellbeing of children from divorced families: Australian research findings', *Australian Psychologist*, vol. 31, no. 3, pp. 174–82, 1996

39 J. Pryor and F. Seymour 'Making decisions about children after parental separation', *Child and Family Law Quarterly*, vol. 8, no. 3, 1996, p. 231

40 K. Funder, M. Harrison and R. Weston *Settling Down: Pathways of Parents after Divorce,* Australian Institute of Family Studies, 1993

41 J. Pryor and F. Seymour 'Making decisions about children after parental separation', *Child and Family Law Quarterly,* vol. 8, no. 3, 1996, pp. 229–42

42 R. Dunlop and A. Burns 'The sleeper effect: myth or reality?', *Journal of Marriage and the Family,* vol. 57, pp. 375–86, 1995

43 P. R. Amato and A. Booth *A Generation at Risk: Growing Up in an Era of Family Upheaval,* Harvard University Press, 1997

44 A. Burns 'Divorce and the children', *Australian Journal of Sex, Marriage and the Family,* May 1981

45 P. R. Amato 'An intergenerational perspective on divorce', paper presented at the Australian Family Research Conference, Brisbane, November 1996

46 E.M. Hetherington, M. Cox, and R. Cox 'The aftermath of divorce', in Stevens, H. and Matthews, M. (eds) *Mother/Child/ Father/Child Relationships,* National Association for the Education of Young Children, 1978

47 R. Dunlop, A. Burns 'The sleeper effect'

48 P. R. Amato and A. Booth *A Generation at Risk: Growing up in an Era of Family Upheaval*

49 P. R. Amato and B. Keith 'Parental divorce and adult wellbeing: a meta-analysis', *Journal of Marriage and the Family,* vol. 53, pp. 43–58, 1991

50 Don Edgar *Men, Mateship, Marriage,* HarperCollins, Sydney, 1997, p. 313

51 E. Kruk 'Psychological and structural factors contributing to the disengagement of noncustodial fathers after divorce', *Family and Conciliation Courts Review,* vol. 30, no. 1, 1992, pp. 81–101

52 Kathleen Swinbourne 'Women won't go back to 50s', *Sydney Morning Herald,* 3 December 1997

53 E. Kruk 'Psychological and structural factors'

54 Australian Institute of Family Studies *A Submission to the Joint Select Committee Enquiry on Certain Family Law Issues,* Melbourne, 1993

55 Janne Gibson *Non-custodial Fathers and Access Patterns,* Research Report No. 10, Family Court of Australia, 1992

56 Family Law Council *Patterns of Parenting After Separation: A Report,* Australian Government Publishing Service, Canberra, 1992

57 Australian Bureau of Statistics *Family Characteristics,* Canberra, April 1997

58 J.B. Kelly 'Current research on children's postdivorce adjustment', *Family and Conciliation Courts Review,* vol. 31, no. 1, 1993, pp. 29–49

59 Janne Gibson *Non-custodial Fathers and Access Patterns*

60 Barry E. Burdon 'Fathers in Families', in Briggs, F. (ed.) *Children and Families: Australian Perspectives,* Allen & Unwin, Sydney, 1994

61 Paul Amato, *Nonresident Fathers and Children's Well-being* Paper delivered at National Forum 'Men and Family Relationships', Canberra 10–11 June 1998

62 Kruk 'Psychological and structural factors'

63 J.B. Kelly 'Current research on children's postdivorce adjustment'
64 Y. Walczak and S. Burns *Divorce: The Child's Point of View*, Harper & Row, London, 1984
65 M. McDonald 'Post-separation conflict and its effect on access patterns in middle childhood', MA thesis, University of Newcastle, 1990
66 Janne Gibson *Non-custodial Fathers and Access Patterns*
67 E. Kruk 'Psychological and structural factors'
68 S.R. Hurst and G.W. Smiley 'The access dilemma: a study of access patterns following marriage breakdown', *Australian Journal of Sex, Marriage and the Family*, June 1984
69 J. Wallerstein and J. Kelly *Surviving the Break-up: How Children and Parents Cope with Divorce*, Basic Books, New York, 1980
    J.R. Johnston 'Children's adjustment in sole custody compared to joint custody: families and principles for custody decision making', *Family and Conciliation Court Review*, vol. 33, no. 4, 1995, pp. 415–25
70 F.F. Furstenberg, S.P. Morgan and P. D. Allison 'Paternal participation and children's wellbeing after marital dissolution', *American Sociological Review*, vol. 52, no. 5, 1987, pp. 695–701
71 J. Wallerstein and J. Kelly *Surviving the Break-up*
72 J.B. Kelly 'Current research on children's postdivorce adjustment'
73 A. Burns 'Divorce and the children', *Australian Journal of Sex, Marriage and the Family*, May 1981
74 Family Law Act, Part VII, Division 5, s. 64 A-W
75 Don Carter '*Fathers, family law and responsibility*', private paper, 1994
76 *Family Matters*, no. 40, Autumn 1995
77 Isolina Ricci *Mom's House, Dad's House: A Complete Guide for Parents Who Are Separated, Divorced, or Remarried*, Fireside Books/Simon & Schuster, New York, 1997
78 C. Ahrons *The Good Divorce*, Bloomsbury, 1993
79 C. Ahrons *The Good Divorce*
80 C. Ahrons *The Good Divorce*
81 Robert Tompkins 'Parenting plans: a concept whose time has come', *Family and Conciliation Courts Review*, vol. 33, no. 3, 1995, pp. 286–97
82 C. Ahrons *The Good Divorce*
83 Phil Dye *The Father Lode*, Allen & Unwin, Sydney, 1997, p. 263
84 Some States have now published more enlightened policies for school principals, e.g. *Family Law and the School*, NSW Department of School Education, July, 1997.
85 Bettina Arndt *Sydney Morning Herald, 4 May 1996*
86 Paul Amato, *Nonresident Fathers and Children's Well-being*
87 Janne Gibson *Non-custodial Fathers and Access Patterns*, Research Report No. 10, Family Court of Australia, 1992
88 Peter Jordan *The Effects of Marital Separation on Men – 10 Years On*, Research Report No. 14, Family Court of Australia, 1996
89 Sharon Wegscheider-Cruse *Life after Divorce – Create a New Beginning*, Health Communications, Florida 1994
90 Paul Amato, *Nonresident Fathers and Children's Well-being*
91 M. McDonald *Children's perceptions of access and their adjustment in*

the post-separation period, Research Report no. 9, Family Court of Australia, 1990

92 American research indicates that in terms of real time, i.e. when a parent is relating to a child *alone*, mothers spend 19.5 hours per week and fathers 5.5 hours. An Australian survey has found that, *in respect of teenagers*, fathers spend less than 15 minutes per day with them.

93 In Janne Gibson's study (see above) over 50 percent of fathers had trouble – some of the time or all the time – in knowing what to do with their children during contact periods.

94 Janne Gibson *Non-custodial Fathers and Access Patterns*

95 Janne Gibson (see above) relates the comments of several separated fathers:

> 'At times I feel access is too painful a reminder of what I no longer have fully in my life.'

> ' . . . the emptiness inside – it makes you feel dead. You have a body but nothing else. It gets worse when you have the kids and you realise what you are missing . . . I think it will end up breaking me.'

> '. . . There is the lack of access to the child during the week . . . to talk of problems eye to eye, or holding and caring . . . The child cannot understand how I am forced to see so little of him . . . It breaks my heart and his too. A child is not a piece of property to be owned by one parent. How can a child's seeing his father more than once a fortnight be so disruptive as to require prohibition with the court's blessing?'

96 E. Kruk 'Psychological and structural factors contributing to the disengagement of noncustodial fathers after divorce', *Family and Conciliation Courts Review*, vol. 30, no. 1, 1992, pp. 81–101

97 M. McDonald 'Post-separation conflict and its effect on access patterns in middle childhood', MA thesis, University of Newcastle, 1990

98 In Sydney the St Vincent de Paul Society and LifeCare both run programs for people with this problem.

99 K. Kressel, S. Forlenza and F. Butler *Essex County Division Custody Mediation Project*, Interim Report, Britain, 1987

100 Janne Gibson *Non-custodial Fathers and Access Patterns*

101 J.B. Kelly 'Current research on children's postdivorce adjustment', *Family and Conciliation Courts Review*, vol. 31, no. 1, 1993

102 A. McMurray and A.M. Blackmore 'Influences on parent–child relationships in non-custodial fathers', *Australian Journal of Marriage and the Family*, vol. 14, no. 3, 1993

103 Bettina Arndt 'Failing our children', a three-part series on the Family Court, *Sydney Morning Herald* and Melbourne *Age*, 12, 14, 15 October 1996

104 R. Gardner *Parental Alienation Syndrome and the Differentiation Between Fabricated and Genuine Child Sex Abuse*, Creative Therapeutics, Cresskill, NJ
G.F. Cartwright 'Expanding the parameters of parental alienation syndrome', *American Journal of Family Therapy*, vol. 21, no. 3, 1993

105 A. Tomison and J. Tucci *Emotional Abuse: The Hidden Form of Maltreatment*, National Child Protection Clearing House: Issues in Child Abuse Prevention, no. 8, Spring, 1997

106 J. Wallerstein and J. Kelly 'The effects of parental divorce: experiences of the pre-school child', *American Journal of Child Psychiatry*, vol. 14, no. 4, 1975, pp. 600–16
     J. Wallerstein and J. Kelly 'The effects of parental divorce: experiences of the child in later latency', *American Journal of Orthopsychiatry*, vol. 46, no. 2, 1976, pp. 256–69

107 Stephanie Dowrick *Intimacy and Solitude*, Mandarin 1993, Melbourne

108 Australian Institute of Family Studies *Settling Down*, Melbourne, 1993

109 The MENDS program is one of the best. See 'Support Groups' appendix.

110 Look under 'Mediators' in your telephone directory.

111 Regarding Parenting Plans, talk to your counsellor, mediator, lawyer or the Family Court. However, beware of plans which still promote the old 'fortnightly father' idea.

112 Andrew Corish *A Guide to Mounting Your Own Case in Family Law Proceedings*, prepared for the Lone Fathers Association, Canberra, July 1997

113 Leonie Star *Counsel of Perfection*, Oxford University Press, 1996, pp. 183 & 207

114 Family Law Council *Interim Report: Penalties and Enforcement*, March 1998

115 *Report of the Joint Select Committee on Certain Aspects of the Operation and Implementation of the Family Law Act*, Canberra, November 1992

116 *Family Law Reform Act 1995*, Australian Government Publishing Service, Canberra

117 Bettina Arndt 'Failing our children'

118 Family Law Act, s. 60B

119 ibid. s. 68F (2)(h)

120 Richards *Joint custody revisited (1989) 19 Family Law 83*

121 Leonie Star *Counsel of Perfection*, Oxford University Press, 1996, p. 205

122 Family Law Act 1975 as amended, Part XIII A

123 *For the Sake of the Kids – Complex Contact Cases and the Family Court*, Australian Law Reform Commission Report No. 73, 1995

124 Family Law Council *Interim Report*

125 Leonie Star *Counsel of Perfection*

126 *ALRC & HREOC Draft Recommendations Paper 3: A Matter of Priority – Children and the Legal Process*, May 1997

127 Bettina Arndt 'Failing our children'

128 *Holmes v Holmes (1988) 12 Fam L R 331*

129 Leonie Star *Counsel of Perfection*

130 Family Law Act, s. 68F

131 *B and B: Family Law Reform Act (1995) 21 Fam L R 676*

132 For example: Steve Biddulph *Manhood*, Finch Publishing, Sydney, 1994

133 A scheme announced in May 1998 by the Australian government

which will provide counselling for custodial parents refusing access, and supervision of contact visits by community workers, is a step in the right direction.

134   Not so in all States. In Sydney about 10 percent proceed to a hearing.

135   Patricia Pearson *When She Was Bad: Violent Women and the Myth of Innocence* New York Viking, New York, 1997

136   Adam Tomison 'Protecting the children: updating the national picture', *National Child Protection Clearing House Newsletter*, vol. 4, no. 2, 1996

137   Felicity Goodyear-Smith *Dunedin Cohort Studies on Inter-partner Violence: A Review*, Department of Psychiatry and Behavioural Science, University of Auckland, May 1998

138   In NSW this legislation is in Part 15A of the *Crimes Act 1900*. The treatment of AVOs in this chapter centres on that legislation. Similar legislation has been enacted in other States and Territories and in New Zealand.

139   Wayne Evans, Stephen Scarlett and John Van Uum, 'A different approach to AVOs', *Law Society Journal*, December 1994

140   Janne Gibson *Non-custodial Fathers and Access Patterns*, Research Report No. 10, Family Court of Australia, 1992

141   A. McMurray and A.M. Blackmore 'Influences on parent–child relationships in non-custodial fathers', *Australian Journal of Marriage and the Family*, vol. 14, no. 3, 1993

142   Australian Institute of Family Studies *Paying for the Children: Parent and Employer Experiences of Stage One of Australia's Child Support Scheme*, Monograph No. 10, Melbourne, 1990

143   J. Bowen *Child Support: The Essential Guide*, Jacaranda Press, 1992, p. 13

144   In 1997 the *Basket-of-Goods Approach* based on the Lovering scale showed that a middle-income family spent $132.14 per week on a teenage child. In the *Expenditure Survey Approach* based on the Lee scale, the total cost of a child 11–13 years for an average family was $243.05.

145   Australian Bureau of Statistics Household Expenditure Survey 1993–94.

146   Australian Bureau of Statistics *Family Characteristics*, Canberra, April 1997

147   Adele Horin *Sydney Morning Herald*, 30 March 1994

148   May 1998 changes in Australian government policy point in this direction.

149   Note however that such benefits may attract the atttention of the Australian Taxation Office.

150   Stephanie Dowrick *Intimacy and Solitude*, Mandarin, 1993, Melbourne

151   ibid.

152   The *MENDS* programme is indicative of a new and positive approach to the wellbeing of separated men.

Book List

The Good Divorce *Constance Ahrons, Bloomsbury 1993*
Good Divorces, Bad Divorces: A Case for Divorce Mediation *Joyce Hauser, University Press of America 1995*
Divorce Hangover: A Step-by-Step Guide to Recovery from a Broken Marriage *Anne N. Walther Cedar 1992*
Fatherhood Reclaimed: The Making of the Modern Father *Adrienne Burgess, Vermilion, London 1997*
Intimacy and Solitude *Stephanie Dowrick, Mandarin 1993*
Forgiveness and Other Acts of Love *Stephanie Dowrick, Viking, Melbourne 1997*
Helping Your Child Through Separation and Divorce *Glenda Banks, Dove, Melbourne 1989*
To-and-Fro Children: A Guide to Successful Parenting After Divorce *Jill Burrett, Allen & Unwin 1991*
Coping with Grief *Mal McKissock and Dianne McKissock, ABC Books, Sydney 1985*
Becoming Single: How to Survive When A Relationship Ends *Hamish Keith and Dinah Bradley, Simon & Schuster 1991*
Private Lives *Bettina Arndt, Penguin, Melbourne 1986*
Taking Sides *Bettina Arndt, Random House, Sydney 1995*
The Father Lode *Phil Dye, Allen & Unwin, Sydney 1998*
A Hard Act To Follow: Step Parenting in Australia Today *Thomas Whelan and Susan Kelly, Penguin, Melbourne 1986*
Manhood: An Action Plan for Changing Men's Lives *Steve Biddulph, Finch, Sydney 1994*
The Wealth Within *Ainslie Meares, Hill of Content, Melbourne 1978*
Relief Without Drugs *Ainslie Meares, Hill of Content, Melbourne*
Men, Mateship, Marriage *Don Edgar, HarperCollins, Sydney 1997*
Real Men *Helen Townsend, HarperCollins, Sydney 1994*
The Road Less Travelled *M. Scott Peck, Arrow 1990*
Child Support: The Essential Guide *Jan Bowen, Jacaranda, Sydney 1992*
Saturday Parent *Peter Rowlands, Allen & Unwin, Sydney 1982*
Political Dreaming: Men, Politics and the Personal *John Andrews, Pluto Press*
When It's Over: A Practical Guide to Separation and Divorce *Marilyn Hauptman and Harold Abrahams, Simon & Schuster*
Parenting Plan and Booklet *Linda Fisher, Relationships Australia*

Self-help Bibliography (a list of self-help books for adults and children who are going through divorce) *Family Court Library*

When She Leaves You *Ian Macdonald, Millennium Books, Sydney 1995*

Dad's Place: A New Guide for Fathers after Divorce *Jill Burrett, Angus & Robertson, Sydney 1996*

Life After Divorce: Create a New Beginning *Sharon Wegscheider-Cruse, Health Communications, Florida 1994*

Parenting Without Custody: A Guide For Survival *Anne McMurray, Angus & Robertson, Sydney*

Men, Sex, Power and Survival *Bill Williams and Gisela Gardener, Greenhouse Publications, Sydney 1989*

Splitting Up: A Vital Handbook for People Facing Separation or Divorce in Australia *Judy Hogg, HarperCollins, Sydney 1996*

Stepfamily Realities: How to Overcome Difficulties and Have a Happy Family *Margaret Newman, Doubleday, Sydney 1991*

Second Chances: Men, Women and Children a Decade after Divorce *Judith Wallerstein and Sandra Blakeslee, Tickner & Fields, New York 1989*

Counsel of Perfection: The Family Court of Australia *Leonie Star, Oxford University Press 1996*

Separation, Divorce and After *Lynne McNamara and Jennifer Morrison, University of Queensland Press 1982*

Fathers, Sons & Lovers *Peter West, Finch, Sydney 1996*

Mothers and Sons *Babette Smith, Allen & Unwin, Sydney 1995*

Research Material

Amato, P. R. 'Contact with non-custodial fathers and children's wellbeing', *Family Matters*, no. 36, December 1993, pp. 32–34

Amato, P. R. and Keith, B. 'Parental divorce and adult well-being: a meta-analysis' *Journal of Marriage and the Family*, vol. 53, 1991, pp. 43–58

Amato, P. R. 'The "Child of Divorce" as a person prototype: bias and the recall of information about children in divorced families' *Journal of Marriage and the Family*, vol. 53, 1991, pp. 56–69

Amato, P. R. *Children in Australian Families: the growth of competence*, Prentice Hall, Sydney 1987

Amato, P. R. and Booth, A. *A Generation at Risk: Growing Up in an Era of Family Upheaval*, Harvard University Press, 1997

Arndt, Bettina *Failing Our Children,* a three-part series on the Family Court, *Sydney Morning Herald* and Melbourne *Age*, 12, 14, 15 October 1996

Australian Bureau of Statistics *Family Characteristics* April 1997

Australian Institute of Family Studies *Parents and Children After Marriage Breakdown*, a survey, 1987

Australian Institute of Family Studies: *'Settling Up' Property and Income Distribution on Divorce in Australia* Ed. Peter McDonald, 1986

Australian Institute of Family Studies *Who Pays for the Children? A First Look at the Operation of Australia's New Child Support Scheme* Harrison, Snider & Merlo Mono no. 9, 1990

Australian Institute of Family Studies *Paying for the Children* Parent and Employer Experiences of Stage One of Australia's Child Support Scheme Harrison, Snider, Merlo & Lucceshi Mono no. 10, 1991

Australian Law Reform Commission *Parent Child Contact and the Family Court*, Issues Paper 14, December 1994

Australian Law Reform Commission *For the Sake of the Kids: Complex Contact Cases and the Family Court*, Report no. 73, 1995

Bordow, S. and Gibson, J. *Evaluation of the Family Court Mediation Service*, Family Court of Australia Research Report No. 12, March 1994

Bowen, J. *Child Support: The Essential Guide,* Jacaranda Wiley, 1992

Burns, A. 'Divorce and the children', *Australian Journal of Sex, Marriage and the Family*, vol. 2, no. 2, May 1981, pp. 17–26

Burns, A. *Breaking Up: Separation and Divorce in Australia*, Nelson, 1980

Cherlin, A.J. and Furstenberg, F.F. *The New American Grandparent: A Place in the Family, a Life Apart*, Basic Books, New York, 1985

Cherlin, A.J., Furstenberg, F.F., Chase-Lansdale, P. L., Kiernan, K., Robins, P. , Morrison, D., and Teitler, J. 'Longitudinal studies of the effects of divorce in Great Britain and the US, *Science*, vol. 252, 1991, pp. 1345–1460

Cooper, J.E., Holman, J. and Braithwaite, V.A. 'Self-esteem and family cohesion: the child's perspective and adjustment', *Journal of Marriage and the Family*, vol. 45, no. 1, February 1993, pp. 153–59

Dudley, J.R. 'Non-Custodial Fathers Speak About their Parental Role', *Family and Conciliation Courts Review*, vol. 34, no. 3, July 1996 pp. 410–26

Dunlop R. and Burns, A. *The sleeper effect: Myth or reality? Journal of Marriage and the Family*, 1995, 57, pp. 386–87

Edgar, D. and Gleezer, H. 'Reconstructing family realities: Men do matter', paper presented at the International Council of Women International Conference, 'Changing Families in Changing Societies', February 1992

Elliott, Ochiltree, Richards, Sinclair and Tasker, 'Divorce and children: a British challenge to the Wallerstein view', (1990) Fam Law 309

Emery, R.E. *Family Processes and Children's Divorce Adjustment*, Sage, 1988

Emery, R.E. and Dillon, P. 'Conceptualizing the divorce process: renegotiating boundaries of intimacy and power in the divorced family system', *Family Relations*, vol. 43, no. 4, October 1994, pp. 374–379

Family Law Council *Patterns of Parenting after Separation*, discussion paper, 1991

Family Law Council *Patterns of Parenting after Separation*, report to the Minister for Justice and Consumer Affairs, 1992

Family Law Council *Interim Report: Penalties and Enforcement*, March 1998

Family Law Reform Act 1995, Australian Government Publishing Service, Canberra

Funder, K. 'Child support – a step towards changing parenting after separation', *Family Matters*, no. 37, April 1994, pp. 70–71

Funder, K., Harrison, M. and Weston, R. *Settling Down: Pathways of Parents After Divorce*, Australian Institute of Family Studies, 1993

Furstenberg, F.F., Morgan, S.P. and Allison, P. D. 'Paternal participation and children's wellbeing after marital dissolution', *American Sociological Review*, vol. 52, no. 5, 1987, pp. 695–701

Gelles, R. and Loseke, D. (Eds) *Current Controversies in Family Violence*, Sage, London, 1993

Gibson, J. *Non-custodial Fathers and Access Patterns*, Family Court of Australia Research Report No. 10, 1992

Gilmour, L. 'Not happily ever after: the implication of marital separation for men', unpublished BA Hons thesis, Macquarie University, Sydney, 1983

Goodyear-Smith Felicity *Dunedin cohort studies on inter-partner violence: a review*, Department of Psychiatry and Behavioural Science, University of Auckland May 1998

Hetherington, E.M. 'Divorce: a child's perspective', *American Psychologist*, vol. 34, no. 10, October 1979, pp. 851–58

Hetherington, E.M., Cox, M. and Cox, R. 'The aftermath of divorce', in Stevens, H. and Matthews, M. (eds) *Mother/Child/Father/Child Relationships*, National Association for the Education of Young Children, 1978

Hilton, J.M. and Macari, D.P. 'Grandparent Involvement Following Divorce: A Comparison in Single-Mother and Single-Father Families', *Journal of Divorce and Remarriage*, vol. 28, nos 1–2, 1997, pp. 203–24

Hirst, S.R. and Smiley, G.W. 'The access dilemma: a study of access patterns following marriage breakdown', *Conciliation Courts Review*, vol. 22, no. 1, June 1984, pp. 41–52

Jacobs, J.J. (ed.), *Divorce and Fatherhood: The Struggle for Parental Identity*, American Psychiatric Press, 1986

Johnston, J.R. 'Children's adjustment in sole custody compared to joint custody: families and principles for custody decision making', *Family and Conciliation Court Review*, vol. 33, no. 4, October 1995, pp. 415–25

Joint Select Committee on Certain Aspects of the Operation and Implementation of the Family Law Act. *The Family Law Act of 1975: Aspects of Its Oeration and Interpretation*, AGPS, November 1992

Jordan, P. 'The relationship chart: a recording and therapeutic process', *Australian Journal of Family Therapy*, vol. 10, no. 2, June 1989, pp. 85–91

Jordan, P. *The Effects of Marital Separation on Men: 'Men Hurt'*, Brisbane Counselling Section of the Family Court of Australia, 1985

Jordan P. *The Effects of Marital Separation on Men – 10 Years On*, Research Report No. 14, Family Court of Australia, 1996

Jordan, P. 'Counselling men confronted by marital separation', *Journal of Divorce and Remarriage*, vol. 18, nos 1/2, 1992, pp. 109–26

Lamb M.E. et al. 'The effects of divorce and custody arrangements on children's behaviour, development and adjustment', *Family and Conciliation Courts Review*, vol. 35, no. 4, October 1997, pp. 393–94

Kelly, J.B. 'Current research on children's postdivorce adjustment', *Family and Conciliation Courts Review*, vol. 31, no. 1, January 1993, pp. 29–49

Kelly, J.B. 'Current research on children's postdivorce adjustment: no simple answers', *Family and Conciliation Courts Review*, vol. 31, no. 1, 1993

Kressel, K. Forlenza, S. and Butler, F. *Interim Report: Essex County Division Custody Mediation Project*, 1987

Kruk, E. 'Psychological and structural factors contributing to the disengagement of noncustodial fathers after divorce', *Family and Conciliation Courts Review*, vol. 30, no. 1, January 1992, pp. 81–101

Marlow, L. *Divorce and the Myth of Lawyers*, Harlan Press, 1992

McDonald, M. *Children's Perceptions of Access and Their Adjustment in the Post-separation Period*, Family Court of Australia, Research Report No. 9, 1990

McDonald M. 'Post-separation conflict and its affect on access patterns in middle childhood', MA thesis, University of Newcastle, 1990

McDonald, P. (ed.) *The Economic Consequences of Marriage Breakdown in Australia; A Summary*, Institute of Family Studies, 1985

McMurray, A. and Blackmore, A. 'Influences on parent–child relationships in non-custodial fathers', *Australian Journal of Marriage and the Family*, vol. 14, no. 3, November 1993, pp. 151–59

McMurray, A. 'Influences on parent–child relationships in non-custodial mothers', *Australian Journal of Marriage and the Family*, vol. 13, no. 2, November 1992, pp. 138–47

Mitchell, A. *Children in the Middle: Living Through Divorce*, Tavistock Publications, 1985

Moloney, L. 'Beyond custody and access: post-separation parenting in the nineties', *Family Matters*, no. 34, May 1993, pp. 11–15

Moloney, L., Marshall, A. and Waters, P. 'Suspension of access attitudes which have influenced the courts', *Australian Journal of Family Law*, vol. 1, no. 1, August 1986, pp. 50–66

National Council for the International Year of the Family, *Creating the Links: Families and Social Responsibility*, Final Report, November 1994

New South Wales International Year of the Family – Advisory Committee *Focusing on Families*, Consultation Report, November 1994

Ochiltree, G. 'The sometimes forgotten parents', *Family Matters*, no. 19, October 1987, pp. 23–25

Ochiltree, G. and Amato, P. *The Child's Eye View of Family Life: a report to respondents in a study conducted in Victoria in late 1982 and early 1993*, Australian Institute of Family Studies, 1985

Parker, S. 'Child support in Australia: children's rights or public interest?', *International Journal of Family Law*, vol. 5, no. 1, April 1991, pp. 24–57

Pearson, Patricia *When She Was Bad: Violent Women and the Myth of Innocence*, Viking, New York, 1997

Richards 'Joint custody revisited' (1989) Fam Law 83

Seltzer, J. 'Relationships between fathers and children who live apart: the father's role after separation', *Journal of Marriage and the Family*, vol. 53, no. 1, February 1991, pp. 79–101

Tomison, A. *Protecting Children: Updating the National Picture* National Child Protection Clearing House, Newsletter, vol. 4, no. 2, Spring 1996

Tompkins, R. 'Parenting plans: a concept whose time has come', *Family and Conciliation Courts Review*, vol. 33, no. 3, July 1995, pp. 286–97

Wallerstein, J. and Kelly, J. 'The effects of parental divorce: experiences of the pre-school child', *Journal of the American Journal of Child Psychiatry*, vol. 14, no. 4, 1975, pp. 600–16

Wallerstein, J. and Kelly, J. 'The effects of parental divorce: experiences of the child in later latency', *American Journal of Orthopsychiatry*, vol. 46, no. 2, April 1976, pp. 256–69

Wallerstein, J. and Kelly, J. *Surviving the Break-up: How Children and Parents Cope with Divorce*, Basic Books, New York, 1980

Walczak, Y. and Burns, S. *Divorce: The Child's Point of View*, Harper Row, 1984

Warshak, *Gender Bias in Child Custody Decisions*, Family and Conciliation Courts Review, vol. 34, no. 3, July 1996, 396–409

Weir, R. *Access Patterns and Conflict*, Family Court of Australia, 1985

Weston, R. 'Divorced parents and child-related orders', *Family Matters*, no. 25, December 1989, pp. 17–21

Weston, R. 'New families, new finances', *Family Matters*, no. 31, April 1992, pp. 26–29

Support Groups

AUSTRALIA

National

MENDS (programs and counselling for separated men)	1300 363 361

ACT

Lone Fathers Association of Australia	(02) 6258 4216 Mobile 0417 668 802
Non-custodial Parents Association	(02) 6292 1121 or (02) 6299 5688

NSW

Credit Helpline	(02) 9951 5544
DADS Sydney	(02) 9721 3177
DADS Springwood	(02) 4759 2178
DADS Coffs Harbour	(02) 6658 5851
DADS Lithgow	(02) 6353 1669
DADS Lismore	(02) 6622 0141
DADS Wagga Wagga	017 970 740 (mobile)
Dubbo Lone Fathers Association	(02) 6889 1036
Family Law Reform Association	(02) 9542 2459
Fathers' Resource Centre	(02) 4758 7672 (02) 9891 2429
Grandparents Support Group	(02) 4341 7640
GRANS	(02) 6554 7268
Macarthur Network for Men	(02) 9607 6464
Men's PhoneLine	(02) 9979 9909
Newcastle Lone Fathers Association	(02) 4943 9634 015 550 964 (mobile)
Wagga Non-custodial Parents Association	(02) 6921 2343

Queensland

Cairns Child Support Action Group	(07) 0515886
DADS Sunshine Coast	(07) 5485 3528
Dysart Lone Fathers Association	(07) 4958 2364
Chelmer Family Law Reform Association	(07) 3379 2871
Gladstone Family Law Reform & Assistance Inc	(07) 4972 5899
Grandparents Support Group	(07) 5535 2907
Mackay Child Support Action Group	(07) 4956 5169 015 156 167 (mobile)
Men's Rights Agency	(07) 3805 5611
Moranbah Lone Fathers Association	(07) 4941 8916
Mount Isa Lone Fathers Association	(07) 430725
Rockhampton Lone Fathers Association	(07) 4927 6448 (07) 4928 2559
Rockhampton and Central Queensland Men's Agency	(07) 4939 5626
Tablelands Men's Help Group	(07) 0954682
Toowoomba Family Law Reform Asssociation	(07) 4638 5850

Northern Territory

DADS Alice Springs	(08) 8952 4485
DADS Darwin	015 615 669 (mobile)
Lone Fathers Association	(08) 8932 3339

South Australia

Child Support Action Group	(08) 8341 1225
Lone Fathers Association	(08) 8370 3169

Tasmania

DADS Tasmania	(03) 6247 7790
Lone Fathers Association	(03) 6239 6140

Victoria

Abolish Child Support and Family Court Party	(03) 9764 8504

DADS Victoria	(03) 9374 2753
Family Law Reform Party	(03) 9387 7044
Grandparents Support Group	(03) 9568 3306
Lone Fathers Association	(03) 9878 6588
Parents Without Rights	(03) 9587 1570
Parent and Non-custodial Children Without Rights	(03) 9753 3356

Western Australia

Family Law and Marriage Environment	(08) 9271 9191
Grandparents Support Group	(08) 9332 5469
Men's Confraternity Inc	(08) 9470 1734
Perth Lone Fathers Association	(08) 9470 1153

Email and Web sites

DADS	DADS.Aust@omcs.com.au
Parents Without Rights (Vic)	gmac@melbpc.org.au
Society for the Best Interests of the Child	http://www.child-justice.dynamite.com.au
Manhood On Line	http://www.manhood.com.au
MENDS	http://www.peerleadership.com.au/mends.html
Mens Health and Wellbeing Association Inc (NSW)	mhwa@peerleadership.com.au http://www.peerleadership.com.au/mhwa.htm
Link Pages for Men	http://www.peerleadership.com.au
Men's Health Network	menshealth@dot.net.au
Men's Rights Agency	http://www.ecn.net.au/~mra
Men's Mailing List	nuance@vicnet.au
Non-custodial Parents Association	ivecm@pcug.org.au
Family Law Reform and Assistance Association Inc (QLD)	smiths@quoin.cqu.edu.au
Family Law Reform Association (NSW)	flra@ozemail.com.au
CERTIFIED MALE (periodical for men) Locked Bag 1 SPRINGWOOD NSW 2777	Pvogel@ibm.net http://www.pnc.com.au/~pvogel/cm

NEW ZEALAND

Christchurch

Father & Child Trust	(03) 372 9140
Caring Fathers, Home & Family Society	(03) 379 5645

Auckland

Men's Centre North Shore	(09) 480 2168
Shore Fathers	(09) 483 2241

Palmerston North

Family Rights	(06) 356 2235

Nelson

Dads Group	(03) 548 9208

Wellington

Widowed, Separated and Divorced Support Group	(03) 548 9208

Men's Groups

For information on men's groups, contact the following:

Far North

Daniel Miller (Kerikeri)	(09) 407 8558

Whangarei

Les Gray	(09) 436 2349

Auckland

Man Alive	(09) 835 0509
Essentially Men	(09) 627 9827
City Fathers	(09) 376 0302
Wellmen	(09) 575 5798
Mens Centre North Shore	(09) 480 2168
Mensline	(09) 522 2500
Mens Studies (Manukau Institute of Technology)	(09) 274 6009
Shore Fathers	(09) 483 2477

Thames
John Finn   (07) 868 5543

Coromandel
Sol Peterson   (07) 866 8972

Hamilton
Graham Harbutt   (07) 856 5778

Hawke's Bay
Colin Littlewood   (06) 877 8634

Wellington
Peter Crossland   (04) 386 4577
Mike Wignall   (04) 478 7477

Nelson/Golden Bay
Jim Horton   (03) 525 9641

Christchurch
Brian Alderdice   (03) 385 1690
Mensline Support Group   (03) 365 4239

Index